Cleopatra's Needles

The Lost Obelisks of Egypt

Bob Brier

BLOOMSBURY ACADEMIC
LONDON · NEW YORK · OXFORD · NEW DELHI · SYDNEY

BLOOMSBURY ACADEMIC
Bloomsbury Publishing Plc
50 Bedford Square, London, WC1B 3DP, UK
1385 Broadway, New York, NY 10018, USA

BLOOMSBURY, BLOOMSBURY ACADEMIC and the Diana logo are trademarks of
Bloomsbury Publishing Plc

First published in Great Britain 2021

Cover design by Catherine Wood
Cover image © Cleopatra's Needle; the machinery for Placing the Obelisk in Position on the
Thames Embankment / Private Collection / Photo © Liszt Collection / Bridgeman Images

A catalogue record for this book is available from the British Library.

A catalog record for this book is available from the Library of Congress.

ISBN: PB: 978-1-3501-9872-2
       HB: 978-1-4742-4293-6
       ePDF: 978-1-4742-4295-0
       eBook: 978-1-4742-4294-3

Series: Bloomsbury Egyptology

Typeset by RefineCatch Limited, Bungay, Suffolk

To find out more about our authors and books visit www.bloomsbury.com
and sign up for our newsletters.

For Richard, Colette, and Alberta, my merry band of translators

Contents

Acknowledgments

When the ancient Egyptians created a monumental statue, it was not the work of a single sculptor. Tomb paintings show teams of artists working simultaneously on a single statue. One sculptor chisels away on a shoulder, another works on a knee, while yet another sands an area smooth. I have had so much help with this book that it is more like an ancient Egyptian statue than one author's work. The variety of the kinds of help I have received is amazing. Perhaps most interesting and rewarding has been in translating.

When I first came to the Long Island University forty years ago, Richard Auletta, a professor in the Department of Foreign Languages, and I began translating texts that I needed for my research. It started with some now-forgotten article in a language I didn't know (I seem to remember Swedish) and Richard came to my assistance. We enjoyed the collaboration so much, that for thirty years we met once a week to translate. More recently, two other colleagues in Foreign Languages, Professors Colette Sumner and Alberta Barga, joined us. The obelisk book had plenty of primary sources in French, Italian, Latin, etc., that needed translating, and many pleasant afternoons were spent in my office over tea and obelisks. Even more recently, an old friend, Armand Thieblot, an engineer and French speaker, caught the obelisk fever and, though unable to join us in person, translated Léon de Joannis's long-forgotten *Campagne pittoresque du Luxor*. A big "Thanks!" to all.

My wife, Pat Remler, served as the "cruel but fair" first editor, and frequently explained that what I had written didn't make sense. She also took almost all the photos for the book, both in Egypt and in Rome on our great obelisk quest. When we discovered we needed a few more Rome photos, Vivian Mosby supplied wonderful images. All the vintage photos came from my own collection with the exception of the tip of the New York obelisk photos that were unearthed by William Joy. The photo of the baton used by the Freemasons at the installation of the New York Obelisk's pedestal was kindly supplied by the Chancellor Robert R. Livingston, Masonic Library of Grand Lodge, New York, N.Y.

Mary Chipman, friend of many years, collaborator on all things Egyptian, and a woman of many talents, served as unpaid, but not unappreciated, "techie." She spent countless hours becoming a master of Photoshop so she could enhance the nineteenth-century images, crop and size the more recent photos, and decide what goes in and what doesn't. I owe Mary, big time.

Armand Thieblot, aside from translating, read the manuscript, caught many of my engineering errors, and improved the text in many ways.

Special thanks go to the Central Park Conservancy who cleaned and conserved the New York obelisk and who erected the scaffold that enabled me to examine the tip of the obelisk. George Wheeler generously shared his written report and other information; Marie Warsh explained the technical details of the cleaning and conservation; and Matthew Reiley unearthed old photos and other information that helped solve the mystery of the obelisk's broken tip.

At the typesetter, Kathy John gracefully supervised the manuscript as it went through publication and was remarkably tolerant of my lack of computer skills. Ian Howe caught my spelling errors and ruthlessly hunted down and annihilated my inconsistencies. Thank you all.

Introduction

It took me a long time to fall in love with obelisks. For years I had seen them in front of Egyptian temples, read about them, lectured about them in my classes, but they just never grabbed me. Then I saw the granddaddy of all obelisks.

If you had to pick the most remarkable object ever produced in ancient Egypt, what would you choose? Tutankhamen's gold mask? Karnak Temple? The bust of Queen Nefertiti? The Great Pyramid? For most people, including Egyptologists, it would be difficult to single one out of all the wonderful objects. For me it's no problem. It isn't even close. It's an obelisk. Lying in a quarry near Aswan is an unfinished obelisk that I believe is the most amazing creation of the ancient Egyptians. It was going to be the largest obelisk ever, by far. It weighs more than 1,000 tons. That's right, more than 2,000,000 pounds, more than two jumbo jets, and they were going to stand it up and balance it on a pedestal. I have been to the quarry more than 100 times and every time I am amazed. How were they going to move it? Stand it up? It is this obelisk that cemented my love affair with obelisks. The stonemasons who were going to move and erect this obelisk were heroes.

The tales of engineering marvels and obelisks don't end in ancient Egypt. They continue in Roman times and into the Renaissance. In the nineteenth century three very large ancient obelisks left Egypt, destined for Paris, London, and New York. The men who transported them faced tremendous difficulties merely trying to move what the ancient Egyptians had created. Lives were lost, one obelisk was lost at sea, and one nearly fell and broke. Some of the men who moved the obelisks left accounts of their trials and tribulations. One was so depressed by the loss of the lives of his men that he never wrote about moving the obelisk and we must trace his actions through newspaper accounts and other sources. The stories of these obelisks in exile are no less remarkable than ones that took place in ancient Egyptian quarries. The events in this book span more than thirty centuries, but it is best to start at the beginning, in ancient Egypt.

How to Quarry an Obelisk

Each year millions of tourists pour into Egypt to see its stone monuments—pyramids, tombs, temples, and obelisks. The ancient Greeks were awed by the Egyptians' skill with stone. Herodotus, the Greek "father of history," visited Egypt around 450 BC and was proud to proclaim, "We Greeks learned to build in stone from the Egyptians." In both the ancient and modern worlds, Egypt was famous for her masonry, but it was not always that way. Before there were pharaohs, there were no stone buildings. Early Egyptians constructed their houses of either reeds bundled together or mud bricks. The choice of material was determined by Egypt's geography.

Egypt is a desert with a river running right down its middle. While the Nile provided enough water to irrigate crops, it didn't provide enough water for forests, so there was little wood for building. Before the pharaohs, even boats were made of reeds bundled together. The lack of wood greatly restricted building and transportation. You can't sail the Mediterranean to trade for goods in a papyrus skiff. But this all changed with the advent of the pharaohs.

Before the pharaohs, ancient Egypt was divided into two kingdoms, Upper and Lower Egypt. Contrary to intuition, Upper Egypt is in the south, below Lower Egypt. This is because the Nile flows from south to north, so you go "up river" when you go south. With Egypt divided into two kingdoms, sometime around 3200 BC, a king from the south named Narmer marched north, defeated the northern king, and unified Egypt into the first nation in history. The story of Narmer's conquest is told on the Narmer Palette, Egypt's equivalent of Magna Carta. Not only does it record Egypt's beginning as a nation, it is probably the first historical document in the world.

Many Egyptians owned palettes on which they ground cosmetics. Take a little duck grease, add some pulverized malachite, mix them together on your palette and you had green eye shadow. If you wanted traditional black eyeliner, substitute galena for the malachite. Because of their function, palettes were smooth, providing a flat surface for grinding and blending. Sometimes they were carved in the shape of a fish or turtle, but for the most part they were simple affairs. The Narmer Palette is different. It is very elaborate, almost every inch is decorated, and it tells the story of Egypt's first pharaoh.

The palette has pride of place on the first floor, just past the entrance of Cairo's Egyptian Museum. Carved from a single piece of slate, the palette is about two feet high and three inches thick. On the front side Narmer is shown wearing the white crown of the south as he defeats his northern counterpart. On the reverse side, Narmer leads a triumphal parade and wears the red crown of the north. He is the first king of both Upper and Lower Egypt. Two mythological creatures with their long necks intertwined symbolize this

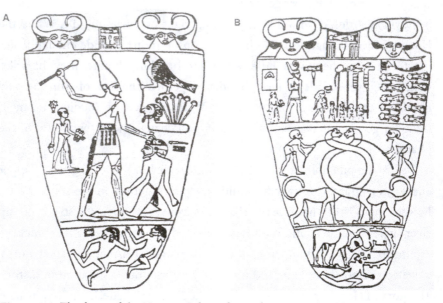

Figure 1.1 The front of the Narmer Palette shows the conquering Narmer wearing the white crown of Upper Egypt. On the reverse, Narmer wears the red crown of Lower Egypt. He is now the King of unified Egypt.

unification; Egypt is a single nation and Narmer is its king. For 3,000 years the icon of Egypt would be the pharaoh smiting his enemy, just as it appeared on the Narmer Palette.

The first building in stone

It is one of those marvelous quirks of history that permits us to know the first significant stone building in the world, when it was built, and even the name of the genius who conceived it more than 4,000 years ago. It was a tomb unlike any other and, to understand just how remarkable it was, we must know something about burials in ancient Egypt.

The earliest Egyptian burials were simple sand pits. Scoop away sand, place the deceased and some of his prized possessions for use in the afterlife in the pit and cover with sand. It is an easy, but impermanent way to dispose of the dead. Eventually winds might blow the sand away; the body is revealed, and perhaps destroyed by jackals. As a solution to the problem, Egyptians began constructing large rectangular mud brick markers above their graves. Egyptologists call these rectangles *mastabas*, which is Arabic for *bench* because they resemble benches often seen in front of modern Egyptian homes. Eventually these mastabas became more elaborate, with chambers inside. The deceased was still buried beneath the mastaba that protected the burial, but now the mastaba also served as a chapel where the family of the deceased could pay its respects. Narmer was buried beneath a mud brick mastaba, as were the early pharaohs who followed him. Then, at the beginning of the Third Dynasty, an architect named Imhotep began building a mastaba for his pharaoh, Zoser.

Like the pharaohs' before him, Zoser's mastaba was large, about the size of a small warehouse, but it was different in one important aspect: it was made of stone. From mud bricks to stone blocks was a bold leap. It was one thing to make a few thousand mud bricks, quite another matter to quarry stone blocks. When Imhotep began Zoser's mastaba, the Egyptians had been manufacturing bricks for centuries. It was an easy matter to mix Nile mud with some straw for strength and then press the mixture into a rectangular wood mold. Lift the mold, let the brick dry in the sun, and they had building material that would

Figure 1.2 Rectangular structures called *mastabas* were placed on top of burials in early Egypt.

last for centuries in a desert climate. Few skills are involved in making mud bricks; many are needed for quarrying stone blocks.

Special tools had to be created to cut the blocks from the quarry—craftsmen had to fashion chisels, hammers, and sleds to pull the stones. And what kind of stone should be used for a mastaba? Egypt has a variety of stones in different colors and densities, each with different properties. Imhotep selected limestone, probably for three reasons: 1) It is plentiful in Saqqara, the area where the mastaba was built. 2) In Imhotep's time, the only metal they had for tools was copper, which is soft, too soft to cut almost any stone but limestone. 3) Once limestone is cut out of a quarry, it hardens, so it is stronger when it reaches the building site than when it was first cut.

While building Zoser's mastaba, Egyptian workmen learned to quarry, dress, and transport stone. If you look closely at the blocks in the mastaba, you can see that the workmen were just feeling their way, learning on the job. The blocks are small, not much larger than the mud bricks they were accustomed to making. Two strong men could heft one block into place. They hadn't yet learned how to cut and move large blocks. It would take a thousand years before their descendants would be quarrying an obelisk that weighed 1,000 tons. Another sign that they were new to working stone is that the edges of the blocks aren't squared off at proper right angles. Still, the pharaoh's stone mastaba was a remarkable advance and must have been the pride of all Egypt. But Imhotep was just beginning.

Egypt's first pyramid

As the mastaba neared completion, Zoser was in good health and clearly would not need his burial place for a while. At this point, Imhotep had the idea to make something even more special; he would build a second stone mastaba on top of the first, creating a two-tiered structure. Clearly everyone was getting more and more comfortable with building in stone, learning as they went along. Over the course of the next twenty years, the mastaba continued to grow; the bottom was enlarged and a total of four higher levels were added to the original mastaba, creating the Step Pyramid of Saqqara. At 200 feet the pyramid was the tallest building on the planet. Stone had given the Egyptians the ability to reach for the sky.

Figure 1.3 The Step Pyramid of Saqqara is the world's first building in stone.

While the pyramid grew, Imhotep had his workmen add a large stone enclosure wall around the pyramid. Inside this wall, just a short walk from the pyramid, he built chapels and shrines of stone where Zoser could perform religious rituals for eternity. One can almost see Imhotep becoming giddy with his new ability to work in this medium of stone. Everyone is getting more and more confident. The enclosure wall and chapels are beautifully carved and polished. Over the course of this twenty-year project they learned the craft of fine stonework. They even created a life-sized limestone statue of Zoser, the first life-size statue in Egypt. Today millions of tourists visit it in the Cairo Museum, just a few steps from Narmer's Palette.

Pyramid mania

Once the skills of working in stone were honed, building became a national mania. Pyramid after pyramid was constructed for successive pharaohs, each trying to outdo his predecessor. After a few step pyramids, a pharaoh—or more probably his architect—decided to fill in the steps and attempt the first true pyramid at a remote site in the desert called Meidum. The Meidum Pyramid isn't just the first attempt at a true pyramid; it is the first pyramid with a burial chamber not beneath the pyramid, but *in* the pyramid. A burial chamber inside a pyramid presents a major engineering problem. With thousands of tons of stone pressing down upon the ceiling from above, how do you keep a large ceiling from cracking? The answer was corbeling. With a corbeled ceiling, the walls narrow as they get higher. As you build the wall out of stone blocks, each level is placed about six inches in from the one beneath it, so it overlaps and looks like an upside–down staircase. Thus, when you get to the top, the block spanning the walls and forming the ceiling is only a few inches wide. A block spanning only a few inches will not crack under the weight above it.

Less than a hundred years after the Meidum Pyramid, the Great Pyramid would be towering above the Giza Plateau. Building had come a long way very quickly, but it wasn't always successful. As architects attempted to build burial chambers inside pyramids rather than beneath them, they ran into problems. Walls cracked, pyramids had to be abandoned, but each step of the way new skills and techniques were developed.

Figure 1.4 Inside the Red Pyramid at Dashour. Corbeling—stepping each stone level inwards—solved the problem of how to span an internal space inside a pyramid.

Disaster in the desert

I love to take my students to the Bent Pyramid at Dashur. Here I can show them that the Egyptians did not always get it right. The Bent Pyramid was built for the Pharaoh Sneferu and had two burial chambers. One was probably intended for Sneferu and the other for his Great Wife, Queen Hetepheres, but neither was buried inside. The pyramid was abandoned without ever having been used, and we know why. About two-thirds up the face of the pyramid, the angle of incline bends, giving the pyramid its distinctive shape and name. The bend is the result of one of the costliest engineering disasters in history. Pyramids are never constructed on sand; sand shifts, blocks move, and the pyramid moves. Pyramids are built on bedrock, and the Bent Pyramid is no exception. However, one corner of the pyramid rested on a layer of gravel, making that one corner unstable. During the early stages of construction there were no problems, but as the pyramid grew taller and its mass increased, the weight pressed down on the blocks on the unstable corner, causing them to shift. This movement was transmitted inside the pyramid and the walls of the upper burial chamber cracked and started moving inward. In a desperate attempt to stop the room from imploding, the ancient engineers wedged huge fifty-foot cedar of Lebanon logs between opposite walls to keep them from collapsing. This stabilized the pyramid, but clearly it was no longer suitable for Sneferu's burial. The pyramid could, however, serve as his symbolic burial, one of the two burials that pharaohs now had, one for Upper Egypt and one for Lower Egypt. The pyramid was completed as quickly and inexpensively as possible, and this is why its angle was changed. Having a gentler slope at the top greatly reduced the number of blocks in the top third of the pyramid and also reduced the weight on the fragile burial chamber. You can just imagine the discussion between the architects when the burial chamber cracked. "You tell the pharaoh." "No, *you* tell the pharaoh." We don't know Sneferu's reaction, but he didn't give up on pyramids; he built another one at Dashur, just a mile from the unused Bent Pyramid.

Figure 1.5 The Bent Pyramid at Dashur was intended as a true pyramid but because it was unstable, its shape was altered.

Figure 1.6 The Bent Pyramid's burial chamber was imploding so huge logs were wedged between the walls to prevent disaster.

Because this pyramid gleams red in sunlight, it is known as the Red Pyramid and it is here that we can see the beginning of the road that would lead to obelisks. The Red Pyramid, like the others before it, is built of limestone blocks cut from quarries with copper chisels. Its two burial chambers, however, are made of huge granite blocks, and this is where a mystery begins. Granite is *very* different from limestone. Limestone quarries are ancient seabeds formed from shells and skeletal fragments of marine organisms piling on top of each other and compressing for millions of years. Limestone varies considerably in quality but all examples are sedimentary and basically calcium carbonate. As found in Egypt, limestone is fairly homogeneous, soft, and splits easily, which is why it can be worked with copper. Granite, however, is another story. Granite is an igneous rock, formed from the cooling of molten rock (magma) beneath the earth's surface. As it cools and solidifies, mineral grains form and produce a matrix. Three minerals usually compose granite: 1) quartz, which is very hard, light gray, and translucent; 2) mica, usually formed in tiny flecks with quartz; 3) feldspar, which if alkali, will be pinkish red, like the granite found in Egypt.

Because granite is composed of different hard materials, it is not easy to split; there are no regular fault lines. If you take a sharp copper chisel to its surface and hit the chisel with a hammer, after two or three strikes the chisel will be blunt and the granite will be virtually unchanged. How did Egyptian stonemasons, having only copper chisels, quarry the granite blocks for the Red Pyramid's two chambers? Some of the blocks are five feet high and weigh nearly ten tons. To answer that question, it will be best to look at the pyramid that followed the Red Pyramid—The Great Pyramid of Giza.

The Great Pyramid of Giza

The Great Pyramid is the big daddy of them all, not just for its size, but also for its complexity. Built for the pharaoh Khufu, the Great Pyramid has three burial chambers and passages connecting them, all of which presented challenges to

Figure 1.7 The weight above the Great Pyramid's burial chamber is diverted from the chamber's ceiling by huge limestone rafters above.

the pyramid's architect, Hemienu. As we have seen, the problem of internal chambers had been solved by corbeling. But Hemienu wanted a flat ceiling and this was where things became dangerous. We take flat ceilings for granted, but inside an ancient Egyptian pyramid it was a miracle. How do you keep the ceiling from collapsing with thousands of tons of stone pressing down on it? Nothing, not even granite, can support such a weight.

The flat ceiling in the burial chamber in the Great Pyramid is formed by nine granite beams that are 24 feet long and weigh between 47 and 63 tons each. Massive stones, but still, Hemienu believed the ceiling could not support the weight of the pyramid above. His solution was to make sure that the beams didn't support the weight above; they form a false ceiling. Above the ceiling he created a small chamber whose roof is also made of nine granite beams. Above this "relieving chamber" is a second one and then above that are two more chambers till we reach huge limestone rafters at the top of the last chamber. Only the rafters support the weight above and, because they are angled, the weight is distributed into the pyramid's solid masonry. The roof of the burial chamber supports nothing.

The Aswan granite quarry

In all, the burial chamber and the relieving chambers required more than sixty granite beams averaging nearly fifty tons each, more granite than Egypt had quarried in its entire history. Hemienu must have dispatched a small army to the granite quarries in Aswan to produce the beams. They left no written account of how they quarried the beams, but it is certain that they didn't use copper chisels—copper is far too soft to cut granite. One clue we have to their method is the hundreds of black stones that can be found, even today, in the Aswan quarries. Made of dolorite, a stone slightly harder than granite, they were used as pounders, a crude and not very efficient method of pounding beams out of the quarry bed. The quarry master first drew an outline of a beam on the floor of the quarry. Then, perhaps twenty workmen ringed the outline, crouched down with their pounders and began dropping them on the outline. Each time the pounder hit the granite, tiny flakes of mica, feldspar, and schist chipped off the quarry floor. After hours and hours of pounding, the outline

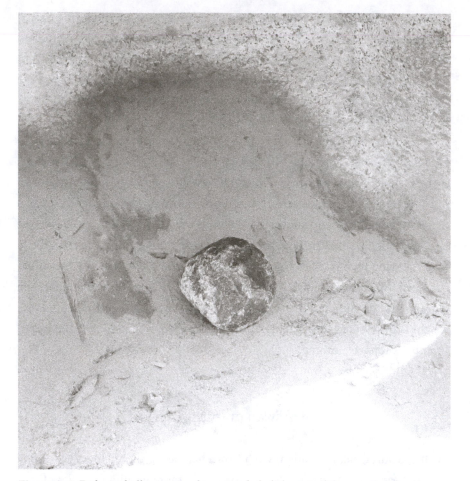

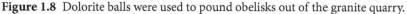

Figure 1.8 Dolorite balls were used to pound obelisks out of the granite quarry.

would have been ringed with indentations looking as if a giant had come with a melon baller and scooped out balls of granite.

As the workers continued pounding, a deep trench formed around the beam, so deep that the men were now totally below ground level. Working shoulder to shoulder in cramped spaces, the pounding continued till the men were more than five feet down in the trench. Now the beam was free from the quarry on all but one side—the bottom, which was still attached to the bedrock. This backbreaking work took its toll on the health of the workers. Aside from squatting, bent over for hours at a time, they were creating clouds of fine

Figure 1.9 The granite quarry at Aswan still shows the effects of blocks having been pounded out.

granite dust that they breathed into their lungs. New Yorkers have learned first hand about "first responders' syndrome," where breathing dust created by the collapse of the Twin Towers ruined the health of many who worked at the 9/11 site. Quarry workers toiled in similar conditions for years on end.

Once the trench around the beam was completed, the workers faced the dangerous task of freeing the beam from the bedrock. At this point they started tunneling from both sides, going beneath the beam, pounding horizontally with their dolorite balls. Eventually both sides met, creating a three-foot-wide tunnel under the beam. Next, a second tunnel was pounded out. With two tunnels completed, two granite blocks, only slightly smaller than the tunnels, were slid into the tunnels, filling them. Next several more tunnels were created and filled with blocks. These blocks supported the beam as the rest of the bottom was pounded away, freeing the beam completely from the bedrock.

The freed beam was still a work in progress; all its surfaces were quite rough, the result of the pounding. You can get a good idea of what a rough beam looked like by wandering through the Aswan Quarry. All along the quarry's floor you can see "melon scoops" left where workers began pounding a beam or obelisk from the quarry. Smoothing the beam's surfaces took hundreds of man-hours. A wet slurry of silica (sand) and granite flakes was placed on the uppermost surface of the beam and used like sandpaper. A small rectangular block of stone would be held in the worker's hand, placed on top of the slurry, and moved back and forth over the beam. With each back and forth movement a bit of the beam's surface was abraded. After days of this, one surface became smooth, so the beam was turned and the next side sanded to near perfection. Dozens of huge beams were prepared in this manner for the roof of Khufu's burial chamber and for the roofs of the relieving chambers above it. In addition to the beams, the walls of the burial chamber itself were made of exactly 100 huge granite blocks, which added to the labor at the Aswan quarries.

The unfinished obelisk

So it was during the Pyramid Age, at the Aswan Quarry, that Egyptians learned how to work large blocks of granite. Centuries later these skills created elegant obelisks soaring more than ten stories into the sky. In the same quarry that provided Khufu's beams lies the largest obelisk ever attempted. It has been roughed out on all but one side; its underside is still attached to the bedrock. The "unfinished obelisk," as it is called, is our greatest clue to how ancient Egyptian engineers cut and erected 500-ton obelisks with such precision that they rest on their pedestals with nothing but gravity keeping them from toppling. Unfinished projects are the best way to learn how something was

Figure 1.10 The unfinished obelisk is the largest block of granite ever quarried.

made. King Horemheb's tomb in the Valley of the Kings was never completed and reveals virtually every stage of tomb building. Some walls have only a painted red grid that guided artists when drawing figures of the gods and pharaoh. Another wall shows how an artist has sketched out scenes and hieroglyphs in black. Some walls reveal where the master artist came and corrected in red roughly drawn figures. Still other parts of the tomb show figures fully carved in raised relief, giving them an added third dimension. Because the tomb is unfinished it is a textbook on how to prepare a king's tomb. The unfinished obelisk is no less instructive; it is a time machine transporting us back to the moment the obelisk was abandoned.

The obelisk is so large that it makes a cameo appearance in Cecil B. DeMille's 1923 silent film *The Ten Commandments* (Charlton Heston is in the 1956 remake). In one scene we see Israelites toiling under the whip of a cruel taskmaster, pulling a large block of stone up an inclined ramp. That incline is the unfinished obelisk! The obelisk is 137 feet long and weighs more than 1,000 tons—heavier than two jumbo jets. Had it been completed it would have weighed more than twice any other obelisk ever erected in Egypt. This was a project of heroic proportions, even for Egypt, and the only reason it is unfinished is because it cracked before it was freed from the quarry. It was a disaster for the men who worked on it, but good fortune for us because it tells the detailed story of its manufacture.

Egyptian obelisks are single pieces of granite, but a perfect block more than 100 feet long is not easy to find. The surface of a granite quarry is irregular, strewn with large boulders, so, to get a long piece, trial pits had to be dug deep into the quarry to see if beneath the surface a suitable block could be found. On one side of the unfinished obelisk we can see the trial pit descending more than 20 feet. As workers pounded it out they watched for cracks in the stone. If they found any, they would have moved on and dug another test pit. If no fissures were found and the quarry master decided to cut the huge obelisk there, the job of removing the rough quarry surface began in earnest. Using dried papyrus stalks as fuel, small fires were lit on top of the irregular surface to be removed. The fire fractured the granite's surface, making it possible to chip away the surface with copper chisels. In the early 1920s, when the quarry was first excavated, Rex Engelbach, an Englishman who was the Chief Inspector of Antiquities for Upper Egypt, found piles of burnt granite chips, the remains of fires set by workmen 3,000 years earlier. Once the surface was smoothed, workers began pounding out the obelisk. Because the obelisk is unfinished we can reconstruct with some certainty how many workers were needed, where they were positioned, and what were the various stages of pounding as the obelisk neared completion.

Like all obelisks, the unfinished obelisk tapers slightly towards its top. At its base, the obelisk is slightly more than 13 feet, so the trench pounded out around the obelisk had to be deeper than that. The trench that now surrounds the obelisk is more than 20 feet deep, 13 feet for the side and another 7 feet to tunnel beneath the obelisk when freeing it from the bedrock. As you look into the trench you can see long individual grooves descending to bedrock where each man squatted with his pounder. Count the grooves and you have a pretty good idea of the number of men who were simultaneously working on the obelisk—130, a sizeable work gang. These poor souls were probably prisoners "sent to the granite."

Today, in Upper Egypt, when workers on an excavation are pulling something heavy, the *rais*, or foreman, chants a line of a work song and the

Figure 1.11 Each groove in the trench along the obelisk is where a worker crouched and pounded out the obelisk.

workmen sing the reply. In this way efforts are coordinated and everyone pulls at the same time. Although obelisk workers were prisoners, one can imagine an overseer, standing above on the obelisk, chanting down to the workers so all pounded in unison. At some point they would have to reverse their positions, to face the opposite direction to pound the other side of the groove. All this pounding created granite chips and powder, so periodically the men would have been told to stop to sweep out the grooves. Otherwise they would be pounding on the debris and not the bedrock.

When Rex Engelbach first excavated the quarry it was full of chips and debris and the obelisk was partially obscured. When the gigantic obelisk was fully cleared, Engelbach had two questions: 1) How long did it take to create such a mammoth? 2) How were the ancient engineers going to move it out of the quarry? To answer the first question Engelbach began pounding. Taking one of the ancient pounders he found in the quarry, he set to work on a block of granite. After an hour's work he had created a depression about a fifth of an inch in the granite. But the area his depression covered was only about one quarter of the surface of one of the grooves the men worked in. So it would actually take four hours to go down a fifth of an inch in the entire groove. Engelbach thought the ancient workers could have done it a bit faster because they were more experienced, so instead of a fifth of an inch each hour they might have gone about a third of an inch. This would mean that every three hours the men bashed out an inch on one quarter of their space. Every twelve hours they would go down an inch. If they worked a twelve-hour day (remember these are prisoners) they would complete one inch each day. The depth of the trench is about 20 feet (240 inches), so the trench would be completed in 240 days or a little more than seven months. This doesn't include undercutting the obelisk to free it completely from the quarry. That is more difficult than creating the trench because the pounding had to be horizontal and you are fighting gravity rather than just dropping the pounder. If we allow nine months for this task, that gives the workers a year and a half to create the obelisk, but the job is not over. They still have to polish it. Because the surface area is so great, this would have added at least another month or two, bringing the entire project close to two years. Some of this is speculation, but a unique pharaoh has left us an account of how long it took to produce an obelisk and we should look at it in some detail.

Hatshepsut's obelisks

The only ancient account we have of how long it took to make an obelisk comes from King Hatshepsut, a woman who ruled Egypt as king. Hatshepsut was the daughter of a king (Tuthmosis I), wife of a king (Tuthmosis II), and stepmother of a king (Tuthmosis III). When her husband died, her stepson, Tuthmosis III, was just a young boy, so Hatshepsut became regent, ruling in his place till he came of age. However, after several years as regent, she declared herself king, wore the pharaoh's false beard of authority, and ruled Egypt as king for more than a decade. Like other Eighteenth Dynasty pharaohs, she built a tomb in the Valley of the Kings, constructed a mortuary temple where she would be worshipped after her death, and erected obelisks, including four at Karnak Temple. During the New Kingdom, when Hatshepsut reigned, obelisks were almost always quarried in pairs. They were placed at both sides of the entrances to the temples the pharaohs built. Their inscriptions usually gave the full five names of the pharaoh and a standard religious text. Of Hatshepsut's four at Karnak, one is still standing, the tallest left in Egypt. The beautifully carved hieroglyphs on its four sides give Hatshepsut's kingly titles and proclaim that she is the daughter of the God Amun.

Like all other large obelisks, Hatshepsut's rests on a single block of granite serving as a pedestal, but, unlike most pedestals, hers bear fascinating inscriptions. She boasts that her two obelisks were cut out of the Aswan Quarry in just seven months, so that gives us an idea that a pair was normally quarried in more than seven months, or she wouldn't be boasting about it. The unfinished obelisk weighs more than both of Hatshepsut's obelisks combined, so Engelbach's estimate of a bit over seven months for just pounding the trenches seems reasonable. But how were they going to get the obelisk out of the quarry and onto a boat on the Nile for transport to its final destination?

We can imagine how the unfinished obelisk was freed from the bedrock, but imagining how the workers were going to move it out of the quarry is far more difficult. The obelisk still rests surrounded by granite, deep in its trench, below the surface of the quarry. There is no obvious path on which the obelisk could have been hauled out of the quarry. There can be no doubt that the ancient engineers had a plan for moving the obelisk once it was quarried; it just isn't clear. It appears as if either the obelisk would have to be raised to the level of the quarry or an incredible amount of granite would have to be removed to create a clear path to the river. Engelbach was the foremost expert on Egyptian stonework and transportation of stones, and he had difficulty coming up with an explanation. The solution he proposed involves raising the obelisk.

Engelbach was convinced that massive levers were used to raise the obelisk out of its trench—probably cedars of Lebanon at least 30 feet long. Placed under the obelisk, with 100 men pulling down on each lever, and with twenty levers on each side, they rocked the obelisk back and forth. As it rocked in one direction, workers slipped small granite blocks under the edge that was off the ground, then the process was repeated for the other side. With many repetitions of this process, the obelisk was slowly raised to the level of the quarry above it.

With the obelisk now at ground level, a smooth path could be created on the surface by heating the rock to fracture it and then chiseling out a smooth track. In this way, a downward slope from the quarry to the desert below was readied for the obelisk's journey to the Nile. Today the modern city of Aswan has grown up around the quarry, but in Engelbach's day one could still see long embankments just north of the quarry that had been prepared to ease the way for various pharaohs' obelisks coming out of the quarry. But how were these obelisks pulled? The unfinished obelisk poses a special problem because it is so big, but we do have records of how the Egyptians moved very large stones.

Djehuti-hotep's colossal statue is moved

Our best representation of Egyptians hauling a large stone is painted on a wall of the tomb of Djehuti-hotep, who governed one of the provinces of Egypt about 500 years after the pyramids were built and just before Egyptian pharaohs began erecting large obelisks. The tomb painting shows a colossal statue of Djehuti-hotep being pulled by 172 men. The statue rests on a sled, and a worker standing by its feet pours water or oil in front to lubricate the way. An overseer stands on the lap of the statue, clapping the rhythm to which the men pull. Moving the statue was not easy, and required considerable coordination. In the painting we see men carrying large wooden beams, perhaps replacement parts in case the sled breaks.

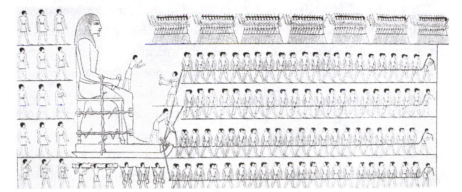

Figure 1.12 The colossal statue of Djehuti-hotep was pulled on a sled by 172 men. Illustration courtesy of Bakha. The artist who did the original drawing of this scene was a young Howard Carter, who later discovered the tomb of Tutankhamen.

The hieroglyphs on the tomb wall tell the story of moving the statue and suggest everyone was happy to participate. Some divisions of the military were called to help, and, in addition, priests hauled on the ropes, locals pitched in, and even the old and infirm. "The aged one among them leaned upon the boy, the strong-armed was with the trembler (palsied). Their hearts rose, their arms became strong." The statue was thirteen cubits (twenty-two feet) high and weighed approximately fifty-eight tons; a large block of stone, but not nearly as heavy as the average obelisk, which weighed in at about 250 tons.

Still, there is no reason why the same techniques used to move Djehuti-hotep's statue couldn't have been ramped up to move 250-ton obelisks. As a matter of fact, we have a scene of two large obelisks on sleds at Hatshepsut's mortuary temple. During the New Kingdom, the era of the great obelisks, most pharaohs built mortuary temples where they would be worshipped after death. They covered the walls of these temples with scenes of the events in their reigns of which they were most proud. Ramses the Great's mortuary temple shows the Battle of Kadesh in great detail, complete with Ramses in his chariot almost single-handedly holding off the Hittite army till support came. Ramses III (no relation to Ramses the Great) was proud of all the donations he presented to the temple of Amun, so the walls of his mortuary temple contain lists of all the cattle, linen, jars of oils and perfumes, and food that he contributed. Hatshepsut's mortuary temple, called Deir el Bahri, is unlike any other and depicts events not seen anywhere else in Egypt.

"Deir el Bahri" is modern Arabic for "Place of the Northern Monastery." Centuries after Hatshepsut died, Christian monks established monasteries on the west bank of Thebes. Some made Hatshepsut's temple their living quarters. Eventually the monastery was abandoned and almost disappeared beneath centuries of accumulated rubble. At the end of the nineteenth century Egyptology was becoming a respected discipline and more and more researchers came to excavate, not for treasure, but for knowledge. Deir el Bahri was one of the first sites excavated by members of London's newly founded Egypt Exploration Fund. Their director of excavations, Edouard Naville, was primarily interested in inscriptions, not objects, and was keen on clearing the temple to learn more about the mysterious Queen/King Hatshepsut. Naville's excavation team included a young artist named Howard Carter who would go on to become an archaeologist and discover Tutankhamen's tomb in the Valley of the Kings, just a few miles from Deir el Bahri. Carter's job was to record the scenes on the temple's walls as they emerged from centuries of accumulated rubble.

The temple is most famous for its scenes of a trading expedition Hatshepsut sent to the land of Punt, somewhere around modern Somalia or Eretria. The carvings on the walls are the first ethnographic depictions of sub-Saharan Africa. We see thatched houses on stilts, the obese Queen of Punt, and Egyptian ships being loaded with frankincense and myrrh, ivory and ebony, and exotic animal skins. These are the scenes that draw millions of tourists each year to Deir el Bahri, but there is another unique scene in an isolated part of the temple that is rarely visited by tourists. It is the only place in Egypt where you can see obelisks being moved.

Hatshepsut was proud of her trading expedition to Punt, but she was also proud of the obelisks she quarried, so she decorated her temple with scenes of two of them being transported from Aswan to Karnak Temple. The carvings are badly damaged, and you must study them for a while before your eyes can discern what is going on, but it is quite a remarkable scene. Most amazing is that both obelisks were placed on one boat. Each obelisk weighs more than 300 tons; why risk losing them both if the ship goes down? Wouldn't it be easier to have separate boats for each? Think about the logistics of maneuvering two obelisks on the deck of one ship. The obelisks are not side by side; they are shown end to end, making their loading even more difficult—the ship has to be twice as long. This is such a remarkable scene that some archaeologists have suggested that the obelisks are not really end to end; they are just shown that way because perspective would have made it difficult to show the two if they were side by side. In Robert Partridge's *Transportation in Ancient Egypt* he says, "In the reliefs, the obelisks are shown end to end on the deck of the barge, but this is assumed to be an artistic convention, which demanded that both obelisks be clearly seen."[1] I think this is wrong. Ancient Egyptian shipwrights really did construct boats that long to transport obelisks. We have confirmation of this in the tomb of Ineni, the architect who served Hatshepsut's father, Tuthmosis I. One wall of his tomb contains his autobiography, where he boasts of his greatest accomplishments. Ineni is most famous for having constructed the first tomb in the Valley of the Kings for his pharaoh. This was a great innovation and he says it was done secretly, "no one seeing, no one hearing." He was also proud of overseeing the erection of two of Tuthmosis's obelisks, and declares that he "built the august boat of 120 cubits in length, 40 cubits in its width in order to transport these obelisks." The boat was approximately 206 feet long, so the carvings of Hatshepsut's end-to-end obelisks were no quirk of Egyptian perspective. They were almost certainly moved on one long boat, just like her father's. Her boat would have been even larger than Tuthmosis I's. His obelisks were about 75 feet long, but Hatshepsut's were nearly 20 feet longer, so her boat would have been more than 250 feet long.

The scenes on the wall at Deir el Bahri provide us with wonderful details of moving the granite obelisks. We see the two obelisks, still on their giant sleds on which they were hauled from the quarry to the Nile. The obelisks lie on the deck with their bases facing each other, the points of the obelisks on the bow and stern of the ship. To ensure that the ship's deck doesn't collapse under the immense weight, the captain has run six thick ropes from the bow, over the masts, and down to the stern. This is called a "hog truss" and takes stress off the deck. Usually Egyptian ships have one rudder at the stern for steering, but this barge is so large it has two. A true barge, it was not self-powered, but was controlled and steered by three rows of nine tugboats each. The ships are not all identical. The three ships closest to the barge have elaborate cabins, decorated with the king's cartouches and paintings of the gods. These three boats housed the officers and officials overseeing the transport. They were within hailing distance of the barge so instructions could be easily conveyed.

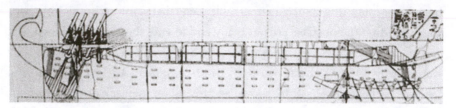

Figure 1.13 A pair of Queen Hatshepsut's obelisks were transported end to end on a single boat.

Each tug has approximately thirty rowers, so when we add to this the pilot ships at the head of each column of tugs and all the officers, we have approximately 1,000 sailors dedicated to bringing King Hatshepsut's obelisks north. The great advantage of going north is that they are going with the current. It might have been impossible to control such a large barge using sail-power against the current. Still, it was a difficult venture.

They would have moved the obelisks during the season of inundation, when the Nile was high and there was less chance of being hung up on a sandbar. Even so, sailors on the pilot ships are shown on the prows of their vessels, long poles in hand, taking soundings. Three smaller boats, not tied to the three columns of tugs but shown near the barge, were probably used to communicate the soundings to the officers on or near the barge. The journey downstream from Aswan to Thebes took several days but the special moment Hatshepsut chose to commemorate for eternity was the fleet's successful arrival at Thebes. The military is out to parade the landing of the obelisks at Karnak Temple.

Pliny the Elder to the rescue

Hatshepsut has provided us with a record of how her obelisks were transported, but she does not tell us how they were loaded onto the barge and taken off, and this was not an easy task. There were no large cranes in ancient Egypt, so the obelisks weren't hoisted into the air and placed on the deck of the ship. There is only one ancient account of how an obelisk was loaded onto a barge, but it is not ancient enough to be reliable. The account comes from Pliny the Elder, a Roman statesman and military man who lived during the first century AD, so he was reporting events that took place more than a thousand years before his time.

In the Preface to his *Natural History*, Pliny says that he covers 20,000 important subjects and has consulted more than 100 authorities. Pliny is, indeed, encyclopedic, but he isn't always right. Sometimes his translations from his Greek sources are a bit off, sometimes he is uncritical of dubious authors, and sometimes he is just confused, but he is always interesting and has something to say about almost any topic. In the end, his curiosity killed him. Pliny was in charge of the Roman fleet at the Bay of Naples when Mt. Vesuvius erupted on August 23, AD 79. Always gathering information for his next work, Pliny sailed across the bay to get a closer look at the volcano. When he landed, poisonous gases killed him almost immediately. He was 57. Pliny loved the unusual, so it is not surprising that in his *Natural History* he talks about Egyptian temples and pyramids and he even gives us an account of how an obelisk was loaded on a barge.

During Pliny's lifetime several obelisks were brought from Egypt to Rome as trophies for the emperors, but the Romans loaded them differently from the Egyptians. Romans had cranes and winches that could lift an obelisk; the Egyptians didn't. Pliny is our only ancient source of how an obelisk was loaded in the time of the pharaohs. He says that once the obelisk was hauled down to the river, a canal was dug from the river to beneath the obelisk, so the obelisk now formed a bridge over the canal. Next, two barges that were to carry the obelisk were brought to the banks of the Nile and loaded with small, one-foot granite cubes that totaled twice the weight of the obelisk. The barges, now low in the water because of their heavy loads, were towed under the obelisk and while in this position the granite cubes were off-loaded. As the ships' loads lightened, they rose in the water till they came in contact with the obelisk and their buoyancy lifted the obelisk off the ground.

When I first read this account I wondered why Pliny was talking about *two* barges for *one* obelisk. How did it work? Was the obelisk half on one deck, half on the other? Were the barges lashed together? It really didn't make sense to me. However, when I read Hatshepsut's account of how she placed two obelisks on one barge, I knew how Pliny got his account. He had read some earlier account and misunderstood/mistranslated it. It wasn't saying two barges for one obelisk; it was one barge for two obelisks. We know the Egyptians did it that way. But would Pliny's account of the canal dug under the obelisk still work for two obelisks on one barge?

Once the first obelisk was on deck, did they load the granite cubes onto the ship and repeat the operation for the second obelisk? It certainly would have been more difficult for two. We know they loaded the barge, we just can't be sure of the exact method. The other unsolved obelisk mystery is what happened to them once they reached their final destination? How were they off-loaded? How were they raised to an upright position on their pedestals? Our man Pliny has something to say about this too, but once again, much is questionable.

We have to remember that Pliny never visited Egypt, so he is relying on hearsay, hearsay that was more than a thousand years old. He offers his readers a remarkable and entertaining account of the erecting of one of Ramses the Great's obelisks. The first of Pliny's dubious claims is the size of the obelisk, a whopping 120 cubits, which would make it more than 200 feet tall, far taller than even the gigantic unfinished obelisk in the Aswan Quarry. Highly unlikely. He got the size wrong, but there are other elements to the story that are even more difficult to accept. He says that Ramses was concerned that the "machine" they were using to erect the obelisk might not be adequate, so he tied one of his sons to the top of the obelisk so the workers would be extra careful when raising the obelisk. It makes a great story, but it is highly unlikely. If you think about it carefully, you realize that Pliny never gives the details of how the obelisk was raised; he just mentions the use of a "machine." I think this is because he figured they did it the same way as the Romans, with a large scaffold and winches and capstans—"machines." But the Egyptians didn't have winches and capstans and couldn't have erected their obelisks in the Roman manner.

The best clues we have are the pedestals on which the obelisks once stood. My students are always amazed when I show them an obelisk on its pedestal and then tell them that the only thing keeping the obelisk upright is gravity. It is a great balancing act. No pins or clamps fix the obelisks to the base. The pedestals are always single blocks of granite, weighing around 50 tons for the larger obelisks. When the Romans took their obelisks to Rome, they left the pedestals behind and these pedestals help us figure out the method used to erect an obelisk in ancient Egypt.

The pedestals are quite impressive in themselves. Most are taller than me, so I have spent considerable time crawling on railings, on top of trash baskets, and on ladders to examine the top surfaces, the ones on which the obelisks rested. Almost all have a groove running across the top. Why?

Imagine the pedestal is in place in front of the temple where we want the obelisk. Now we just have to balance a 350-ton granite needle on top of it. A ramp is built leading up to the pedestal, but high above it, perhaps 100 feet above it. The obelisk is hauled up the ramp bottom first, till the bottom of the obelisk is above the pedestal. Next, the obelisk is slowly lowered down the other side of the ramp till one edge of the obelisk's bottom rests on the pedestal. Perhaps to control the descent of the obelisk onto the base, the pit was filled with sand that was slowly dug out from the bottom, causing the obelisk to descend slowly into position. The purpose of the groove was to engage the lead edge of the obelisk's bottom, so it didn't skid across the pedestal. Once the obelisk's edge was in the groove, ropes fixed to the top of the obelisk were used to pull the obelisk upright.

The quarrying, polishing, transportation, and erecting of massive obelisks in ancient times was a status symbol reserved only for pharaohs, a sign of great wealth and power. Obelisk building reached its peak during the New Kingdom (1570–1086 BC) and the great obelisks tourists see today were erected by New Kingdom pharaohs—Tuthmosis I, Hatshepsut, and Ramses II. After the New Kingdom, Egypt began a long, slow decline and we don't have any massive obelisks from this period. At the very end of the decline, Egypt was ruled by Greek pharaohs, all descended from Alexander the Great's general, Ptolemy.

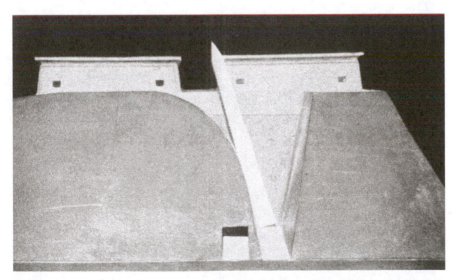

Figure 1.14 Rex Engelbach's theory—that obelisks were pulled up a ramp and then slid onto their bases—is still considered the most probable explanation.

These last pharaohs of Egypt, all named Ptolemy, ruled Egypt for 300 years (305–30 BC). They built large temples in the Egyptian style, including Dendera, Edfu, and Kom Ombo, but we don't have remains of obelisks erected in front of these temples. We do have one small obelisk of this period from Philae temple (it now stands in England) but it is far smaller than the New Kingdom obelisks.

With the death of Cleopatra VII, the last Ptolemaic ruler, the Romans took control of Egypt. The Roman emperors were impressed by the Egyptian obelisks still standing on their pedestals and viewed them as symbols of power. Rather than quarry and erect their own in Rome, they carefully lowered Egyptian obelisks, brought them across the Mediterranean, and re-erected them in Rome. For the emperors they were trophies of war, and thus began 2,000 years of obelisks in exile.

2

Rome's Obelisks

During its long history Egypt was invaded, conquered, and vandalized by foreigners from many directions: the Hyksos, Persians, Kushites, Syrians, Assyrians, Greeks, Romans, Turks, French, and English, among others. For the most part, conquerors from the East tended to destroy what they found; those from the West tended to pillage and loot. Europeans carried home all kinds of spoils because they were exotic and beautiful, but also as symbols of conquest. The largest and most visible of these objects were obelisks, and the conquerors who carried away the most were the Romans.

As we saw in the last chapter, obelisks were difficult to make, move, or erect, being among the heaviest objects ever moved over land in the pre-industrial age. The Egyptians created, moved, and erected them using primitive tools and methods, the details of which are still argued over by academics and engineers. But by the time of the Roman conquest of Egypt, in the last days of the Egyptian Empire but the early days of the Roman Empire—the time of Cleopatra and the Caesars—the technology for moving large loads had advanced considerably. Nevertheless, moving objects up to 100 feet in length and weighing more than 350 tons was a daunting task. And then they had to be placed on their bases. Augustus, who clearly was fascinated by obelisks, was up to the task. First he moved at least two obelisks within Egypt to decorate the Caesarium at Alexandria. Then he took it up a notch and built special transport ships to bring obelisks to Rome, a practice followed by his successors. Because of their efforts, today Rome has more standing obelisks than any city in the world—more than Cairo, Alexandria, and Luxor combined.

We don't know how many obelisks were taken from Egypt, because there was never an inventory of how many existed in ancient times or where they stood, but it was dozens. Probably more than two dozen were hauled off by the Romans with most going to Rome and one to Constantinople. Many lie lost, buried beneath the streets or buildings of Rome. That sounds odd: How could something as large as an obelisk be lost beneath the streets of a bustling city? But we know it is true. Most of the obelisks standing today in Rome were rediscovered under the city. This chapter will trace the history of the Roman obelisks that we do know about, starting with the story of how Rome became involved with Egypt in the first place, conquered it, and turned Egypt into a possession.

For the three hundred years before the Romans took over, the Ptolemies ran Egypt into the ground, extracting as much as they could while putting very little back for the people. The Ptolemies rarely ventured south of their capital city, Alexandria, and as far as we know only one ever bothered to learn the language of the country they governed. If you were an Egyptian who wanted to rise within the bureaucracy, you learned Greek. The last Ptolemy, Cleopatra VII, was different from her ancestors. She cared about Egypt, learned Egyptian, visited the temples, participated in religious rituals, and attempted to restore Egypt to its former greatness. Unfortunately, she shared the throne with her brother, Ptolemy XIII, who was jealous of his sister and raised an army to depose her. With a civil war about to break out, powerful Rome entered the picture.

Caesar and Cleopatra

Egypt was "the bread basket of Rome." With its fertile soil along the banks of the Nile, Egypt produced vast amounts of grain, much of it exported to feed Rome's growing population. Fearing that civil war would disrupt the flow of grain to Rome, Julius Caesar was sent to Alexandria to maintain order. By the time he arrived in Egypt, Cleopatra, fearing an assassination attempt by her brother, had fled the palace and was raising her own army. However, when she heard Caesar had arrived she knew she had to return to the palace before Ptolemy and his advisors convinced Caesar to side with them against her. This is the point at which the teenage queen made her famous entrance into the palace concealed in a rolled-up carpet. This is the stuff of legend, and it's true, but much of the Cleopatra legend is false. After her death she was portrayed by the Romans as a beautiful femme fatale, seducing good Roman men. Contemporary portraits of Cleopatra, however, do not show her to be particularly beautiful, but she was extremely intelligent, articulate, and spoke several languages. These talents may have attracted Caesar to this young queen. Roman women were not usually well educated and certainly none had the power of an Egyptian queen. As worldly as Caesar was, he had never met a woman like Cleopatra and was completely captivated.

Caesar returned to Rome, leaving Cleopatra, now on the throne by herself, and pregnant. (Her brother had conveniently drowned in the Nile.) After she gave birth to Caesarion—"little Caesar"— Caesar sent for Cleopatra and Caesarion, shocking Rome. Caesar had a good Roman wife, so what was he doing with an Egyptian queen? The Roman Senate feared that Caesar was not just enamored with Cleopatra, but also with the idea of ruling as a god/king rather than as a citizen of the Roman Republic. Thus, on the "ides of March," Caesar was assassinated on the steps of the Senate. Alone, in a city hostile to her, Cleopatra fled to Egypt with Caesarion.

The death of Caesar disturbed the balance of power in Rome, creating intrigues. Pompey, the second member of the ruling triumvirate, had been assassinated on his way to Egypt, so a new triumvirate was formed around Octavian, the only remaining member. Eventually Marc Antony, a former ally of Caesar, was selected as a new member of the triumvirate, but it was a triumvirate that couldn't agree on the course Rome was to take. Marc Antony defected and formed an alliance with Cleopatra. Their intention was to defeat Octavian, Rome's rising star, and conquer the world.

Antony and Cleopatra

The war of Antony and Cleopatra against Octavian ended at the Battle of Actium, where the ships of the Egyptian fleet were pitted against Octavian's navy. From the beginning, Octavian's forces were winning and, as the battle raged, Cleopatra turned her ship towards Egypt and fled. Antony, seeing her departure, ordered his ship to follow, leaving his fleet dispirited and soon to be defeated. Both Antony and Cleopatra made their way back to Alexandria.

Antony, depressed, sulked. Cleopatra, knowing that all was lost, planned for the future. She knew that Octavian's troops would soon arrive in the city and that there was no possibility to resist them. She sent her son Caesarion, and his tutor, to the Red Sea with a significant portion of Egypt's treasury. Her hope was that Caesarion would flee to India and found a new dynasty.

The end of the line

As Octavian approached, Cleopatra barricaded herself inside the palace. She knew that if she were captured Octavian would bring her back to Rome to be displayed in chains in a "triumph." With her handmaidens' aid, she committed suicide, probably by the bite of a cobra smuggled to her in a basket of fruit. With Cleopatra's death, the line of Ptolemies ruling Egypt ended. Her son, Caesarion, betrayed by his tutor, was told it was safe to return to Alexandria. When Octavian saw the boy his only comment was "One Caesar is enough," and he had the boy killed. Antony took his own life, so in a sense it is true that Cleopatra led both Caesar and Antony to their deaths, but not in the way Roman historians would portray it. She was an intelligent, well-intentioned ruler who seems to have exhibited true affection for the only two men with whom she allied herself. The Roman version, however, allowed them to resurrect Caesar as a good Roman, seduced by an evil beauty.

How "Cleopatra's Needles" became Cleopatra's

Octavian, now the sole ruler of Rome and consequently of Egypt, changed his name to Augustus and decided to enhance the Caesarium, built to honor Caesar. (Octavian had been adopted by Caesar, so he was actually honoring his father.) To make the temple worthy of the great man, in 12/13 BC Augustus had two of Tuthmosis III's obelisks moved from Heliopolis, near modern Cairo, to Alexandria and re-erected in front of the mausoleum. As centuries passed, the building disappeared, the original significance of the obelisks was lost, and they became known as "Cleopatra's Needles." As far as we know, these obelisks were the first moved by Romans, but they would not be the last.

Augustus wanted obelisks as trophies of war to decorate Rome. Today there are a dozen ancient obelisks standing in Rome, but if the accounts of early geographers and travelers are to be believed, there are at least another dozen or so lost beneath the city's streets.

Piazza del Popolo Obelisk

Figure 2.1 The Piazza del Popolo obelisk, erected by Augustus around AD 10, was the first erected in Rome.

The first obelisk that traveled across the Mediterranean now stands in Rome's Piazza del Popolo. It originally stood in Heliopolis. When that city was sacked by the Persians, dozens of the city's obelisks were ripped from their bases and tumbled to the ground. Strabo, an ancient historian (63 BC–20 AD), describes King Cambyses' destruction of the city, which "partly by fire and partly by iron sought to outrage the temples, mutilating them and burning them on every side, just as he did with the obelisks" (*Geography* 17, I, 27). By the time of Strabo, Heliopolis was deserted. When Augustus wanted an obelisk to grace Rome, he went to Heliopolis. The obelisk was 65 feet long and weighed 230 tons, but the Romans could rely on the experience of Egyptian engineers and sailors for advice. First it was floated down the Nile on a barge to the port at Alexandria. This was not a trivial operation, but had been done many times before. Crossing the Mediterranean was another matter; even the Egyptians had never taken an obelisk across open waters, and here the Romans had to invent new technology.

The special ship constructed to transport the obelisk was such a thing of wonder that, Pliny tells us, "that which carried the first was solemnly laid up by Augustus of revered memory in a permanent dock at Putouli to celebrate the remarkable achievement; but later it was destroyed by fire." There are no contemporary drawings or paintings of this ship so what it looked like is a mystery today. We do, however, have the obelisk, and its hieroglyphic inscription tells us quite a bit about its history. The obelisk was quarried by Seti I, who died before the inscriptions were completed, so his son, Ramses the Great, completed the inscriptions, and thus the obelisk has two different styles of hieroglyphs on its four surfaces.

Augustus erected the obelisk in Rome around AD 10 and inscribed on its base his connection to noble Caesar, as well as establishing the obelisk as a war trophy:

> Augustus son of divine Caesar dedicated the obelisk
> To the sun when Egypt had been brought under the
> Sway of the Roman people.

As centuries passed, the obelisk fell or was taken down and disappeared beneath the ground. Rediscovered in 1587 when Pope Sixtus V's mania for obelisks was at its peak, it was re-erected by Domenico Fontana (we will hear more about Fontana in the next chapter when we see how he moved the Vatican Obelisk). The obelisk is sometimes called the "Flaminian obelisk" because it is first seen through the Porta Flaminia. Augustus brought one more obelisk to Rome. It is similar in size, but has a totally different tale to tell.

The Gnomon Obelisk (Monte Citorio)

Figure 2.2 The Monte Citorio obelisk was used as a gnomon for a sundial inlaid in brass on the pavement. The globe at the top has a slit to allow sunlight through. It never worked.

Augustus's second obelisk bears the same inscription on its base as the first. This, however, is where the similarities between the two obelisks end. It was originally quarried by King Psamtek II of Dynasty XXVI, and is one of the last ever to be erected by an Egyptian pharaoh. Soon after the obelisk was dedicated in Heliopolis, the Persians invaded and for the next 500 years Egypt was dominated by foreigners. Augustus had the obelisk brought to Rome and erected it in the Campo Marzio, where it served not merely as a war trophy but as a gnomon that cast its shadow on a huge sundial laid into the pavement with brass rods. The sundial, with mosaics of the four winds, was so remarkable that Pliny the historian mentions it in his *Natural History*. It may have been marvelous, but it wasn't useful for very long. Pliny tells us that after thirty years it was out of phase with the calendar (*Natural History*, XXXVI, 72, 15).

Although the obelisk didn't work well as a gnomon, it remained standing longer than almost any other obelisk in Rome. It wasn't till the eleventh century that it fell or was pulled down, probably in 1084 when the Norman duke, Robert Guiscard, sacked Rome. The obelisk was discovered in the sixteenth century by a barber digging a latrine behind his shop. He hoped to receive a reward from Pope Julius II (1503–13), but the Pope wasn't interested and the barber reburied it! Julius II was the first of five popes who would become involved with burying or unearthing Augustus's gnomon obelisk. In 1587, just after Fontana had moved the Vatican Obelisk, Pope Sixtus V saw his chance to erect another obelisk and asked Fontana to excavate it. Fontana reported that the obelisk was too damaged to re-erect and a week later his workmen reburied it. In 1647, when work began to extend the Acqua Vergine to supply the fountains in the Piazza Navona, the workmen hit the obelisk and Father Athanasius Kircher was called in to examine it.

The last man who knew everything

Kircher was one of the strangest Renaissance scholars, and that says a lot. Widely acknowledged as a genius, some felt he was also a charlatan. He constructed early computers—"arks" or chests that calculated, made music, and even translated ancient languages. He is even said to have built a mechanical vomiting rooster! Today he is best known for his attempt to translate the hieroglyphs on Rome's obelisks.

Kircher was born in what is now Germany on May 2, 1602, the youngest of nine children. His genius was recognized early and at the age of 16 he entered a Jesuit College, where he studied Greek and Hebrew, the start of a lifelong fascination with ancient languages. At the age of 18 he was admitted to the Society of Jesus and soon began teaching Syriac, Hebrew, and mathematics. When the Archbishop of Mainz visited Kircher, he was so impressed by the young Jesuit's calculating machines that he invited him to Mainz for four years to teach and do research. Kircher asked to be sent to the East as a missionary so he could study Chinese, but because he was so learned, everyone wanted to keep him around.

In 1630 Kircher exhibited one of his most controversial inventions, a "sunflower clock." It was a heliotropic plant, the nightshade, whose seeds, when attached to a cork bobbing in water, supposedly followed the motions of the sun and thus could be used to tell time. Kircher claimed he obtained the seeds from an Arab merchant. French philosopher René Descartes wondered why seeds from Avignon or Rome couldn't do what Arabian seeds could. Descartes concluded: "The Jesuit has a lot of tricks; he is more charlatan than scholar."[1] Descartes was in the minority. Rome was captivated by the brilliant priest. Kircher reciprocated by promising to translate the hieroglyphs on Rome's obelisks. He would unlock the wisdom of the ancients for his new city, just what Rome wanted to hear. Central to the Renaissance was a quest for ancient knowledge, wisdom from which everyone would benefit, and no civilization was older or wiser than Egypt's. Kircher was the right man, in the right place, at the right time, but could he deliver? In 1643 he published *Lingua Aegyptiaca Restituta* ("The Egyptian Language Restored"), where he claimed to have deciphered hieroglyphs, releasing ancient Egyptian wisdom from 2,000 years of captivity. Very few knew how wrong he was.

When Kircher was called to examine the fallen gnomon obelisk, he was fascinated with its former use and reconstructed what the sundial must have looked like, publishing his ideas and drawings in *Obeliscus Pamphilius* (1650)— Pamphili was the Pope's last name—one of the earliest works on obelisks. In 1666 Kircher was called upon by Pope Alexander to completely excavate the obelisk. When Kircher made an inspection he discovered that the obelisk had been broken into three large fragments that along with its original pedestal were now in the basements of houses that had been built over them. Kircher reported to the Pope that if the houses were demolished an excavation was possible, but to no avail. A few years after Kircher's report, the Pope died and the gnomon obelisk once more languished underground till yet another pope became interested in it.

By 1748 the owners of the land in which the obelisk rested had decided to demolish the now dilapidated houses above the three fragments and base. Pope Benedict XIV visited the site and asked the eighty-two-year-old engineer, Niccolo Zabaglia, to resurrect the obelisk. With the aid of new lifting cranes invented by Zabaglia, after centuries underground, the three pieces of the obelisk were finally raised. Today, above No. 3 Piazza del Parlamento is a plaque commemorating the obelisk's original position.

> Benedict XIV dug out with great expense and skill this
> obelisk elegantly inscribed with Egyptian letters, brought
> to Rome by the Emperor Caesar Augustus, when Egypt had
> been brought under the sway of the Romans, dedicated to
> the sun and erected in the Campo Marzio to indicate the shadow
> of the sun and the extension of the days and nights on a
> pavement of stone with inlaid lines of bronze. Broken and

Figure 2.3 Nicolao Galeotti's 1757 engraving shows the Campo Marzio obelisk as it was, in pieces, when it was discovered in 1748.

overturned by inclemency, time and barbarians, buried
under the earth and buildings, Benedict transported it to
a neighboring site for the public good and the support of
letters, and ordered this memorial put up in order that
the ancient place should not eventually be forgotten.

As the plaque shows, Benedict did more than just rescue the obelisk from
obscurity. He wanted to record the history of an ancient monument before it was
lost. So he asked Bandini, an antiquarian/librarian, to write a history of the obelisk.
In addition to Bandini's history of the obelisk the Pope asked James Stuart, a
talented illustrator turned antiquarian, to copy the hieroglyphs on its four faces.

Athenian Stuart

Stuart began his career as an artist by decorating ladies' fans with romantic
scenes, but in 1741 his life changed forever when he decided to walk from
London to Rome! Once he arrived, he studied Latin and Greek, fell in love with
ancient monuments and became an antiquarian. In 1748 he proposed to
publish *An Accurate Description of the Antiquities of Athens*, which earned him
the nickname "Athenian Stuart." Stuart provided the first highly accurate
reproductions of hieroglyphs that capture both their beauty and form, and
Bandini reproduced the drawings in his publication. In a sense, Stuart's copies
of the obelisk's hieroglyphs are the beginning of modern epigraphy—the
careful, accurate recording of inscriptions.

Stuart wasn't just the father of epigraphy; he also improved excavation
techniques. When he excavated the ground where the obelisk stood, he
carefully recorded the levels at which he found objects, examining what later
archaeologists would call "stratigraphy." His most important discovery points
to why the obelisk/gnomon didn't work as a sundial. It was not aligned to the
four compass points, as would be necessary for it to function properly. He
concluded that the obelisk was erected first and then, as an afterthought, a
sundial was laid into the pavement around the obelisk.

In spite of all the attention the obelisk was finally receiving, it still wasn't
erected. It was too badly damaged. The obelisk had been part of Pope Benedict's
plan to beautify the Piazza di Monte Citorio, but since the obelisk couldn't be
erected, he selected instead a different tall ancient monument, the column of

Antoninus Pius. Little did he know that would lead to the destruction of the column and the miraculous resurrection of the obelisk.

Antoninus Pius's column was cut from Egypt's Aswan granite quarries in the sixth year of the Emperor Trajan's reign (AD 105/6) and was erected in the Emperor's funerary temple by the his two sons to commemorate the deification of their father and Faustina, their mother. It has always struck me as ironic that poor Caesar was assassinated because the Romans feared he wanted to rule as an emperor and god. When Augustus crowned himself emperor, the republic was dissolved and from then on the emperors all wanted to be declared gods.

In 1705 the column, along with its spectacular base, was moved to the Piazza di Monte Citorio and was stored in a woodshed to protect it while it awaited resurrection. The base was even more impressive than the pillar. One side showed the apotheosis of Antoninus and Faustina, but it also featured a reclining youth, symbolizing the Campo Marzio, who holds the gnomon obelisk! Another side of the base showed military games held in honor of the deification. The base was set in place on the Piazza to receive the column, but

Figure 2.4 The Monte Citorio obelisk was erected in the Campo Marzio. The base of the obelisk shows a reclining youth, symbolizing the Campo Marzio, holding the obelisk.

before the column was erected the woodshed caught fire, destroying it. Fortunately the base was not kept in the shed, so now the Piazza had a burned pillar, a badly damaged obelisk, and a spectacular base. In 1787 a visit by the German poet, Goethe, gave new lives to all three.

Goethe had an eye for antiquities and realized that the beautiful Twenty-Sixth Dynasty hieroglyphs on the obelisk's three fragments were something special; he had plaster casts of them made for his collection. Goethe's attention created renewed interest in the obelisk, and two years later Pope Pius VI commissioned the architect Giovanni Antolini to join the three fragments and re-erect the obelisk. Pius VI was the sixth pope to attempt re-erecting the obelisk, and now the burned column made it possible. Previous architects faced with the task had pointed out that sections of the obelisk were missing and the three fragments couldn't simply be joined. Replacement segments had to be carved and only the same stone as the obelisk, Egyptian pink granite, would work. Now, with the remnants of the burned pillar, Antolini had a source of pink granite from the same quarry at Aswan that was used for the obelisk. If the shed hadn't burned, the gnomon obelisk might still be lying on the ground.

Antolini's contract stipulated that he had three years to complete the project and he began by getting the massive pillar base out of the way. He moved it to the Vatican, where it can be seen today, in the courtyard of the Vatican Museum. By January 25, 1790 Antolini had the obelisk's original base in place and by September 4 he had the scaffolding needed to raise the obelisk, but then things slowed down. It took three more years to repair the obelisk and cast the bronze ornaments that would be placed on top. As an *homage* to the obelisk's function as a gnomon, the ball on top was cast with a slit to admit a ray of sunlight. Finally, on June 14, 1792 the top piece of the obelisk was put in place. The inscription on the base tells the obelisk's difficult history.

> Cleansed from dirt and with added ornaments,
> Sixtus VI restored to town and heaven King
> Sesostris's obelisk, which Caesar Augustus had
> placed in the campus as an indicator of hours. But
> destroyed by the violence of fire and passage of
> time, had been left by Benedict XVI, after he had
> removed it from the accumulated earth.

The plaque wrongly attributes the obelisk to 'King Sesostris.' There were actually three kings named Sesostris and all lived during the Middle Kingdom (2000–1850 B C), more than a thousand years before Psamtek erected the obelisk. Despite Kircher's claims, hieroglyphs had not yet been deciphered, so no one could read the cartouche containing Psamtek II's name and they guessed it said Sesostris.

Augustus's gnomon obelisk had suffered greatly over the centuries; now, even though it was finally erect again, its trials and tribulations were not yet over. In 1963 one of the bronze ornamental stars fell from the top, prompting the first careful examination of the obelisk in more than 150 years. All the bronze ornaments were badly corroded, but worse, the obelisk was in danger of falling; it was not as it appeared to be. When you look at it from the front, facing the church, you see beautiful hieroglyphs, but as you walk around the obelisk the picture changes. On one side are large patches, and on the back there are practically no hieroglyphs—it's all repairs and it doesn't look solid. Thin sheets of granite are backing the obelisk, and what's behind the sheets began causing problems in the 1960s. When Antolini repaired the obelisk, he used granite from Pius's column, but also bricks held together with iron clamps to fill the inside spaces. The clamps were now rusted and, if one broke, the bricks could shift, sending the obelisk crashing to the pavement. Throughout the 1960s conservators worked frantically, replacing the clamps and stabilizing the obelisk. Today the obelisk's future looks far brighter than its past.

Esqualine Obelisk (Santa Maria Maggiore)

After the death of Augustus in AD 14, two 30-foot obelisks were quarried at Aswan, brought 800 miles down the Nile to Alexandria and transported across the Mediterranean to Rome, where they were erected in front of Augustus's family crypt—a fitting tribute to the first Roman ruler of Egypt, who was so devoted to obelisks. As the centuries passed, the crypt fell into disuse and was robbed. The obelisks were torn down, probably by Christian zealots. By the Middle Ages, the two obelisks had disappeared beneath the ground. In 1519 Pope Leo X excavated one of the obelisks and moved its three fragments to the street in front of the crypt. He intended to join the three pieces and re-erect it, but the fragments remained in the street for more than half a century, a reviled

Figure 2.5 The Esqualine Obelisk originally stood in front of the Emperor Augustus's family crypt.

obstruction to traffic! When Pope Sixtus V came to power, he was keen to erect it; he wanted an obelisk in front of every church "as trophies or spoils of war won from paganism by triumphant religion." But sometimes even popes have to wait. Fontana, "The Pope's Architect," was in the midst of moving the Vatican Obelisk (see next chapter). Finally in 1587 he dismantled the scaffolding in St. Peter's Square and put it into service moving Augustus's obelisk to the Esquiline Square, just behind the Basilica of St. Maria Maggiore.

Quirinale Obelisk

Augustus's second obelisk was discovered in 1549 but disappeared beneath the ground soon after it was found and didn't reappear till 1781, when an alley near the mausoleum was being repaired. Pope Pius VI wanted to erect it at the Piazza del Quirinale, on the highest hill in Rome, where the papal administrative offices stood. The architect Giovanni Antinori was given the job, but before he could erect the obelisk he had to move two ancient monumental horse statues. At first he failed; they wouldn't budge, but finally, with the aid of a winch and sixteen men, he repositioned them. Antinori had chosen white marble for the obelisk's pedestal but it clashed with the darker bases of the horse statues so he suggested re-facing the ancient bases; the frugal Pope told him to stain his pedestal with chestnut water. Antinori may have had an ulterior motive for wanting to re-face the bases. They had been designed by the famous Domenico Fontana, who had carved his name on them. Re-facing them would have removed all traces of the other architect.

The bottom fragment of the obelisk was placed on its base in 1786 and the other two pieces were set in place a few months later. On the south side of the base a very dramatic inscription recounts the obelisk's history:

> I was formerly carved and cut from the mountain of Egypt
> and by Romulean Force dragged through the sea's waves
> that as a pillar of awe, I might stand at the tomb of Augustus
> . . . I lay fallen and broken . . .

So Augustus, the first Emperor of Rome, has six obelisks associated with him, the two first moved to Alexandria and later to London and New York, the two that he moved to Rome, and the two that once stood in front of his mausoleum.

Figure 2.6 The Quirinale Obelisk is the twin to the Esqualine and wasn't re-erected till 1781.

This was just the beginning of a rather steady stream of obelisks that Roman emperors would secure to beautify their city.

Trinità dei Monti (Spanish Steps)

Actually, Augustus has one more obelisk connected to him, although not directly. It now sits on top of the Spanish Steps. We don't know which emperor first erected this obelisk, but he probably ruled about a century or so after

Figure 2.7 The Trinità dei Monti Obelisk sits on the steps above the Spanish Embassy and is a popular tourist attraction.

Augustus. The poorly carved hieroglyphs indicate that the obelisk was carved when such skills were already being lost. In 1666 Athanasius Kircher noticed that the inscription was merely a poor copy of what is on Augustus's obelisk at the Piazza del Popolo. By now the Egyptian language was dying out and whoever was emperor couldn't create his own inscription, so he copied Augustus's.

This obelisk was found in 1544 in the Sallust Gardens, named for the historian Caius Sallustius Crispus, who designed gardens that became part of the palace grounds of several emperors. For two centuries the obelisk lay fallen, until 1786, when Pope Pius VI decided to raise it. It was suggested that it be placed in front of the Church of Trinità dei Monti, at the top of the Spanish Steps—so named because the Spanish Embassy dominated the square below.

Giovanni Antinori, the architect, built a full-sized wood model of the pedestal and obelisk and placed it in front of the church to see how it would look. The Pope approved, and then the intrigue began.

Antinori's rival, Pannini, tried to stop the work by claiming that erecting the obelisk would cause both the church and steps to collapse. The Pope stood firm behind Antinori and the project moved forward, but when Antinori began excavating the foundation for the pedestal, torrential rains fell, flooding and mudslides followed, stopping the work. Antinori was forced to put in a drainage system, but that was just the beginning of his problems.

Bringing the large fragments of the obelisk to the site proved extremely difficult. The space at the top of the steps had little room for maneuvering and Antinori had to build a wooden bridge from the Villa Medici to the top of the steps to create a path for the obelisk. Finally, in April of 1789 the bottom fragment was placed on the pedestal he had designed. But there was a problem. The second piece of the obelisk didn't join with the other fragments; some pieces of the obelisk were missing. Antinori had to ask the Pope's permission to cut replacement pieces from the burned Antonine column before the obelisk could finally be erected.

At the obelisk's inauguration ceremony, a cross was mounted on top, but this was no ordinary cross. It was a reliquary that held a piece of the true cross as well as relics of St. Joseph, the apostles Peter and Paul, and other unnamed saints. Obelisks had now transmuted from Roman war trophies to symbols of Christianity's triumph over paganism. Antinori overcame tremendous political and physical hurdles to erect the obelisk above the Spanish Steps and now that his job was done he was expecting heartfelt congratulations. He was, instead, greeted with universal disdain. Romans felt that the pedestal he had designed was far too large for the obelisk. The size of the base wasn't the only complaint. His critics made fun of the poorly carved hieroglyphs. Antinori just couldn't win!

Today the obelisk is a beloved part of Rome's history and architecture. Had the original base been found, Antinori wouldn't have had to design a pedestal and his work might have been better received. In 1843, a half-century after the obelisk was erected, its base was discovered in the gardens of the Villa Ludovisi. The base didn't fare much better than the obelisk that once stood on it.

In 1883 another obelisk without a base was discovered and it was later suggested to erect it on the Ludovisi base in front of the railway station as a monument to fallen Italian soldiers. The architect refused the offer of the base and it remained neglected till 1926, when it became involved with Benito Mussolini. Fascism was sweeping Italy and it was decided to use the base to commemorate the October 28, 1922 march on Rome that led to Mussolini's first government. Decorated with marble ornaments and bronze plaques, renamed "Ara dei Caduti Fascisti," the base was erected on the Capitoline Hill in a ceremony attended by Mussolini. After Mussolini's fall from power, the ornaments were stripped from the base and it now lies overturned in a garden. The obelisk discovered in 1883 that was erected in front of the railway station didn't fare much better than the base.

The Obelisk at the Railway Station (Viale delle Terme)

The railway station obelisk was the first discovered by a modern archaeological excavation. When Italy became a unified nation in 1870, a commission to supervise archaeological excavations was established. The first place excavated was the site of the *Iseum*, the Temple of Isis, because so many wonderful things had been discovered there in the past. They began digging in 1883 and immediately hit pay dirt. A spectacular sphinx of the pharaoh Amasis emerged from the soil, followed by two life-sized black granite baboons, and then an obelisk. Unlike so many other Roman obelisks, this one was unbroken, in perfect condition, because when it fell it hit accumulated debris and not a hard pavement. Originally erected by Ramses the Great at Heliopolis, it was brought to Rome by an unknown emperor, set up at the Iseum, and later fell and was lost for more than a thousand years. Now that it was rediscovered the discussion began as to where it should be re-erected. In Italy such discussions can take years and this one was resolved in 1887 by an event still discussed by patriotic Italians.

In 1887 Italy was involved in a war with Ethiopia and in January of that year, 548 Italian soldiers fell into an ambush and were killed. It was quickly agreed that the obelisk was to be a memorial to the "cinquecento," as the soldiers were called. Azurri, the architect responsible for the monument, designed a base with bronze lions to symbolize the fallen heroes, whose names were inscribed on a bronze plaque. The public didn't like it. They called it "vulgar" and "inartistic" and complained that it was too small for the large expanse in front

Figure 2.8 The obelisk at the railway station is a monument to 548 Italian soldiers killed in Ethiopia in 1887.

of the railway station. In 1924 the obelisk and base were moved to a nearby park that today is quite shabby. Often the life of an obelisk in Rome was not an easy one.

Bernini's Elephant Obelisk (Piazza della Minerva)

One of the last pairs of Egyptian obelisks was quarried by Psamtek's son and successor, Wa-Ib-Re, called Apries by the Greeks. Following the tradition of earlier pharaohs, Apries raised a pair of obelisks in front of his mortuary temple at Sais in the Delta. During the Roman Period, someone—we don't know who—brought them across the Mediterranean to Rome and erected them at the Iseum. Like so many other Roman obelisks, they toppled and disappeared for centuries beneath the ground.

In 1665 Dominican friars digging a foundation for their garden's wall struck an obelisk. Pope Alexander VII Chigi (1655–67) was thrilled. A humanist and man of letters, he was especially interested in lost knowledge and this was the kind of discovery he loved. He had reorganized the Vatican Library, contributing his own collection of books, and erecting an obelisk would add nicely to what he had already done for the city. The Pope also supported the great artist and architect Bernini, whose works included the colonnade at St. Peter's Church in the Vatican. Bernini was commissioned to design a pedestal for the obelisk that was to be erected in front of the Dominican Church in the Piazza della Minerva.

A large folder in the Vatican Library contains the various design proposals for the pedestal. One shows four dogs at the corners of the obelisk, a pun on "Dominican" and "domini canes"—"the hounds of God" because Dominicans had a reputation for ferreting out heretics. In the end, Bernini's now famous elephant pedestal was selected. The elephant that supports the obelisk is a bit strange; the trunk is too long and the elephant's neck twists so it can see the obelisk. An inscription on the side facing the church explains the symbolism.

> Let any beholder of the carved images of the wisdom of Egypt
> On the obelisk carried by the elephant, the strongest of
> Beasts, realize that it takes a robust mind to carry solid Wisdom.

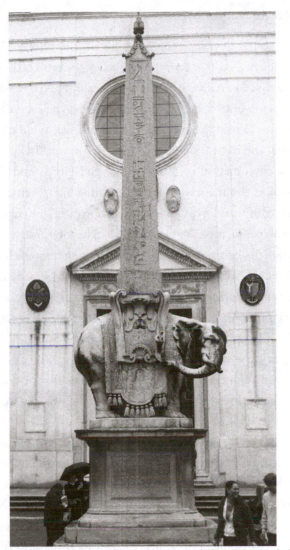

Figure 2.9 During the Renaissance, when the Piazza della Minerva obelisk was re-erected, it was wrongly believed that the elephant was the ancient Egyptian hieroglyph for wisdom. Thus, Bernini designed an elephant base for it!

The idea that inscriptions on obelisks bear the wisdom of Egypt was the result of Kircher's misguided interpretation of hieroglyphs. Obelisk inscriptions are usually dull recitations of the titles of the pharaohs who erected them. This misconception that all hieroglyphic inscriptions contained ancient wisdom was popular throughout the Renaissance, and was aided by the fact that no one could read them, including Athanasius Kircher.

Horapollo leads everyone astray

For nearly a thousand years, scholars were on the wrong track trying to decipher the ancient Egyptian script, and much of the error is due to Horapollo, a Hellenist who lived in Alexandria in the fifth century AD. He is the author of the oldest known work on hieroglyphs, the *Hieroglyphica*, written when the knowledge of how to read the ancient language had just about died. Everything about Horapollo and his work is on the divide of two worlds: Egypt and Greece. His name is a combination of the Egyptian god Horus and the Greek god Apollo; his book is about ancient Egyptian writing but is written in Greek. He had a smattering of how Egyptian hieroglyphs worked, but, like most Greeks, he missed the bigger picture. For example, when he interpreted the meaning of the duck hieroglyph, he got it right, but for the wrong reason. He correctly said that the duck meant "son" but went on to explain why: because the duck fights so fiercely for its offspring. Horapollo had bought into the belief that each hieroglyph is an ideogram, a sign that stands for an idea. This is where he got it wrong. Many Egyptian hieroglyphs are simply phonetic; they stand for sounds, and that's the case with the duck hieroglyph. The duck sign is what Egyptologists call a biliteral, a hieroglyph that stands for two sounds one after the other. The duck represents the sound "sa," and "sa" was the word for "son" in ancient Egyptian.

A manuscript of Horapollo's *Hieroglyphica* was discovered in the fifteenth century and was quickly translated into Latin, becoming the source of countless errors throughout the Renaissance, and may have been the inspiration for Bernini's elephant. Horapollo says, "When the Egyptians wanted to signify a strong man in search of what is beneficial or essential, they drew an elephant with its trunk because the animal probes with its trunk and (thus) becomes master of its fate." This is pure fantasy, the Egyptians never believed anything of the sort, but Bernini believed it, so millions of visitors to Rome are treated to an obelisk on an elephant's back.

Bernini's Fountain (Piazza Navona)

Bernini's elephant was not his only contribution to the obelisks of Rome. In the Piazza Navona, a fabulous Bernini fountain supports an obelisk, but Bernini

Figure 2.10 The Piazza Navona obelisk rests on four sculpted caves, each representing one of the four major continents (Africa, Asia, Europe, and the Americas). Nilus was shown with his face covered because the source of the Nile was yet to be discovered.

was not the first choice to design it. As a matter of fact, it was only because of a devious plan that Bernini got to build his fountain supporting the obelisk. The obelisk in question has a long and strange history, beginning with the Emperor Domitian (AD 81–96) and the goddess Isis.

Domitian's favorite goddess was Isis, an Egyptian deity widely worshipped in Rome during the first century. Isis's rise in popularity was due to a great extent to the Greek philosophers Plato and Aristotle. Aristotelian logic asserted that the world was an orderly place, governed by laws of nature, not by mercurial whims of gods as portrayed in Greek and Egyptian mythology. Aristotle's teacher, Plato, also contributed to the decline of mythology by teaching that the basic truths of the cosmos are unchanging abstract ideas, not subject to temperamental gods. Unlike many other gods, Isis was rational, the devoted wife whose hard work paid off in the resurrection of her husband, Osiris. She was the perfect precursor for Christianity. Because Isis had traveled across the Mediterranean to find her husband's body she was especially popular with sailors, so most Mediterranean harbors had Isis shrines. As the devotion to Isis spread, she became particularly popular with wealthy ladies of Rome. Here was a goddess with whom they could have a close personal relationship, and an Isis Temple, the Iseum, was built. But while Roman ladies loved Isis, the emperors often didn't.

Augustus, Rome's first emperor, banished the worship of Isis when he took over control of Egypt. This is not surprising. After all, Caesar and Antony both had formed alliances with Cleopatra, who had a habit of dressing up like Isis. After Augustus, Caligula reversed the ban and refurbished the Isis Temple, but it burned during the reign of Titus (AD 79–81). Domitian (AD 81–96) rebuilt it, but unfortunately, today no remains of this temple can be seen above ground. Our best indicator of what it looked like is an ancient map, incised on a slab of marble called the *Forma Urbis Romae*. The map shows the temple situated near St. Maria sopra Minerva, which makes sense since Isis was often identified with the goddess Minerva. (On the map the temple is called *Iseum et Serapeum*, indicating that there were two sections, one for Isis and one for her husband, known as Serapis to the Greeks and Romans.) Inside the temple, the map shows a circle and a square—a fountain and a single obelisk. With a little bit of detective work, I believe we can establish that this was the obelisk that now stands in the Piazza Navona.

The obelisk's inscription proclaims that Domitian, the rebuilder of the Isis Temple, erected it and affirms that it is not a member of a pair, so as a singleton it fits the plan on the ancient map. This suggests it was standing at the Iseum two thousand years ago. Although the obelisk was quarried in Egypt, it was probably inscribed in Rome because the hieroglyphs are not well formed. Egyptian hieroglyph carvers would have done a better job. The inscription says that the falcon god Horakhty is Domitian's father, the typical way a ruler in Egypt asserted his divinity. Usually this is followed by the pharaoh's titles; Domitian has merely copied the titles of Pharaoh Ptolemy III, who ruled a few centuries before him. Then the inscription becomes decidedly un-Egyptian; it mentions contemporary people: "Domitian taking over the kingdom of his father Vespasianus from his Elder Brother, Titus, when his soul had fled to heaven." The pyramidion on top of the obelisk is also unusual. Normally we see the king making offerings to a god, or being presented by a god. Here the Emperor is surrounded by a bevy of four goddesses, adoring him! Isis, the Emperor's favorite, presents the crowns of Upper and Lower Egypt to Domitian.

The obelisk stood in the Iseum for two centuries, until AD 309, when Emperor Maxentius's oldest son died and Maxentius appropriated the obelisk for the spina (the central axis) of a circus he dedicated to his son. When that circus fell into disuse the obelisk fell as well, only to resurface in the fourteenth century, broken into four large fragments. The broken obelisk remained prostrate for centuries till 1647, when Pope Innocent X Pamphili decided to commission a fountain to beautify the Piazza Navona. Athanasius Kircher convinced His Holiness to incorporate the obelisk into the new plan for the Piazza. Thus, when the most prominent architects of the day were asked to submit their designs for the Piazza, it was for a fountain/obelisk combo. The great Bernini was not invited. He had been the favorite of the previous Pope, Urban VIII Barbarini, but the Barbarinis had been enemies of the new Pope, so Bernini was out. He was still officially the architect of St. Peter's, but had no work. Even though one of Bernini's specialties was fountains, the commission went to another architect named Borromini. But Bernini had a plan.

On his own, Bernini designed the fountain, executed a model in solid silver, and gave it as a present (or a bribe) to the Pope's sister-in-law. She was to position it in a prominent place in her house, where the Pope would see it when he visited. The plan worked. When Innocent saw it, he was enthralled, studying the model for half an hour. He summoned Bernini and awarded him the contract, forgetting that he had promised it to Borromini. It was now full steam ahead for both fountain and obelisk.

Kircher, told to fully excavate the obelisk, uncovered the four large fragments but was unable to locate the original pedestal. He discovered that some smaller pieces of the obelisk were missing so he went back, excavated some more and found them, but they were too damaged to be incorporated into the obelisk. He copied their inscriptions, then had them carved on new stone so the obelisk could be reassembled. In 1649 the obelisk was erected, but the fountain took another two years to complete.

Bernini quarried travertine marble from Tivoli, near Rome, and carved four romantic caves out of the huge blocks of stone. Each cave represented a continent: Asia, Africa, Europe, and the Americas, each represented by a river with an appropriate sculpture. For Africa, the Nile god cloaks his face because the source of the Nile was not known.

The new interest created by Bernini's fountain and the re-erected obelisk gave Kircher the chance to publish the hieroglyphic translations he had been working on. On the east face of the obelisk the actual inscription reads: "Caesar Domitianus, living forever." But in Kircher's time that meaning had been lost.

Kircher's translation was based on the false assumption that each hieroglyph represented an idea, so he attributed meanings to each hieroglyph, such as the concepts of generating, force, the supernatural, the infernal, emanating from above, and the influence of humors. Kircher's translation was: "The beneficent generative force commanding through supernatural and infernal dominion, augments the flow of sacred humors emanating from above. Saturn, the disposer of fleeting time, promotes the fecundity of the soil, commanding humid nature. For by his influence all things have life force." Pure nonsense.[2]

Almost all of Rome's obelisks were in some way or other associated with either Kircher or Augustus. Most were translated by Kircher, and many of the obelisks were either brought by Augustus or transported from Egypt after his death to grace his mausoleum. But there is one obelisk on the Capitoline Hill that has a unique connection with Augustus. The globe on top was said to contain his ashes.

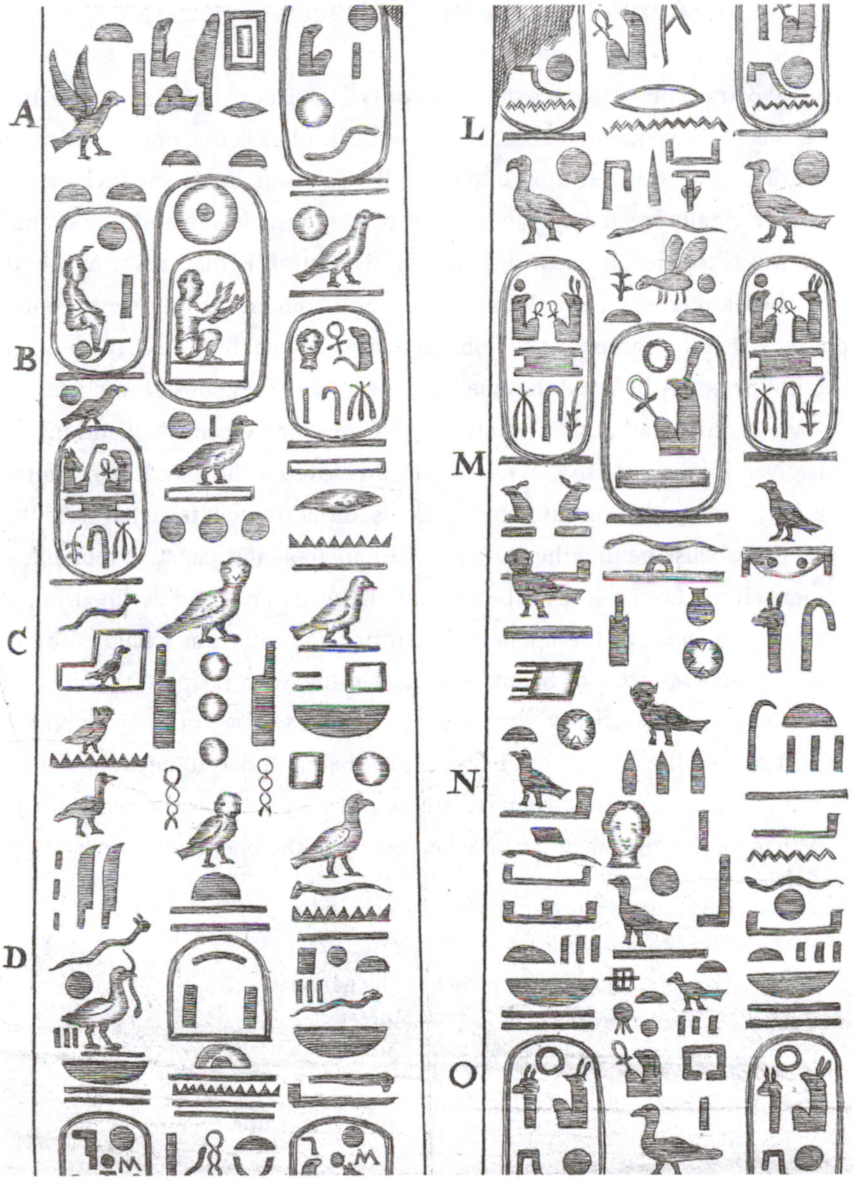

Figure 2.11 Athanasius Kircher's transcriptions of the hieroglyphs on Rome's obelisks were almost as fanciful as his translations.

Capitoline Obelisk (Villa Celimontana)

Several pairs of obelisks once stood in front of the Iseum but they have all been separated; however, some can still be traced. The obelisk that once stood on the Capitoline and was later moved to the Villa Celimontana is one such orphan. It was originally erected by Ramses II, brought to the Iseum and, like so many others, was toppled, broken, and lost. Its distinction is that it is probably the first obelisk re-erected after Roman times. Someone in the fourteenth century placed the top fragment of the obelisk on a new shaft and set it up on the Capitoline. Many believed this obelisk once held the remains of Augustus.

Two centuries after its re-erection, the Capitoline Obelisk fell and in 1582 was given by the state to Ciriaco Mattei, a beloved antiquary. When Fontana finished moving the Vatican Obelisk, he used the timbers from his castello to erect this obelisk behind the Mattei villa in an area landscaped to look like an ancient circus. Over the years the gardens changed hands and declined, but the obelisk remained. In the nineteenth century, the villa was occupied by the exiled Prime Minister of Spain, Manuel Godoy, who restored the villa and gardens. When the obelisk was refurbished in 1817, a workman caught his hand between the obelisk and its base and the hand had to be amputated on the spot. This was considered a bad omen and the obelisk was rarely visited.

When Godoy inscribed the base he preserved the obelisk's history:

> Having first extended the grounds, Manuel Godoy
> Removed hither this obelisk formerly presented
> To Ciriaco Mattei, the ancient owner of the gardens,
> By the Senate and people of Rome. The inclemency
> Of time had almost caused its downfall . . .

The monument is no longer open to the public; it is in a private garden.

Piazza della Rotonda

The mate to the Villa Celimontana obelisk is not far from its twin, in the Piazza della Rotonda. We know very little about its history, only that in 1711 Pope Clement XI re-erected it in front of the Pantheon, incorporating it into a fountain with dolphins that spout water.

Figure 2.12 Pope Clement XI re-erected the Piazza della Rotonda obelisk in 1711, putting it in a fountain with dolphins that spout water.

Rome's last obelisk (Monte Picino)

The last obelisk erected in Rome is a unique bit of Egyptomania, a tribute to the Roman fascination with ancient Egypt. To anyone who knows hieroglyphs, as soon as you near the obelisk something seems wrong; the hieroglyphic inscription isn't quite right. The shapes of the hieroglyphs aren't the way an Egyptian carver would have done it. There's also something about the grammar; it doesn't flow like Egyptian sentences. That' because it wasn't written by an Egyptian; the obelisk was quarried in Egypt during the first century, transported to Rome, and inscribed there by an Egyptophile for the Emperor Hadrian.

The obelisk is a monument to Antinous, Hadrian's lover whose death is still a mystery. The official account is that he accidentally drowned in the Nile while he and Hadrian were touring Egypt, but few people in Hadrian's time believed this account. The historian, Dio, and others believe Antinous was a willing sacrifice who gave his life to ward off an evil omen for his Emperor. Whatever the case, Hadrian had Antinous deified and a new-born star named after him. In Egypt, Hadrian built a Roman-style city in his honor and named it Antinoupolis. Shrines for the cult of Antinous sprung up in Egypt and Rome, with life-sized statues of the handsome Antinous striding forward like an Egyptian pharaoh.

In Rome, Hadrian built a sanctuary for Antinous where he buried his cremated ashes. In front of this sanctuary he erected a 30-foot obelisk, and a Roman scholar of Egyptian hieroglyphs carved an inscription on it proclaiming, "The Remains of Antinous rest here … in the precinct of the goddess of the Luck of Rome." Antinous's obelisk remained standing for two centuries, but, in the beginning of the third century, Sixtus Varius Marcellus had it moved to the Circus Varianus. As centuries passed and Christians pulled down Rome's pagan obelisks, this obelisk also fell and was forgotten. Rediscovered after the Middle Ages, it was described in 1525 as "an obelisk lying on its side, broken in two pieces." In 1570 the obelisk was fully freed from the earth by the two Saccoccius brothers who owned the former circus lands and had it erected in their garden. They carved a plaque commemorating their excavation of the obelisk that can be seen today beneath one of the arches of the Acqua Felice. But the Saccoccius garden was not the final site for the obelisk.

In 1620 Pope Urban VIII's nephew, Cardinal Barberini, took the obelisk to the Barberini's family gardens and had Father Athanasius Kircher transferred to

Figure 2.13 Erected by the Emperor Hadrian (AD 117–38), the Monte Picino obelisk is the last erected in Rome. It was quarried in Egypt but inscribed in Rome to commemorate the death of Hadrian's young lover, Antinous, who drowned in the Nile.

Rome so he could translate the inscription. Kircher was, indeed, a linguist who could read nearly a dozen languages, but, as we have seen, ancient Egyptian wasn't one of them. His translation is once again pure fantasy. Although the obelisk was brought to the family gardens, the Barberinis never got around to erecting it. For more than a century it remained prostrate on the ground. In the eighteenth century, the director of the French Academy in Rome suggested to his king that he purchase the obelisk for France and erect it in Paris. His Majesty replied that the director had too much zeal; an obelisk was an extravagance that the king didn't need. In 1770 the obelisk was given to Pope Clement XIV, but still nothing was done with it. Half a century later, in 1822, it was finally erected in the Viale del Obelisco. Unlike most of the other obelisks in Rome, it bears no cross and it is not in front of a church. Times had changed. The last obelisk raised in Rome is a secular monument, its Latin inscription proclaiming it merely "an extraordinary monument . . . to decorate the delightful Pincio Gardens."

One obelisk standing in Rome has not been described—the Vatican Obelisk. Its history is both so involved and so fascinating that is the subject of the next chapter. But there is one more Roman obelisk to mention here. It is Roman in the sense that the Romans moved it, but it was destined for Constantinople.

The Constantinople Obelisk

Although the Romans erected dozens of obelisks in their city, there is not a single contemporary depiction in Rome of the method they used. The only ancient depiction we have is in Istanbul. The Istanbul obelisk originally stood in Karnak Temple but during the reign of Emperor Constantine it was moved to Alexandria, where it lay on the beach waiting shipment to the new capital, Constantinople. The obelisk languished on the beach till the reign of Theodosius (AD 347–95), who finally had it brought over and erected, the last obelisk moved by a Roman emperor. Sometime during its unfortunate life the obelisk lost its bottom third, so what we see today in Istanbul is only two-thirds of an obelisk. However, on its pedestal is the only ancient representation of an obelisk being raised.

An inscription on the base tells us that it took Proclus, the Prefect of Constantinople, thirty-two days to erect it. The scenes on the weathered base were often reproduced in books of the Late Renaissance. The top two registers show the actual erecting of the obelisk. On the top register the obelisk is lying

The Hippodrom with the Thebean Obelisk and Engines by which it was erected.

Figure 2.14 The base of Constantinople's obelisk bears the only depiction from Roman times of an obelisk being erected.

on the ground being winched along by two capstans turned by four men each. Undoubtedly there were more than two capstans and more than four men per capstan; the scene merely gives a general idea of how it was done. If you look closely at the capstan in the second register, you can see that there are ropes coming from the obelisk in the first register. We are not looking at sequential turnings of the same capstans, but at the simultaneous turnings of four.

Sitting on the ground, near each capstan, someone makes sure that the ropes don't get tangled. In both registers we see someone standing on a platform, probably the overseer of the works calling out instructions. In the bottom register the obelisk is erect and someone dressed in rich robes is handing out rewards. It was not, however, all easy sailing. On the right side of the second register we see someone being carried from the worksite with a woman in anguish to the right. This ancient portrayal of the Constantinople obelisk being raised was the only representation anyone could turn to if he wanted to move or raise an obelisk. This is exactly what was done more than a thousand years later when Domenico Fontana was called upon to move the Vatican Obelisk, to which we turn in the next chapter.

3

God's Architect

Every Sunday thousands of faithful Catholics from all over the world crowd into St. Peter's Square to hear the Pope celebrate Mass. Right in the middle of the throng is an 85-foot red granite spear reaching up to the sky that the Church once thought so powerful that the ritual of exorcism was performed on it. Its history involves two mad emperors, The Book of Revelation, and an archaeologist turned detective, but we still don't know who made it thousands of years ago in Egypt. The Vatican Obelisk has always been a mystery.

Of all the massive obelisks quarried in Egypt, the Vatican Obelisk is the only one uninscribed. No hieroglyphs tell which pharaoh quarried and erected it, and this, in itself, is a puzzle waiting to be solved. Obelisks were erected in pairs at temple entrances to proclaim the pharaoh's power. Carved on all four faces were the king's names and formal titles. This is where pharaoh proclaimed himself "King of Upper and Lower Egypt, Son of the Sun, The Golden Horus, Beloved of the Amun, etc., etc." For an ancient Egyptian king, an uninscribed obelisk was pointless. Why go to the expense and trouble of quarrying and moving a 320-ton shaft of stone and not put your name on it? Perhaps the king died before it could be inscribed, or perhaps it was quarried for a Roman; we will never know for sure. What we do know is that it was brought from Egypt to Rome by Caligula, the modern world's poster boy for a ruler gone mad.

The monster's trophy

Caligula's reputation is well earned. He was a rather strange-looking young man with spindly arms and legs, prematurely bald but with excess hair all over the rest of his body. His name was really Gaius, not Caligula. The *caliga* was a boot worn by Roman soldiers. When he was two years old he wore a miniature soldier's outfit, complete with boots, and was nicknamed "Caligula"—"little boots." He hated the nickname and when he became emperor he punished anyone who used it. He also punished anyone who looked down at his head because they would see he was bald.

As a teenager he had an incestuous affair with his younger sister Drusilla, but this was just the beginning of his excesses; when he became emperor and had unlimited power, Caligula's royal perversions were so great that at one point in his history of Rome, Suetonius says, "So much for Caligula as emperor; we must now tell his career as a monster."

Because he didn't get along with people, Caligula lavished his affections on his horse, Incitatus, who lived in a marble stall and wore royal purple blankets studded with gems. Frequently Caligula held lavish banquets and sent the invitations in the horse's name, and he provided Incitatus with barley crafted from gold. (Caligula had no veterinary training.)

Convinced he was a god, Caligula was particularly fond of Egypt, whose pharaohs were also considered divine. Some time during his brief four-year reign (he was assassinated, much to the relief of most Romans) he decided it would add to his glory to have an Egyptian obelisk in Rome. Not wanting the expense of quarrying one himself, he decided to bring a second-hand obelisk inscribed by Tiberius, his uncle: "Sacred to the God Caesar Augustus, son of the God Julius, and to Tiberius Caesar Augustus, son of the God Augustus." But Tiberius wasn't the original owner of the obelisk either, and this is where, fifteen hundred years later, Professor Filippo Magi, our archaeologist/detective, comes in.

Detective Magi and the case of the uninscribed obelisk

Filippo Magi, Director of Archaeological Research and Scholarship in Vatican City, in the 1960s seemed to know every Vatican statue, painting and monument intimately. If a right index finger was found at an excavation, he knew which statue in the Vatican Museum was missing that finger. He was famous for reconstructing broken statues and vases from bits and pieces.

On a clear December morning in 1961, Professor Magi was standing in front of the Vatican Obelisk looking at the inscription Tiberius had placed on the obelisk nineteen centuries earlier. In the bright, raking sunlight, he noticed dozens of small nail holes within the Latin words. Why were they there? He wondered if they could be the remnants of an even earlier inscription, where individual bronze letters had been nailed to the obelisk. Magi began by tracing the pattern left by the nail holes to see if he could see the outlines of individual letters. He could. Then he made lots of plastic letters to scale and put them where he was certain he knew they belonged. Then, using the rest of the letters like a Scrabble set, combined with some basic principles of cryptology, he moved them around to fill in the blanks that he couldn't read. Finally, he cracked the code: IVSSV IMP CAESARIA DIVI F C CORNELIVS CN F GALLVA PRAEF FABR CAESARIS DIVI F FORVM IVLIVM FECIT. (The inscription is highly abbreviated, for example the "F" stands for "FILII", "son of," and "PRAEF" is PRAEFECTUS, the ruler of Egypt during Roman times.) The inscription proclaims the obelisk was raised by Cornelius Gallus, Prefect of Egypt during the reign of Augustus. Gallus was a renowned writer, praised by the two most famous poets of his day, Ovid and Virgil. But he was also a military man who served under Octavian, who later changed his name to Augustus when he became emperor. Gallus was probably with Octavian when he defeated Marc Antony and Cleopatra at the Battle of Actium. We know for certain that he also led troops in Egypt that defeated Antony. As a reward for his loyal service, Octavian (now the Emperor Augustus) made him Prefect of Egypt, from whence came endless sacks of grain to feed the growing Roman populace. If the Prefect did not keep order and ensure a good harvest in Egypt, Rome could starve. But if it all went well, the Prefect would have been a very rich man.

Gallus served for about four years as Prefect and from ancient Roman historians we know he did some things well, and he was certainly trusted by Augustus. He is even mentioned in Shakespeare's *Antony and Cleopatra* as one of the two friends Augustus sent to bring Cleopatra back to Rome alive so she could be displayed in a tribute in the Circus. It is recorded that Gallus maintained and enlarged the irrigation canals, supported the arts, and increased the papyrus industry. But it seems power went to his head and he spoke disrespectfully of Augustus, never a good idea. The historian Ammianus Marcellinus reports that Gallus plundered Thebes, Egypt's religious capital, and erected statues to himself throughout Egypt. In short, Gallus began acting like a pharaoh, and pharaohs erected obelisks.

The obelisk he erected in the Forum Julium, a public square in Alexandria, fits the picture of someone impressed with himself. It is the largest obelisk ever erected by a non-royal, and may have contributed to his downfall. In 26 BC Gallus was relieved of his position as Prefect and called back to Rome by Augustus because of his conduct. There the Senate convicted him of misconduct, confiscated his estates, and banished him. Soon after his sentence, Gallus committed suicide by his own sword. He was forty years old. Years after Gallus's fall, the Emperor Tiberius removed Gallus's inscription on the obelisk and carved his own name on it, making it his own. So the obelisk that Caligula decided to bring to Rome had quite a history and had already contributed to the downfall of one Roman.

The obelisk soared nearly ninety feet into the sky and weighed more than 300 tons. No existing boat could transport it, so Caligula built a special transport ship powered by three tiers of hundreds of oarsmen. The obelisk was probably secured in the ship's hold by thousands of sacks of Egyptian grain, so it wouldn't shift. After its successful journey across the Mediterranean, the ship was placed on display for all Rome to marvel at it.

Once safely disembarked in Rome, the obelisk was erected in the circus that Caligula was building to further his passion for horse racing. A circus was basically an oval racetrack with a low wall called the *spina* running down the center, around which the horses and chariots would race. Caligula erected his obelisk on the *spina*. We have no contemporary records of how Caligula erected the obelisk, but it must have been different from the Egyptian method. As we have seen from the base of the Constantinople obelisk, unlike ancient Egyptian engineers, Roman architects had pulleys and winches that gave them a mechanical advantage and the ability to lift heavy objects straight up. Caligula's obelisk did not rest directly on its pedestal, as did Egyptian obelisks, but sat on four massive bronze feet each weighing more than 600 pounds. These were fixed to the pedestal in such a way that the obelisk could not have been rotated into position. The Romans must have lifted the obelisk straight up and lowered it onto the bronze feet, but we don't know exactly how. No matter how they achieved it, the obelisk was set on its pedestal so well that it, alone among all the Roman obelisks, remained upright for 1,500 years.

While Rome burned

After Caligula's assassination, his nephew, Nero, expanded and completed the Circus, leaving the obelisk in place. Nero is most famous for having "fiddled while Rome burned." While it is undoubtedly true that Nero was sometimes cruel and sent hundreds of innocent people to their deaths, the fiddling story is not quite accurate and is not so terrible as it sounds. Nevertheless, during the evening of July 19, AD 64 fire broke out in Rome, eventually reducing two-thirds of the city to ashes.

Almost every stratum of Roman society was hurt by the burning of Rome. The wealthy lost their villas and fine possessions and the poor lost their shacks and what little they had; almost everyone lost family members to the flames. During the conflagration, when everyone was doing what he could to help, one group seemed almost to welcome the fire—the Christians. This small group of mostly poor people and slaves followed Paul of Tarsus, a Jew who was a Roman citizen.

Nero sent his agents to investigate the cause of the fire and the Christians who had acted so strangely. He learned that they were awaiting the second coming of their messiah, someone named Christus, who had been executed in Judea a decade earlier. The Christians construed the fire as a divine harbinger that Christ was about to reappear and were thus joyous while other Romans were terrified. Nero failed to share their enthusiasm. He had many Christians rounded up and executed, including Paul of Tarsus.

Witness to martyrdom

Shortly after the massacre Peter, who had now become leader of the Christians, wrote what was to become known as the first epistle. He encouraged the Christians to remain faithful so that "they may be ashamed who falsely accuse you. The end of all things is at hand, therefore watch and pray." Soon after writing this, Nero had Peter arrested and executed at the Circus. Bound to a cross, he asked that he be executed upside down so that his insignificant death might not be confused with that of Christ. When Peter was executed, Caligula's obelisk, which had escaped the fire, was standing nearby. Later in the Middle

Ages, when other Roman obelisks were being toppled by Christians because they were pagan monuments, the Circus obelisk was spared because it had witnessed the martyrdom of St. Peter. It would remain on its pedestal for another 1,500 years till a Pope decreed it should be moved. Thus the Vatican Obelisk owes its longevity to Rome's two most infamous emperors, Caligula and Nero.

For three centuries the obelisk remained in place while the new Christian religion grew. In AD 313 the Emperor Constantine legalized Christianity. He was undoubtedly prompted by his mother, the Empress Helena, who was a devout convert to Christianity. She was also a bit gullible—on a single shopping trip to Jerusalem the Empress bought not only the True Cross but also the bones of the Three Wise Men. Rome became the seat of early Christianity, and in an attempt to make it worthy, Constantine began building. The Circus of Nero, where St. Peter had been martyred three hundred years earlier, was torn down and upon its foundation a basilica for Peter was constructed in the shadow of the obelisk.

Throughout the Middle Ages, as Christianity took hold, the obelisk remained in place. During the Renaissance, when St. Peter's Basilica was now more than a thousand years old and beginning to show its age, a new basilica was begun. The cornerstone was placed by Pope Julius II in 1506, less than a quarter of a mile from the old basilica. The new basilica was spectacular, and soon the old was neglected, and with it the obelisk. Visited by only the most informed and persistent pilgrims, the obelisk's pedestal disappeared beneath accumulated rubbish. The suggestion was constantly being put forward that the obelisk should be moved to the site of the new St. Peter's Basilica where it would be appreciated, but no one was willing to attempt it. When Michelangelo was asked to try he replied, "And what if it breaks?"

There was, however, one brave soul who was apparently eager for the job. Camillo Agrippa was an engineer who in 1583 published a small book, *Treatise by Camillo Agrippa of Milan on Moving the Needle in St. Peter's Square* (*Trattato di Camillio Agrippa Milanese di Transportar la Guiglia in su la Piazza di San Pietro*). Agrippa probably thought his treatise would convince everyone that he could do the job. His idea was to build a giant scaffold to support the obelisk as it was raised by massive levers off its pedestal. Then, while suspended vertically on the scaffold, the obelisk would be moved on rollers to its new location. Agrippa included an engraving of his scaffold, and this may be the reason he didn't get the contract. There is no cross-bracing of the vertical members and the scaffold as designed simply would not have been able to support the enormous weight of the obelisk. As William Parsons put it in his wonderful book *Engineers and Engineering in the Renaissance*, anyone could see that "the main timbers were unsupported at any point in their entire length, that there was no diagonal bracing and that the design was lacking in every essential of sound engineering principles."[1] It would have been a disaster.

Fortunately Agrippa's pamphlet seems to have been ignored, but a year later a new pope, Sixtus V, became Christ's Vicar on Earth and was determined to find the right man to move the obelisk. Sixtus was a Franciscan and took Christ's command to St. Francis literally. (When St. Francis was praying at a small church just outside of Assisi the Christ on the crucifix came to life and said, "Francis, repair my church.") Sixtus intended to complete the dome of St. Peter's Basilica, rebuild Rome, and move the obelisk. Even before he was Pope, as Cardinal Peretti, he was an enthusiastic builder—so enthusiastic that his pope cut off his funds and chastised him for extravagance in building an elaborate villa. The Cardinal was saved by his young architect, Domenico Fontana, who loaned him the money to complete the villa he had begun.

The Pope's prize

Soon after he became Pope, Sixtus formed a committee of four cardinals, a bishop and city council members to select an architect to move the obelisk. Applicants for the job were to submit their plans and appear before the committee to explain their designs. In September of 1585 more than 150 architects and engineers came to Rome from as far away as Greece with plans ranging from the brilliant to the ridiculous. Many did not want to lower the obelisk, fearing it would break when pivoted to the horizontal, and, like Agrippa, suggested it be levered off its pedestal and moved while still upright. The committee selected seven finalists, among them Domenico Fontana. Fontana came from a family of architects and he had worked with his older architect brother, Giovanni, before he moved to Rome. Because he had assisted the Pope when he was still a cardinal, Fontana undoubtedly had the inside track, but he came prepared. He presented an exquisite miniature model of the scaffold he intended to build, complete with a lead obelisk he had cast to scale. His was an extremely detailed plan complete with calculations to determine the weight of the obelisk, and it impressed the committee. Fontana was given the job, but at forty-two years old was considered too young to conduct such an important and difficult job himself, so it was stipulated that he would have to work under the supervision of two senior architects.

Fontana's two supervisors were extremely competent. The seventy-five-year-old Bartolomeo Ammanati was highly respected by everyone and Giacomo della Porta was busy completing the dome on St. Peter's Basilica. Fontana may have been young, but he was supremely confident and wasn't happy about being supervised. He was concerned that the two senior architects would merely take his plans (and the credit) and do the work themselves. He discussed this with his old friend, the Pope, who told Fontana to just go ahead with the project on his own. His supervisors were probably relieved; they had their own projects.

Fontana's book on the project (*Della Transportatione dell'Obelisco Vaticano*) has the only known portrait of the architect. He stares out with a beak-like nose, close-cut thinning hair, and a short beard. In his arms he holds a miniature of the obelisk he moved, around his neck is the medal the Pope awarded to him; resting on a table are the tools of his trade—compass, set square, ink, and quill. It is the portrait of a proud, confident professional.

When the Pope gave Fontana the 'go ahead' for the project, he issued a Privilege to Fontana, the papal equivalent of a builder's contract. It gave the young architect broad powers to conscript land, materials, and manpower needed for the project. Fontana was justifiably proud of the confidence the Pope placed in him, and published the Privilege in his book.

We, Sixtus V, grant the power and full authority to Domenico Fontana, architect of the holy apostolic palace, in order that he may easily and quickly transport the Vatican needle to the piazza of St. Peter's, to avail himself so long as this transport lasts, of however so many workers, laborers, and their things, if they wish, and to compel them if necessary, to lend or sell them to him, satisfying them with due recompense ...

Figure 3.1 The only portrait of Domenico Fontana appears in his book *Della Transportatione Dell'Obelisco Vaticano*. Fontana holds the lead model obelisk that he used to obtain the commission from the Pope to move the obelisk.

That he may (if this becomes necessary) tear down or have torn down houses near the said needle, arranging however the first manner of restoring the damage that will be incurred.

In sum, the said Domenico Fontana is given the power to do, command, execute, and practice all the other things necessary to this end; and moreover, along with his agents, servants, and domestic servants, he may bear any sort of arms . . . in any place and any time.[2]

Fontana was now "God's architect."

His first step was to prepare the new foundation on which the obelisk would rest, and he soon ran into trouble. When he dug down he discovered that the earth was muddy and unstable, and he had to construct his own stable platform nearly twenty-five feet beneath the surface. As a base he used pilings of twenty-foot oak and chestnut logs stripped of their bark that he knew would not rot in water. Once the logs were sunk into the mud, he placed on top of them a mixture of flint chips, broken pieces of pottery and brick as a bed, and poured his cement called *pozzolano*, which sets even when wet. The obelisk's base would last thousands of years.

At each level of the foundation, Fontana placed commemorative medals especially struck for the occasion. One showed St. Francis kneeling before a crucifix by a ruined church; the reverse bore the motto "Go Francis and repair." Others showed Pius V on one side and on the other the personification of either Justice or Religion. The moving of the obelisk was not just a construction project, it was an act of religious devotion. The Vatican needle had witnessed the martyrdom of St. Peter; Fontana had been entrusted with a sacred task and the religious medals would ensure its success.

The *castello*

The new pedestal would have to hold not only the 320-ton obelisk but also the scaffolding or castle (*castello*), as Fontana called it, that would raise the obelisk. The scaffold was a remarkable construction, unlike anything ever built. Composed of hundreds of huge logs held together with specially forged iron bands and chains, it would weigh many tons when completed. Thousand of bolts had to be fabricated; nails couldn't be used because once the obelisk was down, the scaffold had to be taken apart and then reassembled to raise the obelisk on its new foundation. The castle was a giant Erector Set.

With his Privilege in hand, Fontana began ordering and requisitioning the materials he needed for his *castello*. He needed miles of thick ropes that would be threaded through the pulleys and winches that would lower and raise the obelisk. The city of Foligno provided the hemp that was brought back to Rome where rope makers, walking backward, twisted it into the thick cords strong enough, together, to support more than 400 tons. As the rope makers braided the hemp, iron workers at Subiaco, thirty miles out of Rome, were forging the blocks and pulleys through which the ropes would move. So many iron parts were needed that another iron-making town, Ronciglione, was given the job of forging the long, thick iron rods that would encase and protect the obelisk as it was moved.

Prodigious quantities of wood were needed, so an army of woodcutters was dispatched to the oak forests of Campomorto, near the port of Neptune. Hundreds of trees that would become the *castello* were cut, stripped of their bark and hewn into timber. Some of the trees were so large that enormous carts pulled by seven pairs of oxen had to be specially built to haul the logs the twenty-eight miles to Rome. Campomorto wasn't the only forest invaded by Fontana's men. Terracina supplied the elms from which boards to protect the obelisk were cut. Santa Severa provided special oak, suitable for the shafts of the windlasses, rollers, and crossbars.

Considerable architectural, engineering, and managerial skills were needed to direct the army of ironmongers, carpenters, rope makers, and underlings preparing to move the needle, but it took even more than that. Fontana had to also be a politician. Moving the obelisk was not popular with everyone. It had witnessed the martyrdom of Peter and many of the faithful thought it should stay in place. Fontana countered this by explaining that the obelisk "had been largely buried under the earth over the long period of time." He also pointed out that it stood in a muddy, dilapidated area and was not easily found by pilgrims. Fontana published an illustration showing the obelisk at its original site. One feature that strikes the viewer is that it is not "largely buried under the earth." Part of the pedestal is covered, but that's all. You can even see the inscription of Tiberius on the base. Fontana is acting as a lawyer, presenting his case for moving the obelisk. What surrounds the obelisk in the illustration is another indication of Fontana's public relations skills.

In front of the obelisk Fontana shows the other methods of moving the obelisk that had been proposed by his rivals. Some show the obelisk being moved upright; others show it moved at a 45-degree angle. All are impressive, but look carefully in the upper left-hand corner and you will see the winning

Figure 3.2 The obelisk in its original setting, next to the old St. Peter's Basilica. At the top is Fontana's plan for moving it, lifted heavenward by two angels. His rivals' plans are earthbound.

proposal, Fontana's beloved *castello*, supported by winged angels. He was indeed God's architect.

At the very top of the obelisk rested a metal ball. For centuries the inhabitants of Rome believed it contained the ashes of Julius Caesar. Because the obelisk had the inscription DIVO CAESARI DIVE IULII ("Divine Caesar . . ."), in the Middle Ages people believed the obelisk didn't just honor Caesar but that it was his burial place. One twelfth-century guide to Rome refers to the orb at the top of the obelisk and says it is "where his ashes rest nobly in his sarcophagus." Before Fontana lowered the obelisk, he removed the ball and carefully examined it; it was empty. Fontana's examination showed that it is was cast in one piece, so it couldn't have ever contained anything. It did, however, have a few musket ball holes; it was too tempting a target for Roman soldiers. Long forgotten, the orb can be seen today in the Palazzo dei Conservatori on the Capitoline Hill.

One more feature in Fontana's illustration is worth noting. Behind the obelisk is the old St. Peter's Basilica built by Constantine in the fourth century. The round fort-like structure is the church's sacristy. Fontana planned to first lift and then pivot the obelisk horizontally so the point faced east, towards its new destination. This meant that he would have to take down the wall of the sacristy to put windlasses inside so he could pull the bottom of the obelisk from the west. But that's just what Papal Privileges are for; Fontana has opened the wall so the obelisk could be moved.

Man is the measure

To Fontana's many skills we must add mathematics. To lower the obelisk safely, Fontana needed to calculate its weight. Then, and only then, could he determine how many winches, pulleys, and ropes he would need. But determining the obelisk's weight was not a simple calculation. The units of measurement that Fontana used for his calculations were not unlike those used by his ancient Egyptian counterparts who had quarried, moved, and erected the obelisk. It has always been natural for architects to use parts of the body as measurements. The Egyptians used the distance between the elbow and the extended hand as their basic unit of length, the cubit. Cubits were divided into palms and each palm consisted of four fingers. (Our unit, the foot, is a similar practice.) Later the Greeks continued this tradition and used similar units to construct the Parthenon. This is why when the Roman architect Vitruvius visited the Acropolis to see the Parthenon he commented that "Man is the measure." In Fontana's time, Leonardo da Vinci embodied this sentiment in his famous drawing of a man with arms and limbs extended inside a circle. When Fontana began his calculations, his basic unit of length was the *palmo*, the palm, which was about 8.66 inches. For long lengths the cane was the unit, about 5.5 feet. Weight was calculated in pounds (*libri*), but the Italian pound during the Renaissance was about 0.7 of our pound.

When Fontana began calculating the obelisk's weight, he ran into a problem—he first had to determine its volume. The obelisk is not what in geometry is called a regular or Platonic solid. Its sides are not rectangles with right angles. It tapers towards the top, and at the pinnacle is a pyramidion. It is highly irregular. Fontana started by measuring the obelisk at its base and found it was slightly more than twelve palms—about nine feet square. At the top it tapered to a six-foot square. From the top of the obelisk he dropped a plumb bob to get an accurate length of the rectangular shaft—eighty feet. He now knew that he was dealing with a shaft of granite eighty feet in length, six feet wide at the top and nine at the bottom. He had his stonemasons cut a block of granite of one cubic palm and weighed it. Now he needed to calculate how many cubic palms there were in the obelisk, and this is where his mathematical ingenuity came in.

Fontana began by imagining a rectangle the size of the smaller cross section at the top extending downward inside the obelisk. This regular internal column, he easily determined, was 7,024 cubic palms. The hard part was calculating how many cubic palms remained in the rest of the obelisk that surrounded the internal rectangle.

He realized that if he took one wedge-shaped side that was outside the internal shaft and rotated it and then placed one of the other sides on top of it (think about stacking wedges) he would have a regular small rectangular shaft. Do this with the remaining two sides and you can calculate the number of cubic palms. He then approximated the cubic palms in the pyramidion at the top of the rectangular shaft and added all the cubic palms together (rectangular internal shaft + four wedge-shaped sides + pyramidion) multiplied by 86

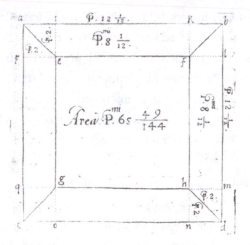

Figure 3.3 To calculate the weight of the tapering obelisk, Fontana divided it into regular solids. This diagram shows cross sections of the obelisk at different heights.

pounds (the weight of the sample cubic palm he had cut) and came to a total of 963,587 pounds, which in modern pounds is 337, 255 tons—just about right.

Once Fontana knew the weight of the obelisk, he calculated that he would need forty windlasses to lift it. Windlasses were traditionally used on ships to raise sails and anchors. The basic element is a gearbox in a horizontal wheel around which rope is wound or unwound. Levers radiating from the wheel give the men turning the wheel a mechanical advantage and greatly increase the weight that can be lifted. Although the windlass is horizontal, the pull can be converted vertically by running the rope through a pulley suspended above the object to be lifted.

Windlasses would be Fontana's main source of power to lift the obelisk off its base but, as a backup, he also intended to insert five huge levers under the obelisk so there would be extra lifting power if the windlasses were not adequate. It was a brilliant plan, but not everyone was convinced it would work. Could forty windlasses be used in tandem? Critics said that the windlasses would not pull evenly, a greater share of the load would fall on a few, and the ropes would break. Fontana himself had never seen so many windlasses used in concert, but he had done tests. He had four large horses pull with all their strength on one of the ropes and saw that they couldn't break it.

From other tests, he knew that when a windlass was overloaded, friction greatly increased and it wouldn't turn; thus the remaining moving windlasses would eventually take up more of the weight and things would even out. Fontana planned to monitor the windlasses as the work progressed. After every three or four turns of the windlasses, work would be stopped so he could feel the tension on the cords to make sure they were not near the breaking point. However, before Fontana could use his windlasses, he had to prepare the worksite.

Fontana had already prepared the foundation at the new site, but he had to shore up the old site around the obelisk because it had to support the weight of the castle. He sunk logs radiating out nearly forty feet from all four sides of the obelisk so the scaffold would remain stable even as it strained under the weight of the obelisk.

The castle was actually two halves on either side of the obelisk that were joined at the top for stability. Think of a giant ladder with the obelisk standing right in the middle. The structure was supported by four "masts" on each side composed of four huge tree trunks that had been hand-hewn into gigantic timbers. These tree-trunk/timbers were held together by iron hoops and massive bolts going through the timbers. For additional strength, wood wedges were hammered between the hoops and the timbers to maintain tightness. If anything shifted during the work, the wedges could be adjusted.

The castle is not easy to visualize, so Fontana provided a wonderful engraving. So that you can understand the basics of the construction, he has not shown all the wood elements. On the outside of the scaffold, forty-eight buttresses kept everything in place when the force of the obelisk being lowered was transferred to the scaffold. Fontana hasn't drawn all forty-eight, but the clearest ones to see are on the right side of the scaffold; they are the very long timbers angled up to the very top.

Now, look again on the right-hand side of Figure 3.4. See those little guys dangling from the ropes? They are pulling on the giant lever that was inserted under the obelisk to give extra lifting power in addition to what the windlasses would supply. In the foreground you can see a windlass being turned by a team of men supervised by two master builders. On the left, Fontana has already opened the sacristy wall of the old St. Peter's so several winches could be positioned inside to pull the bottom of the obelisk towards them.

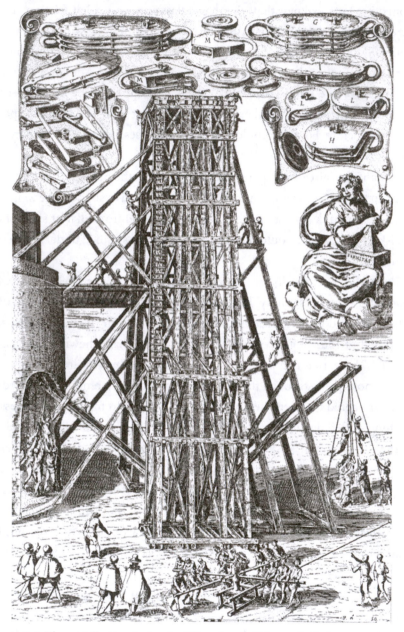

Figure 3.4 The *castello*, the rigging for lifting the obelisk, was built from massive timbers bolted together.

Fontana is never one to leave empty space in his illustrations. At the top he displays all the blocks, pulleys, and tackle that were used to lower the obelisk. The goddess to the right, below the blocks and tackle is Firmitas. The first-century architect Vitruvius said that three things were necessary to build well: commodity, firmness, and grace. Fontana had one of the commodities looking down on his project. The one thing you can't see in the illustration is the obelisk, and that's not an accident. The star of Fontana's book is not the obelisk, it's his beloved *castello*.

You also can't see that the surface of the obelisk was protected by a double layer of wood planks held together by an iron cage composed of strips that were bolted together and ran the full length of the obelisk. The ropes going through the blocks and tackles at the top of the scaffold were attached to this iron cage. When the windlasses turned the ropes were reeled in, pulling straight up on the cage, and the obelisk would rise off its pedestal straight up into the air. At least that was Fontana's plan.

When the Romans first set the obelisk on its pedestal they lowered it onto four massive bronze nodules that Fontana called *gnocchi* (dumplings) but which are traditionally called "astragals" because they resemble bones of the foot. Thus the obelisk wasn't resting directly on its stone base; there was daylight between the pedestal and the bottom of the obelisk and Fontana capitalized on this feature. He threaded his iron cage under the obelisk and up its sides so that when the windlasses turned and the pulleys transferred the forces to the obelisk, it would be pulled from the bottom as well as from the sides. The iron strapping alone weighed 40,000 pounds. The space between the obelisk and pedestal enabled Fontana to insert the immense levers supplementing the lifting force generated by the windlasses. It was a grand plan, well thought out, but would it work? The truth is, no one was sure.

Fontana was clearly worried about the windlasses so he numbered each one so that his foremen on top of the scaffold could shout down orders to the master builders stationed by each one. "Ease up on windlass 32" would thus be guaranteed a quick response. For weeks before the obelisk was to be lowered, Fontana trained his teams. Three or four horses turned each windlass, and one by one they were fine tuned till all had the same tension. Throughout the fall and winter, preparations had gone forward, fashioning the iron straps and pulleys, cutting the timber, pouring foundations, procuring horses, crafting the windlasses, and testing them. Finally, on April 30, 1586 Fontana was ready to lower his obelisk.

Show time

Two hours before dawn, two Masses were said and all workers involved in the project took communion. Even before first light, the crowds had been growing. For six months they had seen endless cartloads of iron and wood come into Rome; this was the biggest show in town and no one wanted to miss it. A barricade was set up around the work area and the entire police force of Rome was called in to keep order. It was explained that any non-worker crossing the barricade was subject to penalty of death. Strict silence was to be maintained by all spectators so Fontana's orders could be heard. To make absolutely certain there could be no confusion of orders, a twenty-foot-high platform was constructed for a trumpeter. When the workers heard the blast of the trumpet, they were to begin turning the windlasses. High on top of the scaffold was a great bell. When it was rung, work was to stop instantly. With a trumpet to signal "begin" and a bell for "stop," there wasn't going to be any confusion on this project.

At one end of the square twenty carters waited with twenty strong replacement horses in case any of the windlass horses tired. At the very base of the obelisk Fontana had twelve carpenters with sledgehammers and wedges ready to hammer in the wedges when the obelisk began to rise. Thus the obelisk would never be supported by ropes alone. These dozen carpenters were supplied with iron helmets to protect them from bolts that might fall from the top of the scaffold. Fontana had invented the hard hat!

Thirty men climbed high on the scaffold to monitor it for movement or signs of weakness. Below, thirty-five men were positioned to work the three levers inserted under the south side of the obelisk and another eighteen to work the two levers at the north end. When dawn finally came it seemed as if all of Rome had gathered to watch *God's work*, as Fontana called it. There were dukes and princes, cardinals, and foreigners who had traveled great distances to see the obelisk move. Every window of every house that faced the square was filled with heads, stretching to see something of the work. The Swiss Guards and light cavalry were spread along the barricade to ensure order and silence.

Fontana asked all assembled, workers and spectators, to kneel and pray for a successful outcome. When everyone rose, Fontana signaled the trumpeter and almost immediately 907 men, 75 horses, and 40 windlasses moved as one. The ground shook as with an earthquake and then a loud crack, like lightning, was heard across the square. Immediately the bell was rung and work halted. One of the iron hoops at the top of the castle had snapped. It was repaired and everything was inspected carefully. Months earlier, when Fontana had dropped a plumb line to measure the height of the obelisk, he had discovered it was leaning slightly. Now, as he examined the scaffold, he saw that the obelisk was perfectly upright. The first turns of the windlasses had moved it; the plan was working.

With the hoop repaired and the scaffold inspected, the trumpeter was told to give the signal to commence and once again horses and men went into motion. Slowly the obelisk rose into the air, but as it inched upward, more and more iron bands snapped. Fontana later said they looked as if they had been made of the softest material that had been cut by a knife. No longer confident that the bands could support the obelisk, Fontana brought in more than a quarter of a mile of the cord his rope makers had fashioned from hemp and wrapped it around the obelisk and its iron basket. Securely encased in its giant net, Fontana was confident the obelisk could once again move safely upward.

Throughout the day the trumpeter sounded, the windlasses turned and the obelisk moved upward. Rope had trumped iron and supported the Vatican needle. At dinner time, baskets of food were brought to the square so the workers would not have to leave their stations. Fontana was not going to worry about rounding up 907 men to begin the work after dinner. By ten o'clock in the evening, after fourteen motions of the windlasses, the obelisk had risen more than two feet above its pedestal. Iron and wood wedges were hammered into the space between the bottom of the obelisk and the pedestal, and with the obelisk resting securely on wedges, everyone returned home. The first day, not without its drama, ended in a resounding success.

The next day the astragals had to be removed because the next step was to swing the obelisk's bottom away from the pedestal so it could be lowered to the ground. The bronze "dumplings" would block the obelisk from swinging freely. As the men began removing the "dumplings," they discovered the task was far more difficult than anyone had expected. First, they were massive, weighing six hundred pounds each. Second, each was cast as a single piece, so it couldn't be taken out in sections. The biggest problem, however, was that on their top surfaces they had projections like rectangular bars that extended more than a foot into the bottom of the obelisk. For four days and four nights Fontana's metalworkers and stonemasons worked to move the bronze dumplings and finally succeeded. One of the supports was brought to the Pope, who was delighted to see tangible evidence of progress; once again the work of moving the obelisk could continue.

While the workers were removing the bronze supports, all the windlasses and pulleys were repositioned for lowering the obelisk. The east side was left completely free because that was where the obelisk was going to be lowered onto its sled. Fontana didn't want the obelisk supported only by the ropes so he cut four 45-foot beams that would support the obelisk as it was lowered. They inserted into the iron fittings that surrounded the obelisk and rested on rollers so they could spread apart, like a tripod, as the obelisk neared the ground. When the obelisk was closer to the ground, four shorter supports would be substituted until the obelisk rested on its sled.

For eight days, Fontana checked the newly positioned windlasses, testing the tensions, making sure they all worked in concert. Lowering the obelisk required even more coordination than raising it straight up, above the pedestal. The windlasses on the west side were attached to the bottom of the obelisk and had to pull, but the other windlasses had to slacken but still maintain tension as the obelisk went horizontal.

On May 7, Fontana was ready to lower the obelisk. When the trumpet sounded, the four windlasses on the west side pulled the bottom and the tip of the obelisk moved eastward. At various times the bell was rung, work stopped, ropes were tightened and the timber supports checked. As the obelisk was lowered, the massive sled on which it was to be pulled to the new site was slid on rollers under it. Fontana provides an illustration of the obelisk at the moment it was lowered to about 45 degrees. Perched on the top, a worker checks the tension on the ropes. At about the midpoint of the obelisk, inside the scaffold, we can see the tripod-like beams (darker wood) that supported the obelisk as it was lowered. The beams rest on the giant sled that has been placed beneath the obelisk. If you look closely—very closely—you will see the ends of the log rollers on which the sled will be pulled to the new site. In the foreground both men and horses turn windlasses. You can also make out two coils of rope, each with its own attendant to make sure the lines don't foul.

Figure 3.5 The obelisk was lowered onto a sled so it could be winched to the new St. Peter's Basilica.

Water on the ropes!

There is a legend that at this point in the operation Fontana encountered his greatest problem. As he continued to lower the obelisk there was too much friction on the ropes and they were getting dangerously hot. As will be remembered Fontana had erected a barrier to keep the onlookers back and had also instituted a policy of complete silence. When the ropes began to smoke, it was clear to all watching that something was wrong. Suddenly, from behind the barrier, a shout shattered the silence: "Acque alle funi!" "Water on the ropes!" The cry came from an old sailor, Bresca di Bordighera, who knew what to do from his years at sea. Water was immediately poured on the ropes, they cooled, and the day was saved.

It is a wonderful story, but the problem is that another version of "Water on the ropes!" appears with respect to a different construction project in a letter written in 1555, thirty years before Fontana moved his obelisk. Fontana's moving of the obelisk was very closely watched by all of Rome and there are no contemporary versions of the story; it doesn't appear in print till the eighteenth century. It simply didn't happen. All indications are that the obelisk was lowered throughout the day without any such drama.

By 10:00 p.m. the obelisk was safely resting on its sled. The crowd had stayed all day and was overjoyed to see their obelisk safely on the ground. Accompanied by drums and trumpets, they paraded the triumphant architect to his home.

Fontana did not rest long. The next day he returned with his workers to dismantle the windlasses, pulleys, and eventually the scaffold. The process took four days. Four of the windlasses were moved to the east side of the obelisk and were used to pull the obelisk on its sled completely clear of the scaffolding. Fontana did not want anything falling and damaging the obelisk as the workmen dismantled the scaffold. The pieces of the *castello* were carefully numbered so they could be easily reassembled when it was time to raise the obelisk.

With the obelisk moved clear of the *castello* and the scaffolding disassembled, Fontana's next chore was to dig out the pedestal from the debris that had buried it for centuries. He soon discovered that the pedestal was actually in three pieces, one large cube on top of another, with a molding in between them. The uppermost block, on which the obelisk had rested, was roughly an eight-foot cube and was totally above ground. It was placed on rollers and moved to the new site at St. Peter's Square. The molding was a thinner, eleven-foot square that rested on the third piece. When Fontana dug out the second block, he was surprised to find that it was slightly narrower than the top block. Almost always a pedestal tapers to the top. He concluded that two architects were involved, one designing the bottom and the other the top. Fontana clearly didn't like the top-heavy pedestal and wanted to make a new one, but there was no stone large enough in all of Rome, and there was no time to quarry one now.

At the new site Fontana was forced to reassemble the three blocks as they had been. This he did on top of the log-and-cement foundation that he had laid earlier. Again, he threw in more medals but this time he added a marble plaque inscribed in Latin with the Pope's name, a brief account of how the obelisk was moved, and the name of Domenico Fontana so he too could be part of this time capsule.

The "transportation" of the obelisk

Once the pedestal was reassembled the "dumplings" were put back in place and the site was now ready for the reassembly of the scaffold. As this took place, the next step was to transport the obelisk the 260 yards (115 canes) to St. Peter's Square, and this is where geography worked in Fontana's favor. St. Peter's Square was thirty feet lower in elevation than the original site of the obelisk—almost exactly the height of the pedestal. Fontana had two choices. Plan A: Pull the obelisk on its sled downhill to the new site and then lift it up thirty feet in the air to set it on the pedestal. Plan B: Build an elevated roadway for the obelisk so that it would remain perfectly horizontal as it traveled. This way, when the obelisk arrived at St. Peter's, it would be just above the pedestal and wouldn't have to be lifted very high.

Fontana chose Plan B, so a causeway seventy-five feet wide at the bottom and thirty-five at the top was constructed of earth, reinforced by wood buttresses. Huge beams were inserted through the width of the causeway and bolted together so the earth wouldn't slide under the great weight it would support. When the obelisk moved on top of it, pulled by several windlasses, it looked something like a railroad trestle. When the causeway reached St. Peter's, it was greatly widened and strengthened to accommodate the *castello*. With the scaffold re-erected, the obelisk, still on its sled, was pulled under it, the ropes attached and run through pulleys and threaded into the forty windlasses that had been repositioned to raise the obelisk. The plan was to raise it with the sled still attached as this would provide an extra layer of protection for the needle.

In the predawn of September 10, 1586 two Masses were celebrated, everyone prayed for a successful outcome, and Fontana's highly trained team took up their stations. Once again, the trumpet blew, the windlasses turned, and the tip

Figure 3.6 The obelisk on the causeway leading to the new location.

of the obelisk began its slow skyward journey. As the tip rose, four specially
positioned windlasses pulled at the bottom of the obelisk so it moved in the
direction opposite to the way the tip was moving. When the obelisk reached 45
degrees, the bell was sounded and food was delivered to the site so the workers
could eat. After dinner the process continued—three turns of the windlasses,
inspection of the scaffold and ropes, and then three more turns. Experience
lowering the obelisk had taught Fontana that he couldn't trust the iron bands
to support it, so this time he began with rope reinforcements and there was far
less drama. It took fifty-two turns of the windlasses, but at 9:00 p.m. the obelisk
was upright and the signal was given to fire cannons to let the city know that
the obelisk was upright. Rome rejoiced, but Fontana's work was not over.

Figure 3.7 Erecting the obelisk in St. Peter's Square was a brilliant piece of planning and organization.

The obelisk still had to be adjusted to its final position on the pedestal. For the next four days, pulleys and windlasses were repositioned for the obelisk's fine tuning. On the final day of the great project, the windlasses were tightened slightly, raising the obelisk just a bit so four massive fifty-foot levers could be slipped under the needle. When a team of men pulled downward on the ends of the levers, the obelisk would rise a bit and wedges were hammered in place. With the obelisk resting on wedges, the sled was finally removed. Now that the obelisk was free of its sled, the 600-pound bronze supports were reattached to the pedestal. Once again the windlasses were turned a bit and the obelisk rose so the wedges could be removed and the obelisk lowered onto its "dumplings." But something new had been added. Fontana really didn't like the dumplings and he commissioned the sculptor Prospero Bresciano to create four recumbent lions for each corner of the obelisk to hide the dumplings. So that it could be viewed with full effect from all angles, each lion has two heads, one for each side of the obelisk. By now it was dark and Fontana and his workers called it a day.

The next day, Fontana suspended a plumb bob from the top of the obelisk to its base to determine true vertical. He then added bronze plates to some of the "dumplings" so the obelisk would be perfectly upright. Finally, with the obelisk securely resting on its dumplings, now hidden by bronze lions, the iron cage and protective wood planks were removed and the obelisk was completely uncovered. Fontana had succeeded in the incredible task of moving the obelisk.

Fontana's accomplishment was one of the great engineering triumphs of the Renaissance, but the goal was not just physical. The obelisk was a symbol of Christianity's triumph over paganism; Rome's needle was seen as a lofty and graceful pedestal for the Holy Cross. The show was not yet over. The Pope had ordered that a ritual of exorcism be performed on the obelisk.

Casting out the devils

The ritual of exorcism is intended to cast out Satan and his demons and was not taken lightly by the Church. Only a specially trained priest could perform it. While the ritual was normally performed on a person, objects too could be exorcised and clearly the obelisk was viewed as a pagan monument that could house malevolent forces. In a sense, there was a double whammy on the obelisk: Egyptian and Roman. The Egyptians had quarried the obelisk, and the church had their gods to contend with. Then there were the early Romans who had confiscated and moved the obelisk to Rome; they were pagans also, so both Egyptian and Roman gods had to be exorcised.

On the morning of September 26, 1586, Bishop Ferratini held a Mass and then led a procession of more than three-dozen cardinals, bishops, monsignors, and other dignitaries up the obelisk's earthwork causeway to an altar that had been set up. Between six giant burning candles, holy water and hyssop had been laid in preparation for the ritual. Hyssop was the herb used by the Israelites to paint their door posts with lamb's blood so the Angel of Death would pass over their homes; it is also used by the church to dab holy water on objects to be purified.

The bishop purified and blessed the obelisk with holy water. Then, with his hand outstretched to the obelisk he began: "I exorcise you . . ." and performed the ritual of exorcism. After the ceremony, part of the exorcism ritual was carved on the east side of the obelisk's base:

ECCE CRVX DOMINI
FVGITE
PARTES ADVERSAE
VICIT
LEO DE TRIBV IVDA
Behold the Cross of the Lord! Flee Adversaries. The Lion of Judea has conquered.

Bishop Ferratini then walked around the obelisk three times and, with a knife that had been blessed, inscribed the sign of the cross on the obelisk's four sides. Next, a gilded seven-and-a-half-foot-high cross was placed on the altar and after it too was blessed, it was hoisted and fixed on top of the obelisk by Fontana's workers. The triumph of Christianity was complete. Trumpets were sounded, prayers recited, and all present received an indulgence of fifteen years!

An indulgence is the remission of temporal punishment for sins that have already been forgiven. Once the sinner has confessed and received absolution, the indulgence can be given for good works or for prayers. During the Middle Ages, pardoners rode circuits visiting those who did not live near a church. A corrupt pardoner is lampooned in Chaucer's *Canterbury Tales* for selling indulgences. The fifteen-year indulgence given by the Pope to those present at the exorcism relieved them of fifteen years' suffering in purgatory, but that was not the end of his generosity. Pope Sixtus V granted a further indulgence of ten years and ten periods of forty days to anyone who passing the obelisk, said an *Our Father* and a *Hail* Mary, and knelt before the cross to pray for the good fortune of the Holy Church and its pontiff.

Today it is still possible to obtain crosses, rosaries, and medals blessed by the Pope with indulgences attached to them. The practice of objects with indulgences attached began with Sixtus V and the Vatican Obelisk but did not end there. After the Vatican Obelisk, the Pope had Fontana erect another obelisk at the Lateran Basilica. Here too some old walls had to be removed, and in the process the workmen found a hoard of ancient coins with the cross on one side and early Christian emperors on the other. The coins were distributed and Sixtus V granted indulgences to those who possessed them. He issued a special Bull, "Laudemus viros gloriosos," on December 1, 1587, spelling out the benefits of these coins.

When the last religious rituals were performed on the Vatican Obelisk, Sixtus had a commemorative inscription cut on the top of the obelisk's west face: "Sixtus V, Supreme Pontiff, consecrates this stone to the Most Holy Cross, this stone torn away and stolen from its original place under Augustus and Tiberius Caesar." The inscription is interesting for several reasons. It is no surprise that it announces the obelisk is now consecrated to the Most Holy Cross. What is surprising is the selection of verbs used to describe the original moving of the obelisk to Rome—"torn away and stolen"—and that he names as the pagan thieves Augustus and Caesar. Caligula, who in AD 37 built the largest ship ever just to bring the obelisk to Rome, had been forgotten.

Another inscription placed on the obelisk indicates the Pope's generosity and appreciation for what Fontana had achieved. On the east face of the obelisk's base is a brief inscription attesting that it was Domenico Fontana who moved and erected the obelisk. Fontana was also made a Knight of the Golden Spur, a papal order of chivalry given to those who have contributed to the glory of the Church, either by feat of arms, writing, or other illustrious acts. Fontana was in good company. Before him, the artists Raphael and Titian had been awarded the Golden Spur and after him it would be awarded to, among others, a fourteen-year-old musical composer named Wolfgang Amadeus Mozart.

Fontana would go on to complete other projects for the Pope, including re-erecting a third, small obelisk. He assisted in completing the dome of St. Peter's, moved an entire chapel in one piece, and constructed an aqueduct to bring water to the highest of Rome's seven hills. When Sixtus died in 1590, Fontana did some work for the new pope, Clement VIII, but fell out of favor and moved to Naples were he died in 1607, aged 63.

When Fontana moved the Vatican Obelisk in 1586 he was the first in more than 1,500 years to attempt such a feat, completing the task in less than a year and with no loss of life. It would be another 250 years before anyone else would attempt to move a large obelisk.

4

Napoleon's Obelisk

Fontana's moving of the Vatican obelisk, one of the great engineering achievements of the Renaissance, was a complicated, difficult, and risky project and took someone with a great ego to accomplish it. When another obelisk finally was moved, it was due, indirectly, to another great ego, Napoleon Bonaparte.

Napoleon on the Nile

In the spring of 1798, Bonaparte was a 28-year-old general fresh from a victorious Italian campaign. He was an undefeated hero and the toast of Paris, but it is dangerous to have an unemployed hero around so the Directory, the ruling body of France, placed him in charge of their "Army of England" which was preparing to invade Britain. Napoleon inspected the ships and troops for the invasion and declared he wanted no part of a major naval battle. He suggested as an alternative that he invade Egypt (which had no navy) and thus cut off England's land route to India, striking a fatal blow to Britain's economy. Although Bonaparte gave solid political reasons for his Egyptian Campaign he had his own agenda. He wanted to follow in the footsteps of his hero, Alexander the Great, and said as much. "My glory is declining. This little corner of Europe is too small to supply it. We must go East. All the great men of the world have there acquired their celebrity." Yes, he would colonize Egypt, but he would do more. He would also reveal the hidden Orient to Europe and thus increase his greatness. Less than three months after his proposal, Bonaparte set sail for Egypt.

Sailing from Toulon on May 19, 1798, Napoleon took with him more than 17,000 troops and 700 horses. To all but a few, the destination was kept secret.

Napoleon had been authorized to occupy Egypt, free her of the tyrannical rule of the Mamelukes, expel the English from the east, take possession of the shores of the Red Sea, and cut the isthmus of Suez with a canal. It was an ambitious plan, but Napoleon intended to accomplish even more. Along with his troops and machinery of war, he brought a second, smaller army of more than 150 engineers, scientists, and scholars to study and describe both ancient and modern Egypt. Many of the savants were distinguished members of the National Institute and they included Gaspard Monge, a physicist who helped assemble the team and who became its leader; Claude-Louis Berthollet, a chemist; Jean-Baptiste Fourier, the mathematician after whom the Fourier equations are named; Déodat de Dolomieu, the mineralogist after whom the Dolomite mountains are named; and the brilliant young naturalist, Geoffroy Saint-Hilaire. With them Bonaparte also brought architects, surveyors, and cartographers to map Egypt and its monuments. There were also artists such as Vivant Denon, who later became the first Director of the Louvre. Officially called The Commission of Arts and Sciences, these men would found the modern discipline of Egyptology.

When the fleet finally landed at Alexandria on July 1, 1798, the troops found a sleepy town in the last throes of decay. They met little resistance, and were soon in control of the city. The next few weeks were spent organizing troops and marching to the capital, Cairo, where they would soon find themselves engaged in a battle that would add to Napoleon's growing legend. A fierce warrior class called the Mamelukes controlled Egypt, and they were not about to give it up. "Mameluke" is Arabic for "bought man." Around the year 1230 the Ayyubid sultan ruling Egypt brought 12,000 youths from the Caucasus Mountains to form an elite corps for his army. They were trained in the art of warfare, given the best of everything, and when they matured they killed the sultan in 1252 and ruled Egypt until the Turkish conquest of 1517. Although the Mamelukes were ostensibly obedient to the Sublime Porte, as Constantinople was called, they ruled Egypt as they pleased and paid Turkey only a small portion of the taxes they ruthlessly extracted from the peasants.

When news reached Cairo that the French army was marching from Alexandria, the Mamelukes massed for battle. Approximately 6,000 mounted Mamelukes and more than 10,000 of their foot soldiers faced an even greater number of French infantry and artillery. The battle presented a striking contrast in combat styles. The Mamelukes were dressed in colorful silks and wore turbans. Each had several pairs of pistols, as well as scimitars, lances, swords, and other hand weapons, many encrusted with jewels. They were followed into battle by servants running behind the horses to reload the spent pistols.

As the Mamelukes pranced in the distance, Napoleon, on his white horse, rode in front of his troops, pointed to the pyramids eight miles in the distance and said, "Soldiers, from these heights forty centuries of history look down upon you." In contrast to the fierce but undisciplined Mamelukes, Napoleon's troops were a well-constructed machine. They formed five battle squares with

Figure 4.1 When Bonaparte invaded in 1798, Egypt was controlled by the Mamelukes, a fierce warrior class.

artillery at the corners, riflemen at the sides, and cavalry inside the squares in case they were broken. The French were instructed to hold fire until the charging Mamelukes were almost on top of them. The first charge was decisive: The French held their fire, the Mamelukes charged, and when the French finally fired, hundreds of Mamelukes fell. The Mamelukes regrouped, made several more attempts to break the squares but suffered even greater casualties. Finally the Mamelukes rode off in defeat, heading south into Upper Egypt. It was clear they were no match for a western army.

The French took control of Cairo, the officers and savants established themselves in the hastily vacated Mameluke palaces, and the soldiers prepared for a long sojourn. Peace did not last long. On August 1 England's Admiral Horatio Nelson sailed into Abukir Bay off Alexandria where Admiral Brueys had anchored Napoleon's thirteen fighting ships and four frigates. Nelson had been searching for Bonaparte's fleet ever since he had heard they had left France, but because the destination was a well-kept secret he had to search throughout the Mediterranean before he found them.

Brueys had anchored the French fleet at Abukir Bay, close to shore to protect the landward side of the ships from attack, and mounted all the cannons pointing seaward so that if the enemy found him, all the firepower was on the enemy. The British discovered the anchored French fleet in the late afternoon and Nelson did two unexpected things. First, he decided to fight right then and there. Normally battles were fought during the day; beginning in the late afternoon guaranteed a night fight. Second, Nelson took the gamble that Brueys had not anchored the French fleet close enough to the shore, and sailed his fleet between the French ships and the shore. With all the French guns mounted seaward and the enemy landward, the French were almost literally sitting ducks.

As Egyptians watched from the shore, the battle continued into the night with cannon fire and burning ships illuminating the sky. Admiral Brueys on the *L'Orient*, the largest fighting ship in the world, had both legs shot off by a cannonball but refused to be taken below to the infirmary. He was placed in a chair, tourniquets tied around the stumps of his legs, and continued to command on the bridge until he was hit and killed by a second cannonball. Brueys was not alone in his heroism.

Throughout the night the British pounded away at the French fleet, sinking ship after ship. The *L'Orient* had been used to store the army's gunpowder and when it caught fire, it was clearly doomed. When the fire reached the powder magazine it exploded with a deafening roar that could be heard fifty miles away, a noise so loud that everyone was shocked and stopped fighting for ten minutes.

With the French fleet destroyed, Napoleon was now cut off from France, reinforcements, and supplies. Nelson simply sailed away, saying that Napoleon was in a jam and would not get out of it. The Admiral had no intention of fighting on land. When Bonaparte received the bad news in Cairo, he issued an Order of the Day. It doesn't mention defeat, merely the glory with which his sailors covered themselves at the Battle of the Nile, as it would come to be known.

In spite of this setback, the savants settled into their tasks. The senior men, Monge, Berthollet, and a one-legged general named Louis Caffarelli, who was in charge of financial and administrative matters, were housed in the palace of Hassan Kashef in Cairo. The botanists set up their experiments in the garden of Qassim Bey's palace. Saint-Hillaire was ecstatic about the space and was soon helping set up chemistry labs and collecting mineral, botanical, and zoological specimens.

As soon as the savants settled into their quarters, Bonaparte wanted something formal to guide their research. On August 21, he held a meeting to found the Institut d'Egypte, the world's first Egyptological Society, but soon Bonaparte had other matters to deal with.

The Turks were massing in Syria to reclaim Egypt, and Napoleon was forced to march to Acre to head off the invasion. On the way, a major battle was fought at Jaffa where more than 4,000 Turks and Moroccans were captured. By this time Napoleon's army was being ravaged by the plague and having difficulty finding food, so there was no way to hold all those captives. Napoleon ordered them to be killed.

On March 17, 1799 Napoleon began the siege of Acre. Djezzar Pasha, who was known as "The Butcher" because of his cruelty, camped his troops inside the fortress that had its back on the water. Normally the siege tactic was to starve out those inside, but the British sent Admiral Sidney Smith to supply rations and expertise from the water, so Napoleon found himself in the unfortunate position of having to attack the fort with inadequate artillery. Trenches were dug, and assaults were repeatedly mounted, but each time the French sustained heavy losses and were forced to withdraw. Finally on May 20,

1799 the French army, now suffering from ophthalmia, an eye disease, and the plague, returned to Cairo. It was Bonaparte's first defeat on land.

The Egyptian Campaign was not going well, but things were also going poorly back in France, so on the night of August 23, 1799 Napoleon, realizing the campaign was a lost cause, secretly sailed for France. He did not even say farewell to General Jean-Baptiste Kléber, for whom he left a letter appointing him Commander-in-Chief of the Army of the Orient. Kléber, a seasoned veteran of war, knew there was no hope for the Egyptian Campaign and began negotiating an honorable peace but was assassinated by a fanatic from Syria. General Abdullah Menou succeeded him. Menou had converted to Islam to marry a bathkeeper's daughter and had the respect of neither the Egyptians nor the French.

For three years, while a hopeless war raged, the savants scoured Egypt looking for temples, tombs, and artifacts to study. They studied the Rosetta Stone, sketched the first accurate plans of Luxor and Karnak Temples, mapped the Valley of the Kings, and, of course, measured and charted the pyramids. But Egypt's obelisks held a special fascination for them. They took the first detailed measurements of the two obelisks at Luxor Temple and the standing one at Alexandria. Their precise, architectural drawings of the obelisks are a far cry from the fanciful engravings produced by Kircher a century earlier. Napoleon's savants took the study of obelisks to a new level, all while working under the most difficult of conditions.

When a treaty with England was finally signed in 1801, one of the terms of the agreement was that the collections formed by the scientists were to be turned over to the English. The savants refused, declaring they would rather burn them than hand them over. The British permitted the scientists to keep their drawings and specimens, but the antiquities were another story. They all went to England and eventually the British Museum. The most famous of all the Egyptian antiquities in the Museum, the Rosetta Stone, is yet another legacy of Napoleon Bonaparte's Egyptian Campaign.

When the victorious British signed their treaty, it was suggested that they bring one of the two Alexandria obelisks home as a monument to the brave soldiers who had lost their lives. The officers and enlisted men happily agreed to donate a percentage of their salary to pay to remove the obelisk. This was the first time the English had thought about bringing a large obelisk home and it was not a carefully thought-out plan. It was soon realized that such an endeavor was well

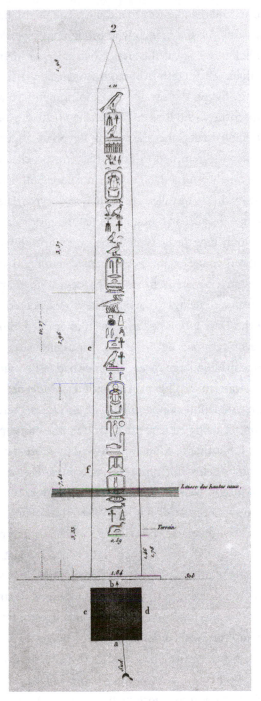

Figure 4.2 Bonaparte's savants conducted the first scientific study of Egypt's obelisks and published their findings in the *Description de l'Egypte*.

beyond their means and the idea was abandoned. The British had won the battle for Egypt, but it would be the French who brought an obelisk home first. The reason was mainly Egyptological: the French had a deeper interest in Egypt and its archaeology than the English. Although Bonaparte's army had suffered a disastrous defeat in Egypt, the savants' accomplishments were an intellectual triumph. They discovered the Rosetta Stone that enabled a Frenchman, Jean-Francois Champollion, to decipher the ancient Egyptian language.

Soon after Bonaparte returned to France he was proclaimed First Consul. When the savants finally returned to France, Bonaparte authorized funds for the publication of their work, to be called *Description de l'Egypte*. The publication was to cover everything—the ancient monuments, natural history, and modern Egypt (*c.* 1800), and was to include the first comprehensive map of Egypt. Edme Jomard, one of the expedition's young engineers, was named editor and solicited drawings, paintings, and research papers from his colleagues. A small army of engravers transferred the savants' drawings to copper plates so they could be printed.

Nothing like the *Description* had ever been attempted. One thousand sets were printed, each containing nearly a thousand large engravings, so approximately one million large sheets of paper had to be made by hand, each page bearing the watermark, "Egypt Ancienne et Moderne." It was not until 1809 that the first installment was published and then there were repeated problems. Bonaparte, losing patience, decreed that the entire project had to be completed by 1811, but that deadline was missed by more than a decade.

To speed production, five different printing companies were used to handle the job and Jean-Joseph Marcel, one of the two printers who went to Egypt with Bonaparte, now Director of the *Imprimerie Nationale*, oversaw the first installments. Because Bonaparte ordered that the maps of Egypt should remain "under the seal of a state secret," the map volume was the last to be published. Even after his exile, the maps were still considered state secrets, delaying their publication until 1828, seven years after the Emperor's death on St. Helena. When the *Description* was finally complete, five massive volumes of engravings depicted the Antiquities, with three volumes for Natural History, and two of Modern Egypt. Here were the first detailed realistic representations of the obelisks of Egypt. France was now in the forefront of Egyptology and would not relinquish that position for more than a century. While all of France was caught up with the fascination for things Egyptian, the British seemed only mildly interested. Still, England, not France, was given the next chance to bring an obelisk home. The offer was political.

As the *Description de l'Egypte* was being published, Egypt herself was not faring so well. When the British evacuated the country in 1803 they left a power vacuum. Ostensibly the Ottoman Empire was once again in charge with the Mamelukes subservient to them, but after Napoleon the dynamics had changed. The Mamelukes returned to Cairo from Upper Egypt to where they had fled, and the Ottoman government sent troops to Egypt to re-establish control. Many of these troops were Albanians who had not been paid for months and were grumbling. With limited funds to pay for its army, the Sublime Porte (the Sultan) disbanded the Albanians in the army in order to pay his own Turkish soldiers. The Albanians turned on the Turks, beginning nearly a decade of civil discontent in Egypt between three factions—Turks, Albanians, and Mamelukes. In the end, an Albanian officer named Mohamed Ali firmly established himself as ruler of Egypt in a brutal coup like something out of the *Arabian Nights*.

After much in-fighting, Mohamed Ali was given the title Governor (Pasha) of Egypt by the Ottoman government, but the Mamelukes, though temporarily peaceful, presented a threat to his power. On March 1, 1811, Mohamed Ali invited 470 Mamelukes to the citadel, an imposing fortress that was his palace/residence, to take part in the installation of his son as Commander of the Army. When the Mamelukes arrived, they were served coffee and then formed a procession on their horses. As soon as they reached the citadel's courtyard, the gates were bolted shut and Mohamed Ali's troops began firing down from the walls on the unsuspecting Mamelukes, slaughtering them all. Legend has it that one escaped by leaping onto his horse from the ramparts. It would have been an incredible feat if true, but what is certain is that Mohamed Ali was now the undisputed ruler of Egypt. He would prove to be a despot, but a progressive one, eager to modernize Egypt and form ties with European powers.

Would the English like an obelisk?

Mohamed Ali realized how much he owed to the British forces and in 1811 asked Samuel Briggs, the British consul, what present would be a proper gift for George III ("Mad King George"). Briggs suggested one of the two obelisks at Alexandria and Mohamed Ali offered an obelisk in gratitude for what the English had done for Egypt, but the British didn't act on it and nothing happened. In 1820 Mohamed Ali again offered an obelisk, this time to George IV, who had succeeded George III. When the British government learned that it would cost 15,000 pounds to retrieve their obelisk, they again did nothing to bring the obelisk to England. In 1831 Mohamed Ali offered the obelisk to

Figure 4.3 Champollion suggested that the French take one of the obelisks in front of Luxor Temple because they were in the best condition. Denon, who was with Bonaparte's expedition in 1798, drew the obelisks as they were then. Thirty-five years later the French took the one on the right to Paris.

William IV, and even offered to move it onto any ship the English sent to pick it up, but again Britain failed to take action.

England was not the only European power that Mohamed Ali was courting and he also offered the French an Alexandrian obelisk. Unlike the British, they sprung into action and accepted. However, Champollion had just made his first visit to Egypt, seen all the obelisks, and suggested that France instead ask

Figure 4.4 Early in the negotiations for an obelisk, the British were given one at Karnak. Even if they had wanted to take it, they couldn't have moved it because it was surrounded by ancient buildings.

for one of the two obelisks in front of Luxor Temple as they were in far better
condition than the pair at Alexandria.

> They are such insignificant little things compared with those of Luxor. If an
> Egyptian obelisk should be seen in Paris, it should be one of those from
> Luxor; there will still remain another one at Karnac, the most handsome of
> all, but I will never give my support to a plan (for which there is no need) to
> cut one of these magnificent monoliths into two or three pieces to move it.
> That would be sacrilege![1]

There were actually two standing obelisks at Karnak Temple but they are
surrounded by other buildings and would have had to be cut into sections to
remove. So, with this report from Champollion, the French turned their
attention to the Luxor obelisks.

Three obelisks are better than one

Baron d'Haussez, acting for the French government, wrote to Mohamed Ali on
November 25, 1829, requesting one of the Luxor obelisks. Mohamed Ali agreed
and the French immediately began designing a ship, the *Luxor*, to bring the
obelisk home. The ship had unique specifications. Because of the shape and
density of its cargo, the usual length-to-width ratio was not possible. Also, the
Luxor, in addition to being seaworthy, had to be capable of sailing on shallow
rivers (the Nile and Seine) and it had to be narrow enough to pass under the
bridges over the Seine. Further, it had to be able to land on a beach to permit
the obelisk to be loaded into the hull. Unlike the British, the French were
enthusiastic when it came to acquiring obelisks. As the construction of the
Luxor progressed, Baron Taylor was appointed Commissioner of the King of
France to the Pasha of Egypt. His mission was to get in writing the gift of more
than one obelisk; as many as possible! The negotiation had its difficulties.
Mohamed Ali had recently promised the Luxor obelisks to Mr. Baker, the
English Consul![2] Taylor worked out an arrangement where in exchange for
their Luxor obelisks the British were given one at Karnak. This probably didn't
matter much to the British, as they didn't seem eager to move *any* obelisk. In
the end, Mohamed Ali granted France both Luxor obelisks *and* the standing

obelisk at Alexandria. Unlike the English, the French moved into action quickly. Even before the *Luxor* was completed, the *Dromadaire* was sent to Alexandria, to lower the standing obelisk and return with it to France.

The *Dromadaire* was not specially built to bring home an obelisk and was too large to sail up the Nile so the only obelisk it could bring back was one on the Alexandrian coast. In their hurry to retrieve an obelisk, the French had not realized that timber was not readily available in Egypt and there was not enough wood for the scaffolding needed to take down a standing obelisk; consequently the plan was abandoned and the *Dromadaire* returned to France with its hold empty. Now French hopes rested on the *Luxor*, which, on April 15, 1831 sailed from Toulon for Egypt, just as Bonaparte had done three decades earlier.

Apollinaire Lebas to the rescue

Apollinaire Lebas, the engineer responsible for bringing the obelisk to Paris, left a remarkable account of its transportation. Perhaps most remarkable is the first sentence. "The brilliant and rapid conquest of Egypt by the French Army is inscribed in the annals of history. . . ."[3] He seems not to know that the French lost! Lebas, however, is not the only Frenchman to wax poetic about Bonaparte's victories in Egypt. Lieutenant Léon de Joannis, second in command on board the *Luxor*, who also published his memoir of the adventure, begins by extolling Bonaparte's achievements in Egypt[4] and also credits Bonaparte with the idea of bringing an obelisk to France.

France was now interested in all the obelisks it could procure and Count de Sebastiani relayed the French government's orders to Lebas.

> If, as I presume, only one obelisk will fit on the *Luxor*, the operation will be made twice, it will be necessary to begin with the one on the right, which was said to be the more precious, as you will see from the copy here appended of a letter by Mr. Champollion the younger, who has recently seen and translated the inscriptions.[5]

Neither Count de Sebastiani nor Lebas realized how difficult it would be to bring one obelisk home, nor that it would be five years before the citizens of Paris would see their obelisk erected in the Place de la Concorde.

Figure 4.5 Frederick Norden's 1737 engraving and caption of Alexandria's fallen obelisk spread the false belief that the obelisk was broken.

When Lebas arrived in Alexandria in the spring of 1831, he had to wait twenty days for the French Consul to return to the city. It would be the first of many delays, but it gave him a chance to visit the two Alexandrian obelisks and to see what he would have to deal with in Luxor. One obelisk still rested on its pedestal, but the second had fallen centuries ago and was half covered with sand. It is widely believed that it fell during the earthquake of 1301, but that is far from established. Because it was covered in sand, many early travelers wrongly believed it was broken. Norden's 1757 illustration of the fallen obelisk bears the caption "A broken obelisk, fallen down, and partly buried."[6]

On June 6 the Consul was finally in Alexandria and Lebas, accompanied by him, met with Mohamed Ali. Lebas was extremely short and the Pasha made a joke of it, pretending not to see him and asking, "Where is the engineer?" Despite the joke, they hit it off very well and Lebas, armed with permissions from the Pasha, was soon on his way to Luxor. The *Luxor* could not sail immediately because the water was too low for it to pass over a large sandbar in the middle of the Nile, so Lebas left with a small fleet of boats and brought with him all the equipment he would need to lower the obelisk. Later, when the *Luxor* caught up with him, he would load the obelisk on board. On his way south he had an audience with the Governor of Cairo, who informed him that there was a crack in the obelisk he intended to take. Neither Champollion nor any books describing the obelisk had mentioned a crack, so Lebas, convinced the Governor was wrong, continued happily on his way south.

Luxor at last

A month later Lebas and his flotilla of small boats approached Luxor. Word had already spread that a fleet of Europeans was near and a crowd awaited him on the bank. Most were begging and simply wanted *baksheesh* from the foreigners, but some asked why they had come. They rarely saw foreigners. Today Luxor is a thriving tourist destination but in the early nineteenth century it was a small village of less than a thousand inhabitants and rarely visited by Europeans. Most visitors came to Egypt on business, conducted their transactions in Alexandria, or on rare occasions went as far south as Cairo. There was no need to go south to Luxor.

Some of Lebas' crew scampered ahead to get a close-up view of the obelisk while Lebas lingered to answer questions. Through his interpreter, Lebas explained that they had come to take the obelisk back to France but the locals would not believe him. They couldn't see the value in an obelisk, and where was the ship large enough to transport it? Besides, everyone knew the obelisk was fixed to the pedestal with a special cement that made it impossible to remove without cutting it in pieces. When asked who was in charge of this supposed project, the interpreter pointed to Lebas, which only added to their disbelief. "Who? That one? My stick is taller than he is! He is not capable of moving even the smallest stone in the temple."[7] The locals were convinced that the obelisk was a pretext. The French were there to lean about the country and the people and then would return to conquer. As this conversation was proceeding, Lebas and his men made their way towards the temple and its obelisks.

The obelisk is cracked!

When they arrived, Lebas found his Italian stonemason, Mazaconi, gently tapping the obelisk on the right with his hammer, intently listening to the sound that resulted. As soon as he saw Lebas he called out in a mixture of Italian and French, "The stone, she is cracked, but I do not believe broken. The sound is good. We will be able to remove it, if it falls slowly, very slowly."[8] The Governor of Cairo had been right! It was cracked.

Lebas was stunned. He couldn't believe no one had spotted the crack, not even the great Champollion. Despondent, he slowly made his way back to the boat, never noticing his exotic surroundings, thinking only about the crack. His fear was that the obelisk might fall apart during the lowering and he would be blamed. The next day Lebas' spirits were better. After all, the stonemason said the obelisk was sound. Preparations could proceed.

The obelisk was covered with ten feet of debris and there were about thirty mud brick huts the villagers lived in that would have to be demolished to clear a path to the Nile for the obelisk. After lengthy negotiations, the huts were purchased for about three times their true value and clearing proceeded full steam ahead.

Lebas began by removing the debris that covered the lower portion of the obelisk and its pedestal. He hired 400 men, women, and children to remove the

Figure 4.6 Apollinaire Lebas cleared the debris covering the pedestal and was the first in modern times to see its decoration.

accumulation of centuries, the men breaking up the debris with pickaxes, the women and children carrying the rubbish away in baskets on their heads. Lebas had no trouble finding workers. He paid them a small salary, but this was far better than what they were used to. When Mohamed Ali needed a workforce, he simply conscripted them with no pay and treated them brutally.

Once the debris was removed, Lebas could see the pedestal on which the obelisk rested, and discovered carvings of sacred baboons that greeted the sun each morning. On two sides of the pedestal were images of bound foreign captives, silent testament to the might of Ramses the Great, who erected the obelisk.

The ship built for one passenger

With the base cleared, the next task was to grade a ramp from the obelisk to the Nile where the *Luxor* would be run aground, facing the obelisk. On August 14 the *Luxor*, having safely navigated the sandbar near Cairo, arrived in Luxor.

Figure 4.7 The *Luxor* was run aground so the obelisk could be loaded onto it.

There was a happy reunion of the ship's crew and Lebas' advance party. They were strangers in a strange land and felt a strong bond.

Captain Verninac ran the ship aground as planned so that its bow lined up with the path the western obelisk would take. The crew immediately began enlarging the living quarters Lebas had established inside the temple. They built rooms out of local mud brick, and used the trunks of date palm trees split in three for roof beams. They planned a garden, set up an infirmary, and built furniture. There was a kitchen, complete with a bakery, and storerooms were built to keep equipment secure. Everyone was in good spirits; this was the adventure of their lives. They were bringing France her obelisk.

Lebas' Egyptian workers carted away 450,000 cubic meters of rubbish, cut through two villages, removed the thirty huts, and graded the quarter-mile path to the Nile. Working fourteen-hour days, it took four months to complete the slope, all the while battling intense summer heat.

On August 27 a ship arrived in Luxor and announced that cholera was raging throughout Alexandria and Cairo. Two weeks later, a Turk recently arrived in Luxor died of cholera. Soon it spread through Lebas' workmen, killing dozens of the Egyptians. Fifteen of the sailors were stricken with cholera but survived due to good care by the ship's doctor. Through it all, work on the path to the ship continued.

A mountain of timber

Lebas had brought from Toulon eight carpenters and two blacksmiths to fashion the capstans, scaffolds, and metal fittings for the project. Nothing like this had been done since Domenico Fontana moved the Vatican obelisk in 1586. Lebas had read Fontana's description of how he did it and knew that Fontana used capstans and horizontal winches, turned by both men and horses, to lower the obelisk. Lebas also planned to use capstans but he had an advantage. The Vatican obelisk had first been moved fifteen centuries earlier, by the Romans who brought it from Egypt. When they re-erected it in the Circus they used bronze pins and fittings at the obelisk's corners to fix it to the pedestal. The pins and fittings caused Fontana considerable difficulty when he tried to lift the obelisk off its base. The obelisk Lebas was moving had been placed on its base 3,000 years ago by ancient Egyptian stonemasons who didn't use anything to attach the obelisk to its base. The 250-ton obelisk was simply balancing on its end and so would be easier to lower.

Lebas constructed two systems for the project—one for lowering the obelisk and one for restraining it. To lower the obelisk, a roller was going to be placed on the pedestal at its western side. Ropes would be attached to the obelisk and when the capstans were turned the obelisk would rotate around the roller, lift off the pedestal and begin to point its tip downward. At the point where the descending obelisk passed through the center of gravity of rotation, the restraining apparatus would come into play to hold back the obelisk and keep it from crashing into the dirt road they had constructed to receive it. The restraining apparatus made use of the second Luxor obelisk standing just 100 feet away. By a system of ropes and pulleys, Lebas could use that obelisk as an anchor to help lower his. He would also use three capstans, each manned by sixty-four men to restrain the obelisk.

For the first few months, before building the lowering and restraining systems, the ship's carpenters trained local workers how to saw planks using ripsaws with precision. First they practiced on the trunks of date palms, then, when proficient, they sawed the oak planks needed for the sheer legs—the 100-foot structures on which the pulleys and rigging were suspended. It was a huge task, but everyone was happy to be working on something so important.

Before the obelisk could be lowered, it had to be clad in wood to protect the beautiful hieroglyphs Champollion had so much admired. A scaffold was created

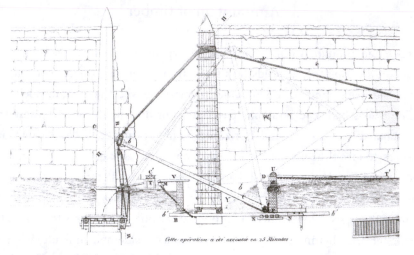

Cette opération a été exécutée en 25 Minutes.

Figure 4.8 Lebas designed an elaborate system of pulleys and rigging to lower the western Luxor obelisk.

and sailors accustomed to rigging were quite happy to climb to the top and attach the French tricolor. They were exuberant and shouted down, "Now it belongs to France. Soon Paris will have this monument." Lebas knew that the most difficult work was still ahead and it was all his responsibility. He responded to the men with a quote from La Fontaine. "Never sell the bear skin without first killing the bear."

In September the cholera epidemic subsided and preparations to lower the obelisk proceeded. The scaffolds, capstans, and riggings were built and erected. Lebas drilled the men on how to turn the capstans, how to hold the ropes and how to follow commands. He had made precise calculations of the forces on the different parts of the system, calculating the friction on the ropes, the forces on the sheer legs, and the strain on the cables as they went through the pulleys. It all worked on paper, but in the back of Lebas' mind there was still a lingering worry about the obelisk's crack. What if it fell apart while being lowered? Still, the time had come to lower the obelisk; it was now or never.

Show time

At dawn on October 23 everyone was in place to lower the obelisk. Sailors quickly scampered up the sheer legs and decorated them with palm fronds and

French flags. One hundred and ninety Egyptian workers waited by their capstans for the order, and at Lebas' command began slowly turning in unison. The ropes went taut, straining under the force, and slowly the obelisk tilted towards the river and began detaching from its ancient base. Then everything stopped. The obelisk, inclined at 8 degrees, needed to rotate through 90 degrees to be horizontal, but it would not budge; it was frozen. The officer in charge of the capstans checked the system and discovered that the anchors stabilizing the system had pulled out of the ground and were dragging across the sand, causing tension on the restraining ropes that were now holding the obelisk back. More rope was played out and once again the obelisk began its slow descent.

The obelisk has landed

When the obelisk reached the center of gravity of the pivot point the restraining system was activated to slow its descent. At 25 degrees the motion was stopped to check tension on all parts of the system. Everything was in order and the obelisk continued its descent to the path. Fifteen minutes later, it was safely resting on a platform built to receive it. With the obelisk down, Lebas, for the first time, could see the top of the pedestal and made a wonderful discovery. Pharaohs frequently chiseled out the names of previous owners on monuments they wanted to claim as their own, and Ramses was one of the most enthusiastic practitioners, so he knew it could happen to him. Before he erected his pair of obelisks in front of Luxor Temple, he carved his name on the tops of the pedestals so that when the obelisks rested on the pedestal they covered the names and no one could get to them. It worked.

Building the platform that the obelisk was now resting on had not been easy. Lebas knew that Egypt had no forests, so he had brought all the oak timbers to build the lowering apparatus from France. His calculation of the amount of wood needed was precise, with little left over, but the plan was that if they needed a few pieces of lumber they could get that from Alexandria. Several times they sent word to Alexandria that they needed more timber, but received no reply, perhaps because the cholera epidemic had reduced communications between cities. They would have to make do with what they had. Lebas had intended to place the obelisk on a giant sled and haul it over the newly constructed pathway

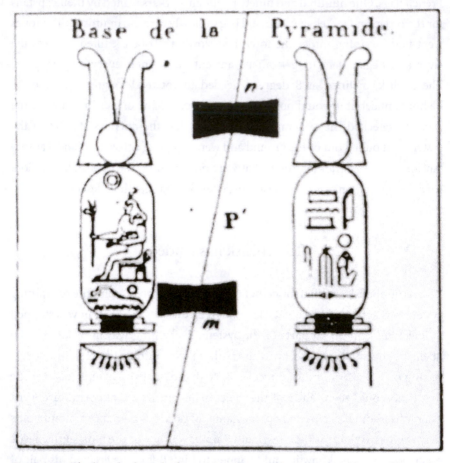

Figure 4.9 The base had cracked in ancient times and was repaired by two "butterfly clamps." Ramses carved his cartouches on the pedestal before the obelisk was lowered onto it so that no later pharaoh would be able to carve Ramses' name off.

to the Nile, but there were no large timbers left to build the sled, only a few small planks. An ingenious solution was needed and the carpenter had it.

The carpenter designed a wood platform composed of three detachable sections that end to end were about seventy feet long. This was the platform onto which the obelisk was lowered. A fourth section was now built out of the scaffolding used to lower the obelisk, which was no longer needed now that the obelisk was down. The fourth section was placed at the front and the obelisk was then winched onto it. As the obelisk moved forward, the rear section could be removed and moved to the front. Thus the obelisk crept towards the beached ship in fits of about twenty-five feet at a time. Crafting the fourth section had exhausted the supply of wood and the master carpenter explained to Lebas, "I have nothing left, not even a piece of wood to make a tongue or bracket that we will probably need during the operation. It is all as you feared, and if any of the planks should break, it will be impossible for me to fix them."[9]

Lebas had succeeded in lowering the obelisk with spectacular success. The entire process took less than an hour, the obelisk was still in perfect condition, and no one had been injured. Now the obelisk had to be hauled on its fragile platform to the beached *Luxor* and loaded onboard.

In the broiling Egyptian sun, workers using four capstans hauled the obelisk down the path that Lebas had so carefully prepared. Once they saw that the platform was holding, it was just a matter of patience. Each time the obelisk moved twenty-five feet, the rear section of the platform was removed, moved to the front, earth packed solidly under it, capstans repositioned, and then the process repeated. By December 19 the obelisk was exactly in front of the *Luxor*.

Figure 4.10 A village had to be torn down to build a road from Luxor Temple to the ship.

The original plan was to cut a hole in the hull large enough to admit the obelisk and winch it in, but this was no longer possible because of the lack of wood. To close the hole would have taken considerably more lumber than they had. The solution was to saw off the entire bow of the ship and, once the obelisk was in, reattach it, which would require less lumber. By now everyone was very experienced with the capstans and their rigging. Once the hull was sectioned and preparations made, within two hours the obelisk was safely inside the *Luxor*. Then came the big wait.

Nubian adventure

The Nile rises and falls once a year and, with the obelisk safely on board, Lebas needed a high Nile to sail for Alexandria, but he had missed it. Not wanting to risk getting snagged on a sandbar, Captain Verninac decided to wait for the Nile to rise in July before sailing for Alexandria. Afraid that the blistering sun would dry the *Luxor*'s wood hull while they waited six months for the Nile to rise, the captain buried the ship in earth and covered the huge mound with reed mats. Each day the vessel, looking more like a hill than a ship, was watered like a plant, to keep it cool.

Figure 4.11 While waiting to sail, the *Luxor* was covered in sand and reed mats to prevent the blistering Egyptian sun from cracking the ship's wood hull and masts.

After months of tension, there was now a sense of relief. The difficult part was done and the obelisk was safely inside the *Luxor*. With nothing to do but wait for the Nile to rise, Lebas, Lieutenant Joannis, and some other members of the crew decided to go south to see the monuments of Upper Egypt and Nubia. As mentioned before, very few Europeans went as far south as Luxor; to go even farther south was an adventure. Both Lebas and Joannis have left their memoirs of the trip. They went as far south as Abu Simbel and were awed by its size and silent beauty. They spent three days exploring the mysterious temple. Lebas, ever the engineer, measured the four colossal statues of Ramses and almost everything else. Napoleon's savants never went south to Abu Simbel so Lebas' professional measurements were a real contribution to Egyptology. On the way back to Luxor they stopped at some of the smaller Nubian temples, including Dandur, which is now in New York's Metropolitan Museum of Art, just a few hundred yards from New York's obelisk.

The temples definitely impressed both Lebas and Joannis but it seems as if something other than the monuments made the deepest impression on the two travelers. Lebas describes one of the itinerant dancers known as the *almees* and in particular one dance. His description is worth quoting.

I will limit myself to recalling a few characteristics of the one they call the *Dance of the Bee*. The *aimée* appears dressed in pantaloons with a skirt on top, a sash, and a belt. Her head is covered by a large veil that falls to the top of her legs. The music starts, and the artist begins to dance and sing while clapping her cymbals. This is a kind of entrance and has nothing to do with the main scene. The first real movements are languid. The face of the *aimée* is motionless. She walks rather than dances. This preamble lasts about a quarter of an hour. After a while, she pretends to hear the buzzing of an insect flying in the room. She lends it an ear, looks, pretends to chase it, continues her steps, and then declares with a painful scream that she is being stung by a bee. Then the two instrument players and her companions come near, screaming at the top of their lungs, AK-AKO! (There it is, there it is!) The movements become much more frenetic. The *aimée* redoubles her complaints, brings her hands to her body, first on one side, then the other, turns and spins in all directions. Her face becomes animated, her black eyes flash and roll. She is suffering from the most violent pains. She squats and her body, enveloped by her veil, rolls on the ground, sometimes pursuing the cruel animal that stings her, sometimes trying to escape from it. Her reiterated exclamations and her most vivid complaints intertwine with cries, AK-AKO, of the assistants who clap their hands in cadence. The beat of the music accelerates more and more. The Basque drums and the piercing sound of the castanets accompany the jerky movements of the *aimée*. Exhausted with fatigue, her voice faint, one only hears the piercing screams of her companions: AK-AKO *embeillaho*: Here it is, here's the bee! The torture she endures is unbearable. Finally she loses all restraint; she throws off her veil; her hair falls in disorder on her shoulder, but the cruel animal persists. It continues to pierce her with its stinger. It takes refuge under the belt and she flings it off violently. It goes under her sash, under her dress. With the same movements, the same intensity, everything is thrown off. Finally it goes under her pantaloons, the last refuge of modesty. The *aimée* brings her hand to it and, torn between the two feelings, she abandons the last piece of clothing and faints to the floor. A veil, thrown by the matron with precision and agility, instantly covers the nudity of the dancer.[10]

Lebas has seen an Egyptian striptease and will never forget it. Lieutenant Joannis also felt compelled to record his impressions of the *Dance of the Bee*. His description is basically the same as that of Lebas. Joannis, however, goes one step farther and becomes the dance critic, comparing the *Dance of the Bee* to ballet, and ballet comes off the loser!

> This dance is really admirable when it is well executed. It is, however, very difficult, because it is necessary to play a pantomime feigning a violent passion, and it is necessary to dance and to sing at the same time, and all of that can't be done without a certain genius.
>
> I recalled, on seeing this original and interesting fiction, our bland ballets, where several pretentious women depress us with leg rounds and jumps while fifty or so automatons are behind looking on.[11]

When the expedition to Nubia returned to Luxor, they removed the earth and mats that covered the *Luxor* and found it in good condition. Towards the end of June the Nile began to rise. Each day they eagerly checked the water level, waiting for the day they could sail. By August 6 the boat just needed another foot of water to float off the bank, but the Nile started to fall and continued to do so for a week. Despondent, they asked the oldest sheikh at the mosque if he had seen anything like this before. If the Nile didn't rise, it would mean famine for Egypt and they would be stranded for another year. The sheikh replied in very serious tones.

Child, don't be worried. Mohamed is good and great, and the lands are not yet flooded. The Nile is like a spirited horse at the start of a long race, breathing to take in wind. In a little while it will be headed up with new vigor. While you are waiting, make an offering of two sheep to the mosque.[12]

Departure at last

On August 12 the Nile began to rise again and on the 25th the *Luxor* began its journey north to Alexandria and the open sea. This time they were navigating the Nile with the current, and often the problem was how to steer the *Luxor* as it sped north with the obelisk in its hold. But because the prevailing winds are out of the north, they could also raise sails and use them against the wind as a brake to slow the *Luxor*.

On October 1 the happy crew arrived at Rosetta, near Alexandria, but there was a problem. The ship was unable to navigate the sandbar and waited for several months for water conditions to change. In late December they heard that a ship loaded with oranges had successfully passed the sandbar and Captain Verninac decided to try. It took three days to rig the *Luxor* for the attempt, but on January 1, 1834 at 11:00 p.m., after scraping the bottom several times, the *Luxor* successfully crossed the sandbar.

Once the *Luxor* had crossed the sandbar, it was met by the *Sphinx*, a steamship sent to tow the *Luxor* to Alexandria and then across the Mediterranean. Because the *Luxor* had been built for a very specific purpose, to navigate rivers with an obelisk in its hold, compromises in its seaworthiness had been made. It had safely sailed across the Mediterranean to Egypt, but then the hold had been empty. As Lieutenant Joannis put it, "To speak more of how *Luxor* comported itself at sea I would be obliged to enter into detailed discussions of little interest to the reader, but I can assure you without contradiction that the lowliest three-masted bark imaginable could be more easily navigated and be more seaworthy."[13] With an obelisk in its hold, the Luxor would have to be towed to France.

On New Year's Day, 1833 the *Luxor*, towed by the *Sphinx*, reached Alexandria Harbor having successfully traveled the 500 miles down the Nile. Now high seas and winter winds worried Captain Verninac and he decided to wait another three months before venturing out of Alexandria's safe harbor. On

April 1, with the *Sphinx* towing the *Luxor*, the obelisk began its international journey.

The obelisk at sea

The first few days were uneventful but then they hit strong headwinds and heavy seas. Afraid that the *Sphinx* might run out of coal at sea from fighting the headwinds, they headed for Rhodes, five days away. After a few days at Rhodes they sailed on, finally reaching Toulon on May 10 at two o'clock in the morning. The obelisk was finally in French territory, but not yet on French soil. The crew was quarantined for twenty days and then Lebas disembarked for Paris to make arrangements for erecting the obelisk. Captain Verninac and the crew made repairs to the *Sphinx* and after 42 days in Toulon, the obelisk continued towards Paris via Gibraltar. At Cherbourg Captain Verninac received orders to dock. The royal family was going to pay the obelisk a visit! The *Sphinx* and *Luxor* were scrubbed in anticipation of the royal visit, which was a great success with Verninac being promoted to Captain of Corvettes.

After the visit, the *Sphinx*, which drew too much water to navigate the Seine, was replaced by the *Heva*, a much smaller steamship. At Rouen, progress

Figure 4.12 The *Luxor* was towed by the steamer *Sphinx* through some high seas on its way to France.

stopped as the river was too low to navigate and, during the three-month wait for it to rise, the *Luxor* was dismasted so it could pass under the Seine's bridges. When the water was sufficiently high, the *Luxor* and its three-thousand-year-old cargo continued on, this time pulled by sixteen horses along the banks. On December 23, 1833 the obelisk reached Paris.

It would be two years before Lebas would attempt to set the obelisk on its pedestal. There were many things to be done and many delays to be overcome. First a dry dock for the *Luxor* had to be prepared so the obelisk could be off-loaded. This could only be done during the season of low water, so that was one setback. Then there was a carpenters' strike, so the obelisk couldn't be unloaded till August of 1834, when the water was low again. This was done with the help of five capstans, each with sixteen bars turned by forty-eight men. Once again, Lebas did all the calculations and figured that the force generated would be almost twice what was needed to move the obelisk. He wanted a cushion to overcome any unforeseen accidents, frictions, or snags. On August 9, 240 artillerymen began turning the capstans and the obelisk moved out of the *Luxor*, onto a cradle prepared for it, and came to rest on the banks of the Seine. It had at last reached French soil, but would remain at that spot for more than a year.

The pedestal had not yet been prepared and there were lively debates about its design and what kind of stone to use. When that was settled, the hull of the *Luxor* was closed and the *Sphinx* towed it to a quarry in Normandy where five huge granite blocks that would form the pedestal were loaded into the *Luxor*. When they returned to the banks of the Seine, once again they had to wait for low water before they could off-load the blocks of granite and drag them to the Place de la Concorde. Once in place, the blocks were assembled and decorated with gilded carvings showing the apparatus Lebas used to lower the obelisk. Now, at last, the obelisk could be moved towards its final resting place.

Raising an obelisk

On April 16 the obelisk began its final four-month journey towards the Place de la Concorde. Now Labas prepared to raise the obelisk onto its pedestal. A stone ramp was built from the ground to the top of the pedestal. The plan was to haul the obelisk up the incline so the foot of the obelisk was level with the top of the pedestal, then rotate the obelisk 90 degrees to set it upright on the pedestal. It would, of course, require much more force to pull the obelisk up an incline than to pull it on level ground, but Lebas had a spectacular plan. He would dispense with the capstans and artillerymen, and would use a new invention that he believed would change the world—the steam engine! There had been considerable resistance to the steam engine, probably because people feared it and just didn't understand it. It had already been successfully used for ships, but on land was another matter. Lebas would promote the use of the new invention and thus help mankind. He said:

> No occasion could be more perfect to brilliantly and solemnly open the eyes of the entire people assembled to the power of this marvelous agent. It would be an incredible spectacle to see a mass of 500,000 pounds rise majestically into space without the help of an animal force and raise itself on its base with the help of the most powerful invention of modern times, perhaps the only one to which the ancients could not claim priority.[14]

But it was not to be. When the steam engine was tested with the obelisk in tow, one of the boilers failed and it was abandoned. Lebas was disappointed, and he was not the only one. Michel Chevalier, a writer for the *Journal des Débats*, gives a wonderful window into how the steam engine was viewed in 1836.

> For some part of the public, the steam engine is an unknown—some sort of mysterious and formidable creation, subject to exploding like thunder. It would have been good to associate ancient monuments and arts with one of the most beautiful products of the inventive spirit of the modern day. It would have been wonderful to show two hundred thousand people one of these machines, so often thought as vulgar, seizing without embarrassment the obelisk of Sesostris and calmly, little by little, with perfect regularity—its firebox, the soul of the machine, fed only by coal—raise it without the help of any living being apart from its driver. These machines are destined to liberate human kind from all work that can be done only by brutal force.... The steam engine is one of mankind's best conquests over nature, at once both serving nature and helping man. It is its destiny to be enslaved, and to be the only slave, the only serf, of the future.[15]

So the obelisk would have to be moved up the ramp and erected by manpower. It took three days for the capstans to be assembled and positioned but then the obelisk, in its cradle, propelled by 120 men and four capstans began slowly moving up the ramp towards the pedestal. In order for the obelisk to come to rest in its proper position on the pedestal, it was crucial that the foot of the obelisk arrive at a precise spot where the ramp met the top of the pedestal. After five hours of capstans turning, the obelisk was at its destination, only two centimeters from its desired position.

For the next two weeks the apparatus for raising the obelisk along with all the rigging and pulleys were set up. The procedure for raising the obelisk would be essentially the reverse of lowering it, with the base of the obelisk pivoting around a roller fixed to the pedestal. On October 24, the day before the scheduled raising, the system was tested and everything worked perfectly— so perfectly that Lebas wanted to continue and set the obelisk on its pedestal! But orders "from above" said "no." Lebas would have to wait until tomorrow.

Figure 4.13 A special medal with the portrait of Louis Philippe was struck to commemorate the erection of the French obelisk.

Early the next morning crowds began to fill the Place de la Concorde and by 11:30 more than 200,000 were crowded together to see their obelisk set on its pedestal. The day was cloudy and cold, but with no rain in sight, which was important as rain would affect the ropes and make things slippery. Before beginning the great maneuver, a small cedar box containing French gold and silver coins of 1836 was placed inside a compartment in the pedestal. In addition to the coins there was a commemorative medal bearing the king's portrait on one side and on the other the inscription "Under the reign of Louis-Philippe I, King of the French, M. de Gasparin, Minister of the Interior, the obelisk of Luxor was raised on its pedestal on the 25th of October, 1836 by the care of M. Apollinaire Lebas, Marine Engineer." Lebas' place in history was established. Now he just had to raise the obelisk.

At 11:30 a.m. Lebas gave the signal, a trumpet blared, and the forty-eight soldiers assigned to each of ten capstans began turning. Ropes from the capstans ran over ten tall masts, five in front of the obelisk and five in back, which continued downward from the masts to chains fixed near the top of the prostrate obelisk. As the obelisk moved slowly towards an upright position the pressure on the wood block around which the 250-ton monolith was pivoting was so great that sap from the fresh timbers squirted out. The obelisk continued its upward journey when suddenly, with no warning, a loud cracking noise sounded through the cold winter air.

Everything stopped so Lebas could check the apparatus. Lepage, Inspector of Works, shouted, "Nothing has moved. You can continue." The immense

CLEOPATRA'S NEEDLE — RAISING THE OBELISK OF LUXOR IN THE PLACE DE LA CONCORDE, PARIS, OCTOBER 25, 1836.

Figure 4.14 On October 25, 1836, 200,000 people watched the obelisk being erected in the Place de La Concorde.

compression of the wood had caused the sound. The turning of the capstans continued and as the obelisk rose, Lebas realized that they had forgotten to adjust the ropes attached to the chains near the top of the obelisk. He had planned to do this as the tension on the ropes changed and the obelisk went upward, but in the excitement of the cracking sound, it was forgotten. Now two marines were called upon to climb up the obelisk and readjust the rigging. This done, the raising continued, but there was a new problem.

Stationed at the base of the obelisk, Lebas discovered that when the carpenters had translated measurements from feet and inches into the new metric system, they had made a mistake. The wooden pivot on which the obelisk was turning was too high for the obelisk to continue its movement. Two hundred thousand amazed spectators looked on as ten strong men with axes in hand hacked a path through the wood so the obelisk could be raised—all this while a band played the "Isis Suite" from Mozart's *Magic Flute*.

Finally, with the king and queen looking on from their decorated balcony at the Ministry of the Marine, the obelisk was erected on its pedestal where it still stands today. The entire operation took three-and-a-half hours, no one was injured, and the obelisk was undamaged. It was a spectacular success. From his royal balcony Louis Philippe applauded and all 200,000 spectators joined him. Lebas was a hero.

While the French basked in their obelisk's glory, the English still didn't have an obelisk, and it bothered them. After all, they had defeated the French in Egypt; they should be the ones with an obelisk. As recently as 1831 an obelisk had been offered to them, but still they seemed frozen, unable to act. It would be nearly fifty years before they would get their obelisk and it would take another major event to set things in motion: the cutting of the Suez Canal.

Cleopatra's Needle Sails for London

With the invention of steamships in the 1830s, sea trade increased and the utility of a Suez Canal became obvious to everyone, except the British. They were using the overland railway route to the Red Sea pioneered by Thomas Waghorn and were not interested in a canal, but former French vice-consul to Egypt, Ferdinand de Lesseps, saw the advantage and pushed hard for France to build it.

The big dig

De Lesseps had been a close childhood friend of Mohamed Said Pasha, one of Mohamed Ali's sons, and when he heard that his old friend had been made Viceroy of Egypt he went to Cairo to re-establish their friendship and discuss the canal. Said was enthusiastic; it would be the jewel in his reign and establish him as a world leader. In November of 1854 an agreement was signed. The Suez Canal Company would be funded by foreign shareholders. Egypt would supply the land and labor and receive 15 percent of the annual profits. Even with the Viceroy on his side, de Lesseps had a difficult time getting the canal going. England did everything she could to sabotage the project, telling the Sultan in Constantinople that it was a plot for Egypt to gain independence from Turkey, and telling the Viceroy that he would have French colonies springing up along the canal. The English efforts failed and finally, with the support of Emperor Napoleon III, the project began to move forward. In 1857, with the Viceroy supplying 20,000 conscripted workers, digging began.

England continued to try to sabotage the canal, starting a campaign against the "slave labor" used in its construction. De Lesseps correctly pointed out that he paid the laborers and treated them well. The canal continued, but Viceroy

Said never saw its completion. He died in 1863 and was succeeded by his nephew, Ismail Pasha. The new Viceroy was even more enthusiastic about the canal, seeing it as a way to increase his power in the world, but ambition eventually cost him his throne.

As the work continued, England put so much pressure on the Sultan to stop the canal that the Sublime Porte told Ismail that he could no longer use conscripted labor and also that he had no right to give Egyptian land to the Suez Canal Company. Under pressure, he stopped supplying labor but an arbitration committee forced him to pay for the labor he was contractually obligated to supply. It was a staggering fee that he could ill afford. In addition, in an attempt to appease the Porte, he bought back all the land given to the Suez Canal Company by Said. To do this he mortgaged the cotton crop for the coming year, a risky proposition.

De Lesseps replaced the loss of manpower by importing huge steam-powered dredging machines and after 1867 most of the canal was dug by these monsters. By 1869, as the canal neared completion, Britain finally realized she could not stop the canal and was now eager to participate in its progress rather than be shut out by France. De Lesseps accompanied the Prince of Wales on a tour of the canal and the Prince confided that he was sorry his government had fought construction of the canal and wished they had an interest in it. Soon he would get his wish. Although Ismail had now been given the loftier title of Khedive and was a major stockholder in the Suez Canal Company, he was about to lose everything he had.

The grand opening of the Canal was Egypt's coming out party and the Khedive planned spectacular celebrations. He built a palace for the Empress Eugénie of France so she would be comfortable during her visit. Later, when she returned to France, Ismail commemorated her visit with murals painted on the palace walls showing Eugénie at the opening and taking a carriage ride through the desert at Ismailia. The palace is now the Cairo Marriott Hotel and still retains much of its old grandeur. In the lobby are murals commemorating the opening of the canal, complete with the Khedive and Empress Eugénie at a banquet and later on a dais at the opening ceremony. The opening was a great social success followed by an economic disaster. The Nile had failed to rise high enough to inundate the fields and the cotton crop failed. Khedive Ismail could not pay Egypt's debts and was forced to sell his shares in the canal to England.

It is a little known fact, but without the Khedive's bankruptcy America would not have the Statue of Liberty. The Khedive had commissioned the sculptor Bartholdi to create a colossal statue for the entrance to the canal that would dwarf ships as they entered. Unlike the Colossus of Rhodes, Bartholdi's creation was an Egyptian woman holding a torch aloft representing "Egypt Enlightening Asia." It was never completed. The Khedive and Egypt were bankrupt; the massive statue was more than the Egyptian economy could afford. The resilient Bartholdi sold the idea of the colossal statue to France; with some minor alterations the French people could give it to America as a gift, renaming it "The Statue of Liberty." Millions of Americans have visited the statue but few know it was originally intended for Egypt.

For most of the twentieth century it was France that had close relationships with Egypt. Her savants published the *Description de l'Egypte*; Lebas brought their obelisk to Paris; and de Lessseps dug the Suez Canal. England had opposed the canal and didn't have a strong bond with Egypt, but once they became a primary partner in the Suez Canal, that all changed. Egypt became a hot topic and, finally, the Brits decided to pick up their obelisk.

The Englishman and the obelisk

In the summer of 1872 a 28-year-old engineer named Waynman Dixon was dispatched to Cairo by his older brother, John, to build a bridge across the Nile at Giza. In October of 1872 John visited Waynman and the brothers went to see the two Alexandrian obelisks. They knew that one had been offered to England years before but nothing had been done to move it. Immediately they began discussing how to transport the fallen obelisk to England. They asked the locals about the depth of the sea in front of the obelisk and on the spot Waynman came up with a plan that would ultimately bring England's obelisk home: Encase the fallen obelisk in an iron cylinder, roll it into the sea, and tow it to England.

John was so excited at the prospect of finally bringing the obelisk home that he wrote to several newspapers, describing the plan, offering to subscribe 500 pounds sterling towards the cost and inviting all patriotic Englishmen to join him. He quickly wrote to Waynman, telling him to clear more sand from the fallen obelisk to determine its condition. If the fallen obelisk was found to be in good condition, they would take that one and not have to worry about lowering an obelisk from its pedestal.

In the past, support for the project had been repeatedly held back by a rumor that the obelisk was in poor condition with most of the hieroglyphic inscription worn away. Much of this was due to Sir Gardner Wilkinson, one of the founders of modern Egyptology. Wilkinson lived in Luxor in the 1830s and had carried out a pioneering study of tombs in the area and is responsible for the current system numbering of tombs in the Valley of the Kings. He simply took a pot of black paint and walked through the Valley painting numbers on the outsides of the tombs! Wilkinson had watched the French lower their obelisk from the front of Luxor Temple and this may have been the source of the widespread belief that the fallen obelisk in Alexandria was in poor condition. The Luxor obelisk is nearly perfect, with all its carved hieroglyphs crisp and clear. The Alexandria obelisks, while in good condition, are not so well preserved. This may have led to Wilkinson's comment after the English government refused to pay for transporting the obelisk to England: "from its mutilated state, and the obliteration of many of the hieroglyphics by exposure to the sea air, it is unworthy (of) the expense of removal."[1] If England's most prominent Egyptologist said it was not worth the expense, who was going to contribute to the project?

A Freemason to the rescue

Waynman quickly hired workmen who uncovered three sides of the obelisk and even dug out the middle section of the underside. It was in quite good condition and Waynman photographed it so John could show potential donors that the obelisk was worthy of England. Armed with the new photographs, John once again began knocking on doors, but his idea of a national subscription to pay for transporting it never took hold. Fortunately, Sir Erasmus Wilson, a famous surgeon and generous supporter of medical charities, became interested in the project.

In November of 1876 Wilson, curious to hear the plan for transporting the obelisk, visited John Dixon in his London office. Wilson had never met the elder Dixon, but knew his reputation as a reliable and resourceful engineer who had recently built the first railway in China. Wilson entered Dixon's office

Figure 5.1 When the Dixon brothers uncovered the fallen obelisk they discovered its hieroglyphs weren't quite so obliterated as Gardner Wilkinson had said. The obelisk was definitely worth bringing home.

with optimism for the project, but what seems to have clinched the deal was that they were both Freemasons. As Wilson put it, "I soon found that Mr. Dixon was a Freemason, hence all formality and ceremony were at once banished."[2] All ceremony may have been banished, but there was still a contract to work out. John estimated that he could bring the obelisk to England for 7,000 pounds sterling; Wilson wanted to think it over. At their second meeting Wilson presented John with an offer that was both generous and dangerous. "The undertaking is not an easy one; you say you can do it for 7,000 pounds; will you undertake to set it up safely on the banks of the Thames for 10,000 pounds; no cure no pay?"[3] The "no cure no pay" meant that John would have to fund the project himself and if he failed the loss would be his. He would only receive the 10,000 pounds when the obelisk was standing upright on a site to be decided. He would have two years to complete the project. It was a tremendous risk. He was a very successful engineer, but 7,000 pounds—the amount he estimated it would take to bring the obelisk home safely—was more than he could afford to lose. Without a second of hesitation he accepted his fellow Freemason's offer. The Dixon brothers would bring Britannia her obelisk.

Building *Cleopatra*

John's first step was to take his brother's plans for the cylinder to the Thames Iron Works. He entrusted the job of constructing the cylinder to a brilliant young engineer named Benjamin Baker who twenty years later would be elected President of the Institution of Civil Engineers. Waynman was in Somalia erecting a prefabricated cast iron lighthouse and his drawings of the cylinder were not finished blueprints, so Baker had to make many important decisions in designing the cylinder. Baker studied previous attempts to move obelisks, including the Romans' and Fontana's repositioning of the Vatican obelisk. The only obelisk that had been moved in modern times that he could study was the one in Paris, and he wasn't impressed.

> Looking at M. Lebas' design now, it appears almost incredible that it should not have occurred to him that a few traversing jacks, costing say 50 pounds, would have done his work more quickly and efficiently than the formidable inclined causeways and capstans, costing many thousands of pounds.[4]

Baker also noted that it had taken the French seven years to finally erect their obelisk. In contrast to the leisurely French timetable, five months after signing the contract all the parts of the sixty-ton cylinder had been shipped to Alexandria for assembly. The cylinder, with its own crew on board, was going to be towed to England by a steamer. When the parts were shipped to Alexandria, Captain Henry Carter, an experienced and highly respected seaman from the P & O Company, would accompany them. He was going to supervise the small crew that would live inside the *Cleopatra*.

It was now time to assemble the cylinder around the obelisk. The obelisk would pass through six internal bulkheads that formed individual watertight compartments so that if one sprung a leak, the others would not fill with water. With Captain Carter working closely alongside Dixon, the bulkheads were placed around the obelisk and then iron plates forming the cylinder's skin were riveted in place. For stability at sea, the obelisk was stowed four inches below the center of the cylinder, but this asymmetry would make rolling the cylinder more difficult. Consequently, twelve tons of iron rails were temporarily added to a groove in the top of the cylinder where a steering cabin was to be added later. To protect the cylinder as it rolled down to the sea, two large wood bands,

Figure 5.2 The cylinder designed to hold the obelisk had six interior bulkheads that formed watertight compartments. If one sprung a leak, the others would not fill with water.

twelve feet long and six inches wide, were attached around the cylinder's circumference. Work went smoothly, but had to be halted in early July when heavy gales pounded the coast of Alexandria. Once the gales subsided work continued. The cylinder's path down to the water was blocked by large stones from ancient temples that had to be removed by Arab workmen, who also shifted tons of sand to create a clear incline down to the sea. Finally, the old seawall was taken down, removing the cylinder's last obstacle on shore.

Down to the sea

Divers sent down to clear the seabed to receive the cylinder found the remains of a huge wall with blocks weighing up to twenty tons. Using dynamite they blew up the wall in order to remove its shattered stones. For all we know, they dynamited the remains of Cleopatra's palace!

Launch day was August 28 and John Dixon, his wife Mary, and Benjamin Baker had sailed to Alexandria for the occasion. Thick steel cables were wrapped around the cylinder with the two free ends played out to two small steamboats off shore. The cable ends were attached to onboard winches and when the signal was given, the winches turned, slowly pulling the 300-ton cylinder down to the sea. Progress was painfully slow, and by noon the cylinder had moved only one revolution—about fifty feet. The problem was that the two ships could not find secure anchorage on the coast's rocky seabed, so it was decided not to use winches. Rather, the anchors were pulled up, the cables were attached to the sterns of the ships, and then the tugs slowly steamed seaward, pulling the cylinder down the prepared slope to the Mediterranean.

By 5:30 p.m. the cylinder with the obelisk inside was nearing the water's edge. Now screw jacks pushed from one side as tugs pulled on the other, and just before 7:00 p.m. the cylinder made its final turn and came to rest in three feet of water. At last, the obelisk was in the water. The next day they would tow it nine miles to Alexandria's deep harbor.

At dawn the operation began again. The two tugs, with their cables attached to the cylinder, headed out to sea, but the cylinder barely moved. As the August sun rose high in the sky, the tugs tried and tried, but by noon the cylinder, now in seven feet of water, had moved only one revolution and would not budge any further. Slackening the cables, the tugs went full steam ahead and tried to jerk the iron tube free but it still wouldn't move. At sunset the dejected engineers pondered the situation. Benjamin Baker calculated that the cylinder needed nine feet of water in order to float. Though the depth was very close to that, it just wasn't moving. All agreed that at first light they would carefully inspect the cylinder.

Early the next morning, Waynman Dixon was rowed out to inspect the cylinder. He opened the hatch and discovered that the tube was half full of water! Was it leaking? The first thing was to pump the water out so he could go in and see what the problem was. Sixteen men were required to work the huge

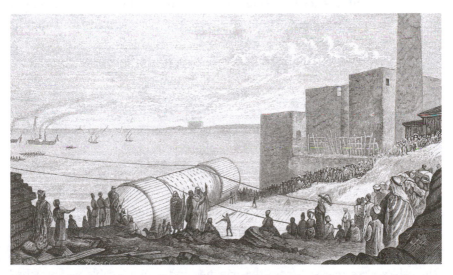

Figure 5.3 The completed cylinder with the obelisk inside, ready to be rolled down to the sea.

hand pump, but as hard as they pumped, the cylinder would not empty. Water was coming in as fast as they pumped it out. A second team relieved them, and then a third, all with no success. Obviously, somewhere there was a large hole through which water was rushing in.

A diver was sent down and found that an ancient building stone weighing several tons had pierced the cylinder, creating an eighteen-inch gash, and was now firmly lodged in the hull. But why had the entire cylinder filled with water? The bulkheads were designed to be watertight, so if one compartment was breached the others would hold, allowing the cylinder to float. The answer was simple: no one had closed the bulkhead doors! With three engineers (the two Dixons and Benjamin Baker) and an experienced Captain (Henry Carter) supervising the operation, not one of them had thought to check that the doors had been closed! Now they had a difficult repair. The cylinder had to be turned so the gash was out of the water and could be repaired, but it was not going to be easy moving a cylinder half full with water. John Dixon came up with an ingenious plan.

First the stone was cut out of the hull. He then had workmen build a huge nine-foot-square wood box that was open at the top. This crib was sunk next to the cylinder on its seaward side. The box was then filled with scrap iron and rocks, fixing it firmly to the seabed. A powerful jack was wedged between the box and the cylinder and expanded, rotating the cylinder towards the coast till the hole was above water. On September 5 the hole finally saw the light of day and all the water was pumped out. The torn iron plate was replaced and the cylinder, now named *Cleopatra*, was once again seaworthy. It is not recorded, but undoubtedly the bulkhead doors were closed.

Out to sea

On September 7 the tugs once again began towing the *Cleopatra* out to sea. This time it was easier, and slowly but surely the cylinder approached the critical nine-foot depth where it would float. Just before noon the *Cleopatra's* movements changed dramatically; it was rising and falling with the swells in the harbor—she was afloat. Adjustments were quickly made for normal towing. The cables were released from the winches and a single cable was attached from the bow of the *Cleopatra* to the stern of the tug *Champion*. The second tug was brought alongside the *Cleopatra* to assist at turns. The next day the cylinder was towed to Alexandria's dry dock but the seas were particularly rough. The tugs bobbed up and down violently, but the cylinder took the waves far more easily, barely rising or falling, a reassuring sight for the *Cleopatra's* captain and the three engineers.

Once in dry dock the cylinder received its final fittings and preparations for its first and only voyage on open seas. The twelve tons of counter ballast that had been placed on top to roll the cylinder to the sea were removed and transferred to the bottom of the vessel as ballast. Then a steering deck with an iron catwalk around it was riveted in place. Beneath the cylinder, two forty-foot-long keels were riveted in position to make sure the *Cleopatra* didn't roll in high seas. A mast was fitted, to be used in an emergency, and a third keel was attached to the stern. The final preparations were done in ten days with Captain Carter and Waynman Dixon overseeing every step. On September 19, the daughter of Admiral McKillop Pasha, the English officer in charge of the harbor, broke a bottle of champagne over the iron cylinder; the *Cleopatra* was formally christened. Mr. and Mrs. John Dixon hosted a luncheon for 150 dignitaries, officers, and prominent expats from the Alexandria community. They had worked very hard to get to this point, but their work was not yet over.

Waynman had designed the *Cleopatra* so the obelisk could lie below the geometric center of the cylinder, the low center of gravity giving it more stability on open seas. Now, while in dry dock, an additional twenty tons of scrap iron railings were laid in the bottom of the *Cleopatra*, lowering the center of gravity even more. With this ballast, two-thirds of the *Cleopatra* would be submerged during the voyage. The ballast was held in place by wood flooring laid over it.

Captain Carter hired seven men for his crew: his second in command, the boatswain; five Maltese seamen; and a carpenter to make any necessary repairs at sea. Carter had to pay a bit above the going wages for such a crew; many seamen were hesitant about signing onto such an unusual vessel for four weeks on the open seas. It would, indeed, be a voyage they would never forget.

A British steamer, the *Olga*, was about to sail from Alexandria with a load of grain destined for England. Captain Carter thought the *Olga* suitable for towing the *Cleopatra*. Powered by a 130-horsepower steam engine, she was 251 feet long, only seven years old, and commanded by an able captain. Carter struck a deal with Captain Booth, who agreed to tow the *Cleopatra* to Falmouth for 900 pounds sterling, half to be paid in advance, half upon arrival. Everything was in place for the great adventure.

The *Cleopatra*'s odyssey began on September 21 when Captain Booth, commanding the *Olga*, slowly towed the cylinder and obelisk out of Alexandria Harbor and into the open Mediterranean. On the deck of the *Olga* was Waynman Dixon, who intended to accompany his cylinder all the way to England and would be available to oversee repairs if needed. Onboard the *Cleopatra* were Captain Carter and his crew. Several systems had been worked out so the two captains could communicate throughout the voyage. During calm seas a megaphone could be used, but for rough weather Captain Carter would stand on the steering bridge and use a blackboard to communicate his needs. At night, a system of lights was employed.

Figure 5.4 Captain Carter on the *Cleopatra* communicated with the tow-ship *Olga* via a blackboard.

The *Cleopatra's* early behavior greatly reassured everyone. She sailed calmly through the waves with her steering house splitting those waves that washed over the low-in-the-water cylinder. The biggest problem was Carter's second in command, the boatswain, who became ill the second day at sea, forcing Carter to stand watch all night, every night, and catch snatches of sleep during the day when possible; but Carter had plenty to do during the day too.

Every six hours he checked the bulkhead compartments to make sure there were no leaks. First he would open a small hatch in the floor of his cabin and, carrying a candle, would slip down into the darkness. He would check the first compartment, open a tiny door to the second and, holding the candle in his teeth, would squeeze through and inspect that bulkhead. This was repeated for each of the seven bulkheads and then he made his way back to the first compartment and the hatch to his cabin. Once, while freeing both hands so he could push himself through one of the doors, he held the candle in his teeth and it began to burn his nose! The candle fell, went out, and Carter was stranded in the dark with a singed nose. It took more than half an hour to feel his way back to daylight, and after that experience he took a crewmember along to hold the candle.

Otherwise, the first week was uneventful, with clear skies and calm seas, as all England followed the progress of their obelisk in *The Illustrated London News*. Although it was late in September, the temperature in the tiny cabins was brutally hot and stifling, with several of the men preferring to sleep nights, as best they could, on deck by the steering house. On day six they had half the Mediterranean behind them and were off the coast of Malta. There was no stop scheduled, but Carter's Maltese crew begged for a layover; Carter, fearing they would desert, continued on.

One night the lookout on the *Olga* saw a flare go up from the *Cleopatra* that was followed by lights signaling "STOP." The cable had detached and the *Cleopatra* was being left behind. Captain Booth quickly turned the *Olga* around, came alongside the cylinder and began hauling in the cable, which took several hours. The fitting attaching the cable to the *Cleopatra* had broken but at daybreak it was replaced and the two ships were on their way.

Off the coast of Algeria they hit bad weather and, since they were using more coal than Captain Booth had anticipated, they put in to port. The crew of the *Olga* was given shore leave (they got drunk) but Carter, fearing his *Cleopatra* men would jump ship, kept them on board. In less than 24 hours the *Olga* had

Figure 5.5 All of England followed the voyage of Cleopatra's Needle.

taken on coal and the two vessels were on their way. They reached Gibraltar on October 7, their first scheduled stop, and put in to port for supplies. Waynman wrote letters home telling of their progress. The *Cleopatra* was performing admirably, but he was worried about Captain Carter, who was exhausted from his lack of sleep. At Gibraltar Carter had his first full night's rest in two weeks and, refreshed and refueled, the armada of two pressed on.

On October 9 they passed Portugal, rounded Cape St. Vincent and headed north into the Atlantic. The waves were a bit bigger than in the Mediterranean but the *Cleopatra* took them in her stride. Continuing north they passed the northern coast of Spain and entered the Bay of Biscay, their route to the English Channel. The Bay was notorious for bad weather, but the two ships needed only three more days of reasonable weather and they would be safe. On October 15, their luck ran out.

Hurricane, then disaster

At 9:00 a.m. rains began out of the south-southwest and within a few hours reached gale force. The waves were building rapidly and for the first time the *Cleopatra* was going to be tested. Waynman watched her closely from the *Olga's* deck. At 10:40 a.m. he wrote in his log: "'Olga' rolling 10 times per minute 10 degrees to port 5 degrees star'd. It is really wonderful how 'Cleopatra' rides out the heavy sea—hardly a roll in her!" For the next few hours the barometer continued to fall and winds were now at hurricane force. Captain Booth continued to steer the two ships into the wind, then, amid thunder and lightning, the wind suddenly shifted and both waves and wind came at right angles to the *Cleopatra's* steering house. The winds and waves were so strong that Carter feared they would rip the deckhouse right off the cylinder. He signaled Captain Booth to "Prepare to Heave-to, Head to Wind." He wanted some slack so they could turn into the wind. Booth replied "Greater Risk to Tow-Line if Hove-to." He was afraid of snapping the cable connecting the two vessels.

For an entire day, gale and hurricane forces had tossed them about, and now it was getting dark. It seemed almost impossible, but the weather was worsening. Carter, fearing the next wave might wash him off the deck, again signaled "Heave-to" and Captain Booth, sensing the desperation, complied, skillfully moving the *Olga* into the wind. As Carter tried to steer the *Cleopatra* to follow the *Olga's* lead, a tremendous wave hit the deckhouse, capsizing the *Cleopatra*. As the cylinder went over on its side, Carter, clinging desperately to the railing, felt and heard something moving deep inside the *Cleopatra*. He immediately knew what it was.

The timber work which secured the iron rails used as ballast gave way, the rails shifted, and the vessel lay over at an angle of more than 45 degrees from

Figure 5.6 The *Cleopatra* caught in a hurricane.

the perpendicular. I soon opened the man-hole door in the cabin, and got my crew into the hold to right the ballast. I found the vessel was taking water at the upper bolt holes; the gale was at its height, and the sea breaking completely over. I made signals of distress to the *Olga*, but still kept working at the ballast. In a few hours a good proportion of the ballast had been replaced, and the vessel became a little more upright, but a heavier sea than usual again threw us over, and the ballast went back to its former position.[5]

Carter, sensing they could not reposition the ballast, decided their best hope was to abandon ship. He lowered their little lifeboat but, before they could get into it, a huge wave sent it crashing into the hull, smashing it to bits. Captain Booth slowed engines and tried to maneuver the *Olga* closer to the *Cleopatra* and heard, "Foundering, send a boat." Booth said to his men, "What can we do, no boat will live in such a sea." William Askin, the second mate, replied, "We must lower a boat and try, we can't leave the poor fellows to drown." Five other brave crewmen volunteered and with great difficulty descended in one of their lifeboats to rescue the *Cleopatra*'s crew.

It was now 9:20 p.m. and the storm was still raging. Captain Booth could see the lifeboat slowly fighting its way through the turbulence towards the *Cleopatra*. As it neared the cylinder, Booth lost sight of it in the darkness. The

Figure 5.7 In a valiant effort to save the crew of the *Cleopatra,* six brave men lost their lives.

Cleopatra's crew was on deck, clinging to the railings. Over an hour later, Askin and his crew reached the *Cleopatra*. A line thrown to them was caught, but was pulled out of the sailor's hands as the boat was battered by the waves. Then, before the line could be thrown again, a giant wave reared up, crashed down on the little boat, and it disappeared.

The six men brave men were never seen again, and Carter and his terrified crew would have to survive the night on their own. He brought the crew inside and they descended below the flooring for one last attempt at repositioning the ballast. For several hours they worked in incredibly cramped conditions, all the while being thrown around by the waves. They had nearly completed their task, the *Cleopatra* was almost upright, and, amazingly, she was headed into the wind, and it looked as if they might succeed. Then a huge wave crashed into the side of the *Cleopatra*, scattering ballast and capsizing the cylinder once again. It was midnight and on the *Olga* Captain Booth could see little but by now he knew his six crewmen who had not returned were probably lost.

On the *Cleopatra* Carter's spirits were extremely low. His log entry reads: "The swells high and confused, and the *Olga* seems determined to tow us through the water or under it. I wish she would break down, for the quick pitching motion is almost unbearable." Still, he encouraged his men to keep trying to reposition the ballast, but one by one they fell to exhaustion. In such heavy seas, there was the horrible possibility that the two vessels would collide, so around 1:00 a.m. Captain Booth cast off the towing cable, setting the *Cleopatra* adrift. Waynman Dixon volunteered to take a second boat to the *Cleopatra*, but no one followed his lead. On the *Olga* Captain Booth kept his ship as close to the *Cleopatra* as possible. At 2:00 a.m. he tried to send a buoy with a line attached to the *Cleopatra*. With 100 fathoms of line attached, he steamed around the *Cleopatra*, dragging the line so it would cross on top of the cylinder and be grabbed by the men, enabling them to be hauled on board the *Olga*, but the sea was too rough. Booth signaled that they would have to wait for daylight and Carter replied he didn't think the *Cleopatra* would float that long. Another attempt was made at 5:00 a.m. and that too failed, but finally it was getting light.

Booth tried to maneuver the *Olga* close enough to the *Cleopatra* to throw her a line, but was worried that a wave could send him crashing into the cylinder, sinking both ships. He got as close as possible and heaved a line. It missed. He tried two more times with no success. Finally a line went across the *Cleopatra*'s stern and was grabbed. The *Cleopatra*'s crew closed all bulkhead doors, hatches, and manholes in preparation to abandon ship. This was their last chance. Using the line they had thrown, the *Olga* sent an unmanned lifeboat to the foundering *Cleopatra*. In high seas, one by one the *Cleopatra*'s crewmembers jumped into the boat, Captain Carter last. The boat was quickly hauled into the *Olga*. Finally all hands were on board.

Booth now steamed off to search for his six missing sailors. Around 1:00 p.m., after not finding anyone, he gave up and returned to where they had left the *Cleopatra*. He still intended to bring their obelisk home, but was also concerned that the 300-ton cylinder would be a hazard to navigation. But it was gone. Everyone concluded it must have filled with water and was now at the bottom of the Bay of Biscay.

What began as a wonderful patriotic adventure had ended in disaster. Six brave men were dead and the object for which they had lost their lives lay beneath the sea. Captain Booth reset the *Olga*'s course for Falmouth, reaching it two days later to deliver their sad news. John Dixon had been waiting anxiously at Falmouth. He had received a telegram that the *Olga* had been sighted—without the *Cleopatra* in tow. He rushed on board and was relieved to see Captain Carter, but his spirits fell when his brother told him of the six drowned sailors and the lost obelisk.

Lost at sea

As they stood on board, none of the sad company had any inkling that the *Cleopatra* was still afloat. While Captains Carter and Booth battled the hurricane, several other captains on the Bay of Biscay were doing exactly the same thing. One was Captain Evans of the *Fitzmaurice*, who had sailed from Middlesbrough bound for Valencia, Spain with a cargo of pig iron. As he entered the Bay he hit the same strong winds that the other ships encountered and, just like Carter and Booth, he fought the hurricane, keeping his ship into the wind for a full day. When the storm finally died down, Evans and the *Fitzmaurice* resumed course for Valencia. Carter and Booth had lost the *Cleopatra*, but now she was about to be found.

Around 4:00 p.m. the *Fitzmaurice*'s lookout spotted what looked like a capsized ship. Through his binoculars Captain Evans made out the letters on the hull: CLEOPATRA. He had read of the *Cleopatra*'s voyage in newspapers and knew exactly what she was. Getting as close as possible, he hailed her but was not hailed back. There was no sign of her crew. She had been abandoned.

According to maritime law, if Evans could secure a line to the *Cleopatra* and tow her to a port, he would be entitled to payment for his work and also the value of the ship and its cargo. The *Cleopatra* was salvage and, given her unique cargo, it could be worth a considerable sum. The problem was going to be getting a line on her. Although the gale had subsided, the *Cleopatra* was partially submerged and rolling from side to side in rough seas. Some of the *Fitzmaurice*'s crew would have to be lowered in a lifeboat onto the churning seas, then one would have to jump onto the half-submerged bucking cylinder, catch a line thrown to him and tie it to the *Cleopatra*. It was a dangerous proposition and no one volunteered, but when Captain Evans offered a share in the prize, four men agreed. Just lowering the boat in swells was difficult, but boarding the *Cleopatra* proved nearly impossible. One man tried to jump from the boat onto the *Cleopatra*'s steering deck, the only place with railings to hang on to. With the vessel bobbing up and down, it was like jumping onto the back of a bucking iron horse and he fell into the cold water. His comrades pulled him back in by the rope they had tied around his waist, but now he was cold, shivering, and not eager to try again. One by one they tried till, finally, one of the men made it and secured a towing rope to the *Cleopatra*. The prize was theirs; now they just had to tow it to safety.

Figure 5.8 The *Cleopatra* was found abandoned at sea and towed to Ferrol.

With her steering deck half submerged, it was a difficult tow, but Captain Evans managed to do it. When the *Olga* was towing the *Cleopatra*, a specially made steel cable was used, but Evans only had thick rope and after a few hours it snapped. Fortunately the seas were calming and now it was not difficult to attach a new line and continue towards the nearest port, Ferrol, on the Spanish coast. On the second day the winds built again to gale force and the tow ropes separated. The ship was within sight of Ferrol and the captain and crew weren't going to give up their prize now. By heroic efforts they managed to reconnect the tow ropes and brought the *Cleopatra* into the safety of the harbor.

Captain Evans immediately saw that shifting ballast had caused the *Cleopatra* to be abandoned. He later commented that, from the way it had been stowed, "it appeared to be the work of soldiers, and not sailors."[6] Captain Evans quickly contacted the British vice-consul and left the *Cleopatra* in his custody. The vice-consul telegraphed London and all of England soon knew their obelisk had not been lost. The two illustrated newspapers of the day, *The Graphic* and *The Illustrated London News*, ran articles about the loss and recovery of the *Cleopatra* and the death of the six crewmembers. London knew they would be getting their obelisk, but at a terrible price.

The *Fitzmaurice* continued on to Valencia, dropped its cargo of pig iron, and picked up a new cargo bound for Liverpool. When Captain Evans docked, Captain Carter was waiting to ask about the condition of the *Cleopatra*. Evans had brought Carter's log book and some of his navigation instruments, but almost everything else was gone, scavenged by the *Fitzmaurice's* crew, including a collection of ancient Greek and Roman coins Carter had assembled while in Alexandria. Carter was told that with some refitting the *Cleopatra* would be seaworthy, but before they could begin the salvage claim had to be settled.

What's an obelisk worth?

Carter returned to London and with John Dixon set off to Scotland to deal with the owners of the *Fitzmaurice*, Burrell & Son of Glasgow. Mr. Burrell demanded 5,000 pounds sterling to release the *Cleopatra*, which was an extraordinarily high figure. John Dixon countered with an offer to write a check for 600 pounds on the spot. Burrell wouldn't budge; the matter would be settled in court.

The claim went before Sir R. J. Phillimore in the Admiralty Division of the High Court. In a salvage case, there are three amounts that must be determined: 1) actual cost of the salvage; 2) value of the rescued ship; and 3) value of the cargo. Once these three figures are determined, a judge awards the salvers some portion of the total sum. Dixon agreed to pay all costs for the salvage, so that was not a problem, nor was the value of the *Cleopatra*. It was designed for only one voyage and was now worth only its value as scrap iron. The problem was the cargo. What was Cleopatra's Needle worth?

Burrell & Son suggested it was nearly priceless. They pointed out that France had spent the equivalent of 80,000 pounds sterling to bring their obelisk to Paris and certainly other European capitals would be willing to purchase such an ancient and unique antiquity if they had the opportunity. On the other extreme, John Dixon proposed that the obelisk should be viewed as a load of stone, valued by the ton! Justice Phillimore didn't buy Dixon's view. He praised Dixon's patriotic intention to bring England an obelisk, but explained that it would play no part in the valuation of the claim. He commended the crew of the *Fitzmaurice* for their bravery in boarding the *Cleopatra* and agreed that the obelisk was a unique ancient treasure. But what was it worth? After an adjournment for lunch, he finally assigned a total salvage value of 2,500 pounds for the *Cleopatra* and her cargo. Now he had to determine what portion of that should be the award. He awarded a total of 2,000 pounds plus costs, with 1,200 pounds going to the owners, 250 pounds to Captain Evans, and the rest distributed among the crew according to their rank, with double shares to the four brave men who first boarded the *Cleopatra*. Just as Erasmus Wilson had predicted in his meeting with John Dixon, it had proven to be a difficult undertaking with unexpected expenses.

With legalities settled, Captain Carter set out to repair the *Cleopatra*. It was now mid-December and with a new crew hired in Liverpool, he boarded the Spanish steamer, *Nina*, for Ferrol and the disabled *Cleopatra*. One of the crewmembers, Josiah Matthews, was an experienced riveter who would carry out many of the repairs. Stowed in the hold of the *Nina* were tons of rivets, iron plates, steel cables, and anything else they might need to repair the cylinder. As soon as they arrived, Carter inspected his injured vessel. Internally it was in remarkably good condition. It had remained watertight throughout its battering so, aside from repositioning and securing the ballast, there was little to be done. The exterior was another matter. For three weeks the crew worked to replace the mast, install a new tiller, repair the smashed rudder and refit the steering deck that had taken the brunt of the storm. When everything was in order, John Dixon hired the *Anglia*, one of the largest and most powerful deep-sea tugs in the Port of London, to tow the *Cleopatra*. The *Anglia* specialized in towing distressed ships and had a crew of seventeen plus two captains, one to steer the *Anglia* and one to supervise the ship being towed. Dixon wasn't taking any chances on losing the *Cleopatra* again.

The *Anglia* arrived in Ferrol on January 12 and for two days the three captains conferred, with Carter familiarizing his two colleagues with the *Cleopatra*. Carter had seen what bad weather could do; they would wait till the forecast was for a considerable period of fair weather before setting out to sea. Britain's Meteorological Department provided daily forecasts and John Dixon checked these against forecasts telegraphed to him each day from the *New York Herald*. All indications were that there should be clear sailing for the immediate future so it was decided to depart on January 16, a few days before a full moon on the 19th. Usually a full moon heralded good weather and they wanted it in the middle of their journey across the Bay of Biscay. However, the weather forecasts were so optimistic on the 14th that all agreed to push up the departure date to the next day. At 7:00 a.m. on January 15, the *Anglia* gently moved out through Ferrol harbor with the *Cleopatra* in tow. The forecasts were accurate and for two days the weather was unusually fair for the Bay of Biscay in January. On the morning of the 18th they rounded the tip of France and entered the English Channel. They were halfway home with only 350 miles to go.

Home at last

While crossing the Channel, the *Cleopatra's* steering failed and had to be repaired. After a while it failed again, but fortunately the full moon forecast was working; the waters were unusually calm and lack of steering posed no problem. On January 21 at ten o'clock in the morning, they reached Gravesend and the *Cleopatra* docked off English soil. Mr. and Mrs. John Dixon were waiting to greet the two ships. The two vessels cleared customs quickly and by 1:00 p.m. they were slowly sailing up the Thames. After a few hours the ships were met by a small local tug, the *Mosquito*, that replaced the *Anglia* for the final few miles. As the sun was setting the *Mosquito* gently guided the *Cleopatra* into her berth at the East India Docks; the long journey was over at last.

Although Cleopatra's Needle was finally in London, it still hadn't been decided exactly where in the city it would be erected. Various competing camps had differing philosophies as to the best location for an ancient Egyptian obelisk. Some favored the middle of a public square, much like France's obelisk at the Place de la Concorde. Others felt that, because the ancient Egyptians put obelisks at the entrances to temples, the obelisk should be near buildings. The two men who had paid for the obelisk's journey, John Dixon and Sir Erasmus Wilson, had the privilege of making the ultimate decision. The contract they signed had stipulated that it would be on the Thames Embankment, but now both felt a better site would be in front of the Houses of Parliament. John went so far as to erect a full-scale wood model of the obelisk to show how it would look. The site was vetoed by some unexpected players—the Directors of the Metropolitan District Railway. Unfortunately, the proposed site was above a train route and the Directors were afraid the train's vibrations would topple the obelisk, causing it to crash through the top of the tunnel and onto a train. Dixon suggested that iron beams could be used to reinforce the tunnel, but this was

Figure 5.9 A full-scale wood model of the obelisk was built to see how it would look in front of the Houses of Parliament.

not convincing. The Directors wanted a perpetual indemnity and no insurance company would take that risk, so Cleopatra's Needle was still in need of a site.

Eventually it was decided that the original site agreed upon by Dixon and Wilson was best and John quickly dismantled his wood obelisk and re-erected it at the Adelphi Steps of the Thames Embankment to show Londoners how their obelisk would look when finally set upright. He next had the *Cleopatra* towed from the East India Docks to a dock opposite the Houses of Parliament so that it could be visited. For the four weeks that this unusual vessel remained docked, curious Londoners were permitted to go on board and some adventurous souls even descended beneath the floor to catch a glimpse of Cleopatra's Needle. London was caught up in obelisk fever.

While London was meeting and greeting its obelisk, the site at the Embankment was being readied to receive London's newest and oldest monument. The location by the Adelphi Steps was basically a platform supported by four giant arches that would have to be filled in if they were to support the 230-ton obelisk. For two months, workers mixed and poured thousands of tons of concrete, filling in the arches, creating a massive support, all paid for by John Dixon. How right Erasmus Wilson was when he predicted unforeseen expenses! But it was now time for the *Cleopatra* to make her last voyage.

On May 30 Captain Carter supervised the towing of the *Cleopatra* to the Adelphi Steps, where an ingenious dry dock awaited her. A wood cradle was anchored to the riverbed so that when the tide rose it would just barely be submerged. The *Cleopatra* was floated above the cradle, and when the tide went out, she came safely to rest in her dry dock. The dock's anchor was then pulled up so the cylinder would be permanently out of the water, enabling a swarm of ironworkers to dismantle her. First the steering deck that Captain Carter and his men had clung to in the hurricane was stripped off for its scrap value. Next the uppermost iron plates were removed and workers descended

Figure 5.10 Londoners were permitted to crawl beneath the floorboards of the *Cleopatra* for a glimpse of the obelisk.

into the hull, removing the cabins and flooring, exposing the obelisk to the light of day for the first time since it left Egypt. One wonders what John Dixon thought as he watched his cylinder being destroyed.

The tops of the bulkheads were removed so the obelisk could be lifted out of what remained of the *Cleopatra*. Four pairs of hydraulic jacks were placed beneath the obelisk and slowly lifted the granite monolith a few inches at a time. As the obelisk inched upwards, timbers were placed under it, the jacks were raised a bit, and the process was repeated till the needle was hovering on timbers and jacks above the *Cleopatra*. Now it had to be hauled up the steps leading from the dock to the embankment some thirty feet above.

The obelisk was clad in wood to protect it as it ascended the stairs. The needle was raised and pulled up at the same time—raised by the hydraulic jacks and pulled up by four screw traversers. Traversers are basically four-inch-wide screws that are slowly retracted by men working giant winch-like levers. With the obelisk's point aimed up the stairs, the wood casing was attached to the four screws on the steps above. As the jacks elevated the obelisk's bottom, the screws were retracted and pulled the monolith up. When the obelisk gained a few inches, beams were placed under it and the journey continued. It was painstaking work, taking nearly two weeks to elevate the obelisk thirty feet up to the Embankment, but finally it rested horizontally on a bed of timbers. The final step was to raise the obelisk onto its new pedestal of granite blocks.

Benjamin Baker, who had created the *Cleopatra* at the Thames Iron Works, was called upon to fashion an iron mechanism that would support the obelisk in a horizontal position fifty feet above the ground and then swing it into position on top of its pedestal. Before the obelisk began the journey skywards, an iron sleeve was fitted over its middle at its exact center of gravity. This jacket was attached to iron beams so that, once the obelisk had been raised horizontally fifty feet into the air, it could be rotated from its horizontal position to vertical, and then lowered onto its pedestal. Throughout the summer, teams of carpenters nailed and bolted together a giant wood scaffold to support the obelisk and its turning mechanism as it was raised aloft. Now they had to raise the 300-ton combination of granite and iron fifty feet into the air.

The same hydraulic jacks that had lifted the obelisk out of the *Cleopatra* and up the Adelphi Steps were now placed beneath the iron beams supporting the obelisk. Using the same system of jacks and wood beams, the obelisk rose four

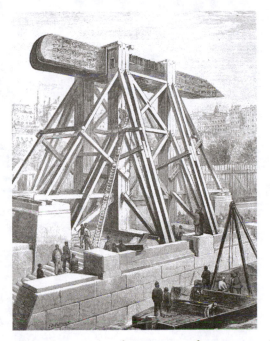

Figure 5.11 Throughout the summer of 1878, teams of carpenters nailed and bolted together the mechanism that was needed to turn the obelisk to vertical and place it on its base.

inches in ten minutes. Then the lifting was halted, timbers were placed under the obelisk, the jacks were repositioned, and another four inches could be gained. This continued throughout August and by early September the obelisk, like a magician's assistant, levitated fifty feet above the ground, ready to be swung to the vertical and placed on its pedestal.

John Dixon announced to the public that he would lower the obelisk onto its pedestal at 3:00 p.m. on September 12. This gave him a few days to test his system and make sure everything would go smoothly. The day before the big event, he removed the iron pins that locked the obelisk into a horizontal position and discovered that he had calculated the obelisk's center of gravity so accurately that just his own muscle power, pulling on a cable, could move the obelisk towards vertical. Satisfied, he replaced the pins and waited for the next day. All of London was in a buzz.

People started gathering around the obelisk early in the morning to get a good viewing spot. For months Londoners had been following the saga of Cleopatra's Needle. Both the *Graphic* and *The Illustrated London News* had

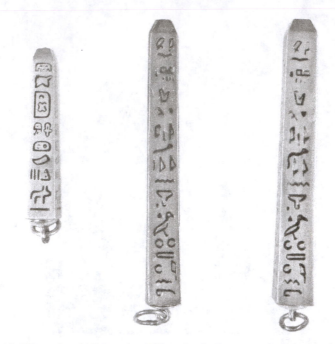

Figure 5.12 When the obelisk arrived, Victorian ladies wore obelisk pencils around their necks.

chronicled building the cylinder, the loss at sea, and the deaths of six seamen. Now that the obelisk was finally in London, everyone felt invested in its safety and its successful erection on the banks of the Thames. All Londoners wanted to be part of history. Hawkers sold an assortment of souvenirs; one of the most popular was a lead pencil in the shape of an obelisk that ladies could hang on a chain around their necks. Pamphlets offering translations of the obelisk's hieroglyphs were offered for a penny, and there was even a song called "Cleopatra's Needle Waltz" that was dedicated to Erasmus Wilson.

As the crowd grew so did anticipation, and by noon everyone was eager to see their obelisk finally on its pedestal. Then, as if the obelisk hadn't had its fair share of bad weather, rains came—heavy rains that began at 1:00 p.m. and kept falling, scattering the crowd, forcing everyone to seek cover. Finally, after an hour of downpour, the rain stopped, the sun broke through the clouds, and the crowds gathered again.

A few minutes before three o'clock John Dixon gave the signal to remove the pins that held the obelisk in a horizontal position. Steel cables running from the obelisk to two pairs of winches on either side of it steadied the stone shaft.

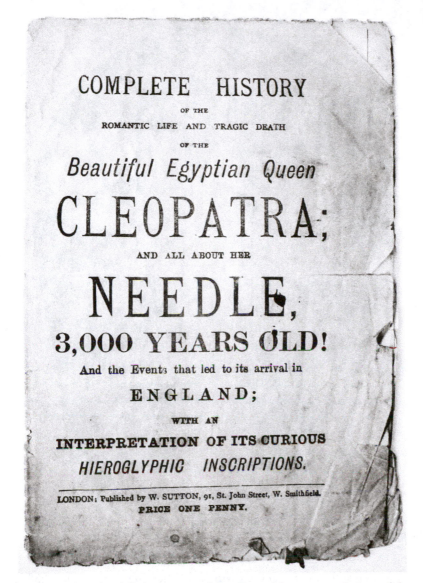

Figure 5.13 When the obelisk was erected, hawkers sold penny translations of the obelisk's hieroglyphs.

When John Dixon gave the signal, four men on each winch started turning, drawing in the cables, and the 230-ton obelisk began slowly rotating through the air. The packed, wet crowd stood transfixed, amazed at how gracefully the massive stone moved. After ten minutes of breathless silence the shaft of granite was at 45 degrees—halfway to vertical. A few minutes later it was at 60 degrees,

Figure 5.14 London went wild with obelisk mania and one could dance to the "Cleopatra's Needle Waltz."

with the men still straining at their winches. When Big Ben sounded 3:30 p.m., the obelisk was upright, hovering just four inches above its pedestal.

Dixon had calculated that the obelisk could balance on its pedestal with nothing fixing it to the base, just as the ancient Egyptian engineers had done. As they looked at the suspended monolith, one of the engineers felt it didn't look quite right; it didn't appear to be perfectly vertical. They decided to wait till morning to check the angle of the obelisk and then lower it. When they announced to the crowd that the day's work was over everyone burst into applause. It had been an exhausting day for Dixon, Wilson, and everyone else involved in the obelisk's erection, but it had been a rousing success.

The following day the obelisk was found to be perfectly vertical and was lowered the final four inches onto its pedestal. For the next few weeks the site was cleared. The iron jacket around the obelisk's middle was removed, the huge timbers for the scaffolding were taken down, and the iron turning mechanism was dismantled. Commemorative plaques were added to the pedestal that can still be read by visitors today. One tells the obelisk's ancient history and then recounts its more modern adventure:

> THROUGH THE PATRIOTIC ZEAL OF
> ERASMUS WILSON F.R.S
> THIS OBELISK
> WAS BROUGHT FROM ALEXANDRIA
> ENCASED IN AN IRON CYLINDER
> IT WAS ABANDONED DURING A STORM
> IN THE BAY OF BISCAY
> RECOVERED AND ERECTED
> ON THIS SPOT BY
> JOHN DIXON C.E.
> IN THE 42ND YEAR OF THE REIGN OF
> QUEEN VICTORIA
> 1878

Most visitors to the obelisk see this plaque but there is another, on the side facing the Thames, that is usually missed. There is an ancient Egyptian expression, "To say the name of the dead is to make him live again." Whenever I visit the obelisk, I walk around to the riverside and read the plaque.

> WILLIAM ASKIN   MICHAEL BURNS
> JAMES GARDINER   WILLIAM DONALD
> JOSEPH BENBOW   WILLIAM PATAN
>
> PERISHED IN A BOLD ATTEMPT
> TO SUCCOUR THE CREW OF THE
> OBELISK SHIP "CLEOPATRA" DURING
> THE STORM OCTOBER 14TH 1877

The Oldest Skyscraper in New York

Bringing an obelisk to London had cost England the lives of six brave men, but in spite of that tragedy, America was now determined to have its own obelisk. Paris and London had theirs, so why not New York? The idea of an American obelisk was not new. In 1869, when the world gathered in Egypt for the opening of the Suez Canal, the United States was offered an obelisk, not out of generosity and friendship, but out of desperation. Egypt was bankrupt, but the preparations for the canal's opening had been made, the invitations to the world's rulers had been sent, and the Empress Eugénie's palace had been completed, so in spite of financial difficulties, the festivities had to go forward. The only problem was that Egypt no longer owned the canal. It was in the hands of receivers, owned by the powers of Europe who had loaned the funds to build it. It was under these difficult circumstances that William H. Hurlbert, editor of the *New York World*, was introduced to Egypt's ruler, Khedive Ismail, at the opening ceremonies. Khedive Ismail, eager for an ally to save him from his European creditors, suggested to Hurlbert that America might want an obelisk, but nothing was done and the offer was soon forgotten. Eight years later, in 1877, when London erected its obelisk and New York was suffering from obelisk envy, Hurlbert would have gladly accepted the Khedive's offer, but did it still hold?

In 1877 a friend of Hurlbert's chanced to meet in London John Dixon who, along with his brother, was in the process of moving London's obelisk. Dixon informed Hurlbert that Egypt was willing to offer America an obelisk and that, for 15,000 pounds sterling, Dixon could bring the upright Alexandrian obelisk to the United States. Hurlbert was ecstatic; not only would America get an obelisk, he had a news scoop. He quickly published an article telling New Yorkers that they would soon have an obelisk. The Commissioner of Parks,

Henry G. Stebbins, contacted William Vanderbilt to ask him to head a committee to raise the necessary funds. Vanderbilt, caught up in the obelisk mania, offered to pay the entire bill. New York had to have an obelisk.

Things moved quickly. Vanderbilt contacted Dixon to work out a contract to move the obelisk, Stebbins contacted the Department of State to ask for assistance in dealing with the Khedive. E. E. Farman, United States Consul-General in Cairo, was instructed to get the gift in writing. New York eagerly awaited news of when the obelisk would arrive, but there was one problem; the Khedive now had no intention of giving away another obelisk. It was all a mistake, something like the game of telephone where the whispered message gets garbled through numerous transmissions. Dixon hadn't said anything about Egypt's willingness to give away an obelisk. He merely suggested that if the United States could get an obelisk, he could bring it to America's shore.

Does the offer still hold?

This all became clear when Consul-General Farman received his instructions to secure the gift of the obelisk. The 46-year-old Farman had only recently been appointed Consul-General but he was a brilliant man with considerable talents. He had studied International Law in Heidelberg and Berlin, and these skills were critical to his job in Egypt, a country being pulled in all directions by foreign powers. His photo shows a handsome man with dark, attentive eyes and a short but untrimmed brown beard.

Farman was in constant contact with the Khedive, but had never heard mention of an obelisk, so he knew something was wrong. Soon a letter arrived from Dixon explaining the confusion. "This is all very proper but my name has been mixed up with it as though I were a purveyor of obelisks to H.H.!! I believe it was founded upon a casual remark of mine that if the U.S. wanted an obelisk, I thought it possible that one might be obtained."

So there was no offer of an obelisk, and once the confusion was straightened out, Farman received no further communications about obelisks from the State Department, or from anyone else. If America was going to have an obelisk, the Consul-General would have to start from square one and do the work on his own, but did he want to do that? Around this time, a tourist from the United States arrived and helped him decide—General Ulysses S. Grant.

The great Civil War hero had just completed his second term as President of the United States and had declined to run for a third. After three decades of public service, he was ready for some relaxation, and on May 17, 1877 sailed from Philadelphia to begin a grand tour around the world. By the time he arrived in Alexandria, Egypt on February 4, 1878, he had already seen Europe and was eager to encounter Egypt's antiquities.

Grant was welcomed by Farman, the Governor of Alexandria, and representatives of the Khedive, who informed the General that the Khedive would be pleased to provide a palace in Cairo to lodge his group and also a steamboat for their trip up the Nile—just the kind of generous hospitality that was bankrupting Egypt. When the travelers reached Cairo, a large welcoming party of officials and civilians had formed. Grant was wildly popular wherever he went and Egypt was no exception. Among the throng was William Loring, with whom Grant had served more than thirty years earlier. Loring was amazed when his old comrade picked him out of the crowd and warmly greeted him.

The Khedive gave a reception and proudly showed Grant the murals in Eugénie's palace commemorating the opening of the Suez Canal. In the evening Farman hosted a dinner at the New Hotel. Grant, a sharp judge of character, quickly sized up the young Consul-General and commented to a member of his party that "America had in Mr. Farman a most excellent representative, who could not but do honor to consular service." Farnam would indeed prove to be a credit to his country. A few years later he would help restructure Egypt's judicial system and serve as a judge in its Mixed (International) Courts. The young Consul also had a sense of humor.

While the party was in Cairo they traveled to see the tree under which the Holy Family had supposedly rested during their flight into Egypt. Loring was with the group and mentioned to Farman that he intended to make a welcoming speech for the General and tried it out on Farman. Just as Loring was ready to make his presentation, Farman stood up and gave the speech, almost verbatim. Loring was literally at a loss for words. It was all in good fun, and Loring took it that way, but the next day he got his revenge. The party was visiting the Pyramids of Giza where a group photo was going to be taken. Loring later recounted, "My friend, the Consul-General, placed himself near the ladies to good advantage. I was talking to some Bedouins when I noticed the operator fixing the camera. Immediately I rushed between the Consul-General and the instrument. The picture was taken, and I completely blotted him out. This was how I got my revenge out of him for stealing my speech. Grant was very amused at the incident."

Which obelisk is ours?

When General Grant's party started up the Nile on the Khedive's steamer, Consul-General Farman was with him. He was good company, intelligent, witty, and officially responsible for General Grant's safety and comfort in Egypt. He also had an ulterior motive for joining the group. He had been thinking about how America could obtain an obelisk and needed to determine which one would be most likely to be given and transported, should the Khedive agree for one to leave Egypt.

There were only five large obelisks left standing in Egypt, and Farman knew two of them well. One was in the Heliopolis section of Cairo, but this one had its own special problem. It was the oldest obelisk in Egypt, centuries older than the other four erect ones, and clearly Egypt was not going to give away its senior obelisk. He was also quite familiar with the single standing obelisk at Alexandria—the mate to the one the British had recently taken. It was right on the coast and stood alone, perfectly situated for removal, but Farman knew there was a political problem with this obelisk. The inhabitants of that city might protest too much. When the British took their obelisk there was an outcry about Egypt's treasures being stolen by foreigners. Now, taking the second one might be difficult. That left the three still upright in the south of Egypt. As he steamed south with General Grant's party Farman would have a chance to examine the three southern obelisks first-hand and assess which might be best for America.

General Grant on the Nile

The nucleus of the group of travelers consisted of General Grant, his wife and their twenty-year-old son Jesse and Consul-General Farman. Also along was

John Russell Young, a 37-year-old journalist whom Grant had sent on missions to Europe for the State Department, but on this trip he was the unofficial historian, sending telegraphic dispatches to the *New York Herald* describing the trip so readers could follow the General's adventures abroad. Young would later write a two-volume chronicle titled *Around the World with General Grant* and in 1897 would be appointed Librarian of Congress by President McKinley.

The General had also invited three officers from the *Vandalia*, the ship that brought them to Alexandria. In addition, Farman had brought his consulate's majordomo, Hassan, who was an object of wonder for the group. Hassan dressed in Arab style, complete with turban and scimitar, and possessed two wives! He also took pride in his service and wore a gold American eagle pin. The Khedive also sent his trusted majordomo, Sami Bey, to make sure things went smoothly as the General and his party steamed up the Nile. Perhaps the most important member of the group was Emile Brugsch, a high-ranking official in the Antiquities Service who served as the group's guide. Brugsch's older brother Heinrich, also an Egyptologist, was director of the newly created Egyptian Museum in Boulaq, a district of Cairo.

There was excitement within the band of travelers. Those who had not seen Egypt's ancient monuments were eager; those who had were thrilled to be traveling with the General. It was a compatible group, happy to leave Cairo. The city was too French for their taste, not Middle Eastern enough. The walls of the palace the Khedive had provided were covered with French wallpaper, there was French dinnerware, French food. The Service des Antiquités was run by the French; even official governmental correspondence was in French. Now on their steamer *Zinet el Bohren* ("Light of Two Rivers") they could have a proper oriental adventure.

They enjoyed being tourists, bought fezzes to go *à la Turque* and rode donkeys to the sites to be visited. It was all great fun. As they steamed south and visited the temples and tombs along the way, anticipation was growing. They were nearing Luxor, the holy grail of all Victorian travelers to Egypt. This ancient religious capital of Egypt held more spectacular monuments than any other city in the world—Luxor and Karnak Temples on the east bank, and on the west were the Valley of the Kings, the mortuary temple of Ramses the Great, and the temple of Deir el Bahri, built by Queen Hatshepsut who ruled Egypt as pharaoh. It would be a grand adventure.

By the time the *Zinet el Bohren* docked at Luxor the travelers were far more sophisticated about ancient Egypt than when they began their journey. At first they asked Brugsch only questions relating to the Bible: "Was this temple of the time of Moses or of Abraham?" "In which city were the Israelites held in bondage?" The Bible was their sole reference point to ancient Egypt; Sunday school was the only place anyone learned about Egypt. Under Brugsch's tutelage they soon learned that many of Egypt's tombs and temples were far older than either Moses or Abraham. Now they were asking "Which Ramses built that pylon?" "Was Hatshepsut married to Tuthmosis II or Tuthmosis III?" They delighted in the way Brugsch made the monuments come alive, telling the stories behind the stones. The journalist, John Russell Young, later commented in his book *Around the World with General Grant* that Brugsch "knows every tomb and column in the land."

The party was pleased to have reached Luxor, but Consul-General Farman had his own secret reason to be happy. He was going to have a chance to examine the obelisks at Luxor and Karnak Temples to determine which could best be sent to America. Two were still standing at Karnak Temple, one erected by Hatshepsut, the female pharaoh, and the second raised by her father Tuthmosis I. When the party visited Karnak, Brugsch translated the inscription on the base of Hatshepsut's obelisk, telling how it and its now broken twin were quarried and transported in just seven months. As Farman listened to Brugsch tell the obelisk's story, he must have realized that the Egyptians would never let Hatshepsut's only standing obelisk, and the tallest obelisk in all of Egypt, leave the country. There was another reason why the obelisk would not be coming to America. Both Hatshepsut's obelisk and that of her father just a few yards away were smack dab in the middle of the temple, hemmed in by other buildings, and it would be very difficult to lower them from their pedestals. When they were first erected they stood at the entrance to the temples, but throughout the following centuries other pharaohs had added their buildings in front of the temples, surrounding the obelisks. The sharp-eyed Farman also noted that the Tuthmosis I obelisk had a crack and it would have been dangerous to try to lower it. No, the Karnak obelisks were out. That left the one at Luxor Temple.

When the group approached Luxor they were surprised to see the British flag flying above the temple. The British consulate had been built inside the

Temple of Luxor! The group noted that it was totally out of place and asked Brugsch why this had been permitted. "The Khedive doesn't want to offend England. They only regard these monuments as reservoirs from which they can supply their own museums." Indeed, all along the trip Brugsch had expressed his view that the French and English were vandals. One can only wonder what he would have thought if he had read Farman's mind as he stood in front of the obelisk.

As Farman stared up at the beautiful, pristine shaft of granite erected by Ramses the Great he had visions of this gem coming to the United States. It was in beautiful condition, and the French had removed its mate in 1833, so clearly it was possible for American engineers to lower and remove this one. It was a real possibility. But there was also the obelisk at Alexandria that was closer to the sea and perhaps easier to move. He had two possibilities; could he get one of them? But first he had to answer the question, *should* he ask for an obelisk?

As the United States' Consul-General to Egypt, Farman's job was to assist American citizens in Egypt and to implement policy sent from Washington. Once the confusion about an obelisk being offered to the United States had been cleared up, he hadn't heard a word about obelisks, not from Secretary of State William Everts nor from the New York contingent that had been so eager for an obelisk. Once everyone learned that no obelisk had been offered, it was a dead issue. Undoubtedly New Yorkers would still like one, and Vanderbilt was almost certainly still willing to pay for its transportation, but should Farman, without orders from Washington, ask for one? He wasn't sure, but there was someone who would know what to do—the former President of the United States of America, Ulysses S. Grant.

Farman explained to the General the history of the misunderstanding and the correspondences that had gone back and forth concerning the obelisk and asked about the propriety of attempting to obtain an obelisk on his own initiative. Grant replied that he saw no objection and advised Farman to procure one if possible. It was a go. As the group sailed south to Philae Temple and then back to Cairo, Farman worked out his strategy. He would approach the Khedive with his request and present the case why it would be good for Egypt to give an obelisk to America.

The group reached Cairo in the beginning of February and on February 9, 1878 Grant and his party left Egypt to continue their tour around the world.

On March 4, 1878 Farman had an audience with the Khedive at the Abdin Palace, the sprawling winter residence of the royal family. He was ready to present his request. When Farman asked His Highness about the possibility of Egypt giving America an obelisk the Khedive was surprised. Farman expected this, since neither Dixon nor anyone else had discussed the matter with His Highness. Farman explained that Paris and London had obelisks but New York, a far bigger city, had more people who would see an obelisk there, and Egypt's tourist business would increase. He had two possible obelisks in mind, the one at Luxor and the one at Alexandria. He suggested the Alexandria obelisk would be the better of the two since it would be the easiest to move. The Khedive replied that he was favorably inclined to offer America an obelisk, but there were problems. He felt the Alexandria obelisk would be out of the question as the inhabitants of that city would protest too much. But he did say he would consider the request, and with that the audience was concluded. The Khedive was indeed inclined to give an obelisk to the Unites States because his country needed all the friends it could muster. He had just been forced to sell the Gizira Palace to a hotel chain to pay some of his European creditors and there was a movement on the part of France to depose him. It would not hurt to have the United States of America on his side.

Serious negotiations

Several days later the Khedive hosted a dinner party at the Abdin Palace for several dozen guests and invited Counsel-General Farman. Also present was Ferdinand de Lesseps, the builder of the Suez Canal, who had become a close friend and advisor to the Khedive. After dinner, the guests were standing in small groups in one of the palace's ballrooms when the Khedive walked up to Farman and said, "Well, Mr. Farman, you would like an obelisk?" Farman replied that America would like one very much, but before the conversation could continue, others joined them, ending that discussion.

Later in the evening Farman was sitting talking with de Lesseps about Egypt's debt. This was a particularly difficult time for Egypt and the Khedive. Egypt owed European investors one hundred million pounds and was unable to pay even the seven percent interest. The Nile had not risen that year and the crops had failed. Egypt was still using the same system of irrigation used by their ancient ancestors. Each year when the monsoons arrived in Ethiopia the Nile swelled with the runoff. As the river entered Egypt in the North, it overflowed its banks, depositing rich silt over the land. When there was a low Nile, water was too scarce for irrigation, the land was not fertilized, and famine occurred. Just as it had sometimes occurred in ancient times, Egypt was now suffering from a low Nile. With no crops to export there was no way to pay the debt. De Lesseps was appointed by the Khedive as head of a commission to restructure Egypt's debt and determine a new interest rate. As Farman and de Lesseps were discussing the country's finances the Khedive walked over, sat next to the two men and, interrupting the conversation said, "Mr. Farman wants an obelisk." De Lesseps replied, "That would be an excellent thing for the people of the United States." He then paused, thought a moment and continued: "And I do not see why we could not give them one. It would not injure us much, and would be a very valuable acquisition for them." The Khedive replied, "I am considering the matter," and walked away.

Farman was encouraged. The Khedive, not he, had raised the subject. Why would the Khedive raise the subject if he weren't favorably inclined? Three days later Farman called on the Khedive and was informed that His Highness had decided to give America an obelisk, but not the one at Alexandria, because there were too many political problems with that one; it would have to be another one.

A few days later, Farman was attending a ball at the palace and was approached by Heinrich Brugsch, the older Brugsch brother who was the Museum's Director. "I learn you are trying to obtain an obelisk to take to New York." Farman heard the disapproval in Brugsch's voice and replied, "Why not? They have one in Paris and one in London, and the people of New York wish one also." The Egyptologist was not impressed.

> You will create a great amount of ill feeling; all the scholars of Europe will oppose it. The Khedive has asked me to give a description of the obelisks remaining in Egypt, and to state which one can best be spared; I shall not designate any to be taken away, for I am totally opposed to the removal of any of them.

Brugsch's feeling towards the antiquities of Egypt was shared by many others. The rape of Egypt was over and Farman was trying to get an obelisk at the wrong time. Many now felt that Egypt's antiquities should remain in Egypt. As an Egyptologist, Brugsch realized that each obelisk remaining in Egypt was different, had been erected by a different pharaoh, and told a different story. To Farman, they were all the same: tall, silent slabs of granite.

This question of what should be done with Egypt's patrimony continues today. There are constant reports of Dr. Zahi Hawass, former Secretary-General of Egypt's Supreme Council of Antiquities, asking the British Museum to return the Rosetta Stone, or demanding the Berlin Museum return the bust of Nefertiti. Should they be returned? It is not an easy decision. If an object is freely given, isn't it OK to keep it? This was precisely Farman's position. The Khedive was the ruler of Egypt and the obelisk was his to give, though he didn't attempt to convince Brugsch of that. Brugsch had told the truth when he said others would oppose any obelisk leaving Egypt. Farman thought the opposition was coming from foreigners, Europeans who already had their share of Egypt's treasures. No, he would continue to work towards securing an obelisk for America, but he had yet another unpleasant surprise ahead of him.

Farman had been told by the Khedive that the Alexandria obelisk was out of the question, so it seemed that the Luxor obelisk was the only real possibility left. Word had gotten around Cairo that Farman wanted an obelisk, and soon after the disturbing conversation with Brugsch, the British Consul-General informed Farman that the Luxor obelisk had been given to the British many years ago, and although the British didn't intend to take it soon, they objected to anyone else removing "their" obelisk. Farman checked with the Khedive and, indeed, it was true! When the Khedive's grandfather, Mohamed Ali, gave the French their obelisk, he gave the British the second obelisk at Luxor. Now they had approached the Khedive and reasserted their claim to it. The Khedive told Farman that his hands were tied and he couldn't offer the Luxor obelisk to the United States. To Farman it seemed as if all of Europe was conspiring to ensure that he didn't get an obelisk. He was right.

Weeks passed with no mention of an obelisk, partly because the Khedive had asked Brugsch to select the obelisk that could be most easily spared, and Brugsch was not going to do anything of the sort. Finally, in the spring of 1878, the Khedive opened the discussion again and said that though he had not yet selected an obelisk, he intended to do so soon. There was hope!

As prospects for obtaining an obelisk were finally looking up, Egypt and the Khedive were sliding downward towards hard times. Egypt was bankrupt and thousands of peasants in the south had died of starvation the previous year. Once again, Egypt could not pay its debts, and England and France notified the Khedive that in April they would insist on payment for the debt coupons they held. To pay the debt, the Khedive was forced to pledge the wheat that was now growing in the south. It was a desperate gamble. If the harvest were not exceptionally good, there would be another famine.

In June a commission formed by European nations to oversee the finances of Egypt demanded that the Khedive and his two brothers surrender their private estates as collateral for further debt payment. The royal family signed over 25,000 acres of land to the government that were then mortgaged to secure a loan from the Bank of Rothschild. Times were grim. Many government officials were dismissed because there were no funds to pay them, as were many Americans who were in the Khedive's military service. Most were Civil War veterans, brought to Egypt to help modernize Egypt's army. These soldiers had back pay due them for their services and it was Farman's job, as their representative in Egypt, to press the Khedive for payment, while at the same time he was trying to obtain the Khedive's permission to acquire an obelisk. It was an impossible position, and with the oppressive heat of summer settling in on Cairo, he asked for a leave of absence and returned to the United States.

When Farman returned to Egypt in November, he found a new government in power. An Anglo-French Ministry was now running the country. The Khedive was still the nominal head of Egypt, but foreign powers controlled the purse and internal workings of the country. If Farman was to secure an obelisk, it was this Ministry that would have to give it, and they were Europeans. To make matters worse, a very powerful force was telling them not to give away an obelisk.

Brugsch Bey (Bey was a title given to high government officials) had already said that he would not select an obelisk to be taken out of the country. Now he was joined by Auguste Mariette, the Director of the Service des Antiquités, who sent a memorandum to the Ministry stating that he was strongly opposed to any obelisk leaving Egypt. The memorandum explained the uniqueness and importance of three of the obelisks—the two standing at Karnak Temple and the one remaining in Heliopolis. He knew that the one at Luxor was protected by the British and the Alexandrian obelisk was off limits because of the uproar any attempt to move it would cause.

It is ironic that Mariette was now the defender of Egypt's treasures. As a young man in the 1850s he was first sent to Egypt by France to purchase ancient manuscripts. While he was waiting for the deal to be struck (it never was) he explored the sites of Egypt. At Saqqara he discovered the ancient burial site of the sacred Apis bulls, took his manuscript money and used it to excavate the tombs, and packed up everything that wasn't nailed down and shipped it back to the Louvre. Soon after, he was asked to leave the country for pillaging. Much later he was appointed Director of the Antiquities Service and was now defending Egypt's treasures! In Egypt there is an expression that the only thing that is permanent is change. Farman was experiencing this every time he thought he had an obelisk in his grasp.

Certainly at this point things were bleak for America's obelisk. The Khedive, though in favor of giving the obelisk, was powerless. The Ministry, which had the power to give it, was being lobbied by foreign powers and the two highest-ranking Egyptologists in the country not to allow any obelisk to leave. Just as things seemed utterly hopeless, sunlight entered through an unexpected crack.

The head of the Ministry was Nubar Pasha, who had recently fought and won a heroic battle to reform Egypt's antiquated judicial system. To do this he went throughout Europe convincing foreign powers to agree to participate in a system of Mixed (International) Courts in Egypt. One expert on the Mixed Courts said, "Nubar's struggle is entitled to be ranked among the foremost diplomatic achievements of modern history."[1] Nubar, who was now acting as Egypt's first prime minister, informed Farman that he was fully aware of his negotiations for an obelisk and, since the English claimed the Luxor obelisk, and Mariette was opposed to the Karnak and Heliopolis obelisks being removed, he would give America the obelisk at Alexandria! He even drafted a memorandum to the Minister of Public Works to put the gift in motion. Farman was elated, but then things changed again.

Details of the famine in the south reached Cairo and Egyptians were furious because the Commission had sold their grain to pay the government's debt and now people were starving. A mob, led by former officers and soldiers who had been fired without pay, attacked Nubar and other government officials in the street. They were held prisoner till the Khedive personally came to free them.

The Khedive took advantage of the anti-European sentiment and moved quickly. For the safety of the country, he asserted, Egypt must have Egyptian rulers.

He disbanded the Commission and appointed a new, entirely Egyptian, Commission. For President of the Commission he selected Cherif Pasha, a man admired by all for his honesty and intelligence. From an aristocratic family, Cherif had been educated in Europe, but chose the life of an Egyptian public servant, beginning his career in the army and quickly rising to the rank of colonel. Now he was Egypt's most powerful government official during Egypt's most difficult time. Soon, under his stewardship, the government began to stabilize and function again, largely because everyone had confidence in this noble man.

Farman and Cherif knew and respected each other, and after a few weeks of political calm, Farman screwed up his courage to ask about the obelisk. Cherif's reply was that he would have to speak to the Khedive; Farman could check with him the next day and he would have an answer.

"We have concluded to give it to you"

The next day Farman called at the palace and was told Cherif Pasha was in a meeting with the Khedive. Farman dropped in on the Khedive's seal-bearer and found him chatting with the Khedive's two brothers. The three invited the Consul-General to join them for coffee and, just as Farman settled in, a very agitated Cherif Pasha walked in. Farman sensed there were governmental problems again. Cherif said something in Arabic to the seal-bearer and then indicated by a nod that Farman should follow him outside. Cherif walked silently with Farman down a long hallway and then descended a grand staircase leading to the door, where Farman's carriage was waiting. As they walked through the doorway Cherif Pasha asked, "It is the obelisk in Alexandria that you prefer, is it not?" The Consul-General explained that it would be the easiest to remove. "Well," said the Pasha, "we have concluded to give it to you."

Farman was pleased, but not elated. He had been promised the obelisk several times—by the Khedive, by Nubar Pasha, and now by Cherif. Cherif was an honorable man, but how long would *he* stay in power? Farman thought quickly and suggested he should have something in writing. He also requested that the obelisk be given directly to the City of New York, not to the United States. Vanderbilt was paying for the obelisk's transportation because it was coming to New York. If it were given to the United States, Congress would have to decide which city got it and there were guaranteed funds only for New York. "We give you the obelisk, do as you wish with it." Cherif paused and then added,

> Write me a note, indicating what you wish to have done. State that all the expenses of removal are to be paid by the United States or by the City of New York, if you prefer. Hand the note to my Secretary-General, and tell him to prepare an answer confirming the gift in accordance with the suggestions you give, and bring it to me for my signature.

Farman jumped in his carriage, rushed back to the consulate, drafted the letter, and two hours later handed it to the Secretary-General of the Department of Foreign Affairs. He was afraid the Khedive and Cherif might be out of power before he could get something in writing. The following day the letter was in Cherif's hands.

MR. FARMAN to CHERIF PACHA, Minister of Foreign Affairs

Cairo, May 17, 1879

EXCELLENCY: Referring to the different conversations that I have had the honor to have with your Excellency, in which you informed me that the government of His Highness the Khedive is disposed to present to the city of New York, to be transported and erected there, the obelisk of Alexandria, I should be pleased if your Excellency would have the kindness to definitely confirm in writing the gift of this monument.

It is understood that its transportation is to be effected at the expense of certain citizens of the said city of New York.

I beg to assure your Excellency, in advance of the warm thanks of my government for having thus favorably responded to the representations I have made to the government of His Highness the Khedive, in accordance with the instructions that I had received on the subject.

I have every reason to hope that the monument, which is thus soon to be transported and set up in the city of New York, will always be a souvenir and a pledge of the friendship that has ever existed between the government of the United States and that of His Highness the Khedive.

I beg your Excellency to accept the renewed assurance of my high consideration.

E.E. FARMAN[2]

The next day Cherif's reply, which had been drafted by Farman and put into the jargon of Middle Eastern diplomacy by the secretary, arrived.

CHERIF PACHA, Minister of Foreign Affairs, to Mr. FARMAN

Cairo, May 18, 1879

Mr. AGENT AND CONSUL-GENERAL: I have taken cognizance of the dispatch which you did me the honor of writing me on the 17th of the current month of May.

In reply, I hasten to transmit you the assurance, Mr. Agent and Consul-General, that the government of the Khedive, having taken into consideration your representations and the desire which you have expressed in the name of the government of the United States of America, consents, in fact, to make a gift to the city of New York of the obelisk known as Cleopatra's Needle which is at Alexandria on the sea-shore.

The local authorities shall therefore be directed to deliver this obelisk to the representative of the American government and also to facilitate, in everything that shall depend upon them, the removal of the monument, which, according to the terms of your dispatch, is to be done at the exclusive cost and expense of the city of New York.

I am happy, Mr. Agent and Consul-General, to have to announce to you this decision, which, while giving the great city an Egyptian monument, to which is attached, as you know, a real archaeological interest, will also be, I am as yourself convinced, another souvenir and another pledge of the friendship that has constantly existed between the government of the Unites States and that of the Khedive.

Be pleased to accept, Mr. Agent and Consul-General, the expression of my high consideration.

CHERIF[3]

It was a done deal. New York would have its obelisk and take its rightful place alongside the great cities of London and Paris. It was wise that Farman had acted so quickly. France had been insisting that the Khedive resign and was reluctantly seconded by England. Soon other European nations joined the call for abdication. On June 27, just one month after Farman had secured the obelisk, the Khedive resigned, and passed the throne to his son, Mehmet Tewfik Pasha. Three days later, when the Khedive sailed into exile, Farman had in his hand the letter giving the obelisk to New York, but now it was from a government that no longer existed! Immediately foreign powers began putting pressure on the new Ministry that was formed to negate the gift of the former regime. The matter was debated twice and the Council of Ministers finally decided that the gift held; a legitimate government had given it. New Yorkers would have their obelisk; all they had to do was pick up the gift.

When Hurlbert was notified that the obelisk was indeed available, he contacted Dixon to reaffirm that if Dixon would bring the obelisk to New York he would be paid 15,000 pounds sterling. Dixon had just experienced his difficulties in bringing London its obelisk and replied that the fee would have to be raised to 20,000 pounds. When Hurlbert heard the fee was increased he refused. He just didn't do business that way. Now someone else had to be found who could bring Cleopatra's Needle to the shores of New York.

The right man at the right time

The June 17, 1879 issue of *The World* carried the announcement that America had been given an obelisk, funds were available for its transportation from Egypt, and all that was needed was the man to do the job. Lieutenant Commander Henry Honeychurch Gorringe was convinced he was that man. At six feet tall with piercing blue eyes, Gorringe was impressive in his naval uniform, but he did not have a particularly impressive beginning. His father was an Anglican missionary posted to Barbados where Henry Honeychurch Gorringe was born in 1841. Barbados in the 1840s was a sleepy island, but soon the family moved to the even sleepier Tobago, where Henry, his older brother, and two sisters grew up. Living on a small island, Henry grew up around boats and sailing and was comfortable on the water. By the time he was fourteen he had had enough of both education and Tobago and convinced his father to arrange a position for him as a cabin boy on an acquaintance's ship. Henry's first voyage on the open sea was like something out of adventure novels, involving a shipwreck on the way to India, being marooned in the Indian Ocean, rescued and transported to Cuba, eventually arriving home at Tobago.

Rather than being discouraged, Henry was elated by his adventures and committed to the life of a sailor. With little formal education, his intelligence and drive served him well and by the time he was twenty-one he was offered command of his own ship, but he chose to enter the United States Navy instead, and when the Civil War broke out he served under Admiral Farragut, where he was promoted three times for gallantry in action. By the time he was 26 he was a Lieutenant Commander.

After the Civil War the United States began using its navy for nonmilitary projects, mapping coastlines in what were called hydrographic surveys. America wanted its own depth charts, maps of currents, and anything else that would aid navigation and make commerce more profitable. Gorringe was given command of the *Gettysburg* and was dispatched to the Levant to chart coasts and current and sound depths. His navigator, Seaton Schroeder, a lifelong friend, in his autobiography gives a rare first-hand assessment of Gorringe's personality.

> Captain Gorringe and I had become great friends, and in later years we became very intimate; he had such sterling qualities as to endear him to any one who could pierce the crust of an unfortunate sensitiveness which seemed at times to indicate a nature very foreign to what he really was. . . . A natural element in his character was the most absolute, unquestioning self-confidence; never was it "Can this be done?" but only "How shall it be done?"[4]

Self-confidence is one thing, but Gorringe seemed fearless. Once when he and Schroeder were mapping rocks that might be navigational hazards off the coast of Tripoli they were placed in a difficult position.

> [A]n elderly sheik came to us and said that he understood what we wanted and had no objection to it personally, but that he could not answer for his young men, and must ask us to go; which we did. But after nightfall, there being no moon, we pulled noiselessly ashore in a little boat with the instruments and dark lantern and made some careful and satisfying observations of stars within sound of the Arabs' camp; then we stole back to the ship without detection.[5]

Mapping the coast of the Levant allowed Gorringe to experience antiquity, and he was enthralled. In Turkey he walked the site of ancient Troy, recently discovered and excavated by Schliemann. In Egypt his first opportunity to actually own a bit of antiquity presented itself when an Arab offered to sell him a handful of ancient coins. Schroeder was present and comments that they both agreed that the price was very high, but Gorringe was fascinated and paid it. A year later Gorringe took the coins to the British Museum for authentication. One was an extremely rare coin from the time when the Greek Ptolemies were ruling Egypt; it sold at auction for twenty times what he had paid for the entire lot. Like a novice gambler who wins at his first attempt at the slot machines, Gorringe was hooked and collected ancient coins for the rest of his life.

When Gorringe read the announcement in *The World* asking for someone to move New York's obelisk, he couldn't believe it. He and Schroeder had visited the Alexandrian obelisks during their hydrographic survey days and had thought about moving one to America. The obelisks were unappreciated, amid the garbage of a squalid neighborhood. Some of the locals made money by taking a sledgehammer to the obelisk to chip off souvenirs for tourists. Now Gorringe could rescue the standing obelisk and bring it to New York, but he had to submit a plan that would convince Hurlbert he could do it.

Gorringe began planning how he was going to move the obelisk. First he studied the methods the French and English had used to transport their obelisks. The French didn't have to navigate the Atlantic. Once the *Luxor* reached Alexandria, it was a straight sail across the Mediterranean to Toulon and this allowed the *Luxor* to be towed. Also, the *Luxor* had been specially constructed to hold the obelisk and navigate the shallow Nile. Gorringe wasn't going to construct a special ship for his obelisk. He would buy one inexpensively and then reconfigure it for the obelisk.

The British also didn't have to cross the vastness of an open ocean far from sheltered harbors when they towed their obelisk to England. Still, even with their special vessel, the *Cleopatra*, constructed to house the obelisk, and no vast, open seas, it was lost at sea. There was a limited amount of experience Gorringe could glean from the two previous ships that had transported Europe's obelisks. He had a far more daunting task ahead of him. Towing was not an option for him. He had to sail America's obelisk across the Atlantic. He would need a different plan, but he was sure of one thing: he needed a ship that was self-powered and could navigate heavy seas with a 250-ton obelisk in its hold. Up to this time, the largest object ever put in the hold of a ship was a 100-ton cannon manufactured in England and shipped to Italy. To put the gun on board special hydraulic cranes had to be constructed, and they cost a fortune—more than the entire allotment Gorringe had to move the obelisk. Since super cranes were out, it would not be possible to lift the obelisk onto the ship. Gorringe planned to open the hull, slide the obelisk into the ship's hold, and then replace the planks that had been removed in opening the ship, a procedure similar to what Lebas had done seventy years earlier at Luxor.

He would also have to move the obelisk over land, first from where it stood in Alexandria to the transport ship and then from the ship when it docked in New York to its final site in Central Park. As he searched previous attempts at moving heavy weights over land, he found an earlier engineering feat that would become his model, but it wasn't an obelisk that was moved. It was something much heavier—the immense base for a statue of Peter the Great in Russia. Now largely forgotten to history, it was a remarkable accomplishment by a remarkable man.

Count Carburi moves the rock

The year was 1768 and the Czarina Catherine the Great was planning a statue of Peter the Great to grace the new city of St. Petersburg he had created. The statue was going to be a massive bronze of Peter on his horse galloping up a steep craggy rock. Since the figure of Peter was going to be more than eleven feet high, the base had to be huge. To make the statue and base even more impressive, it was decided that the base should be a single stone.

The task of finding and transporting such a stone was entrusted to a shadowy aristocrat going under the name of Chevalier de Lascari. Actually, he was Count Carburi from Cephalonia in the Peloponnese. As a young man he was involved in an altercation that ended in a death and he had to flee his native land and change his name. Carburi must have earned a reputation for engineering skills as he was entrusted with transporting the largest stone ever moved in modern times.

A Russian peasant told Carburi about a rock in a swamp outside the village of Lachta near the Gulf of Finland. Carburi found the rock overgrown with moss but very impressive. By probing beneath it he estimated that it was approximately 42 feet long, 27 feet wide and 21 feet high. Like the Egyptian obelisks, it was granite, and because of its massive dimensions it weighed 600 tons, more than twice the weight of the obelisk Gorringe would be moving a century later. Carburi returned to St. Petersburg to design the capstans that would be used to haul the rock, and after testing various models concluded none of them would be adequate. In the summer of 1768 he returned to the mosquito-infested swamp to begin the first step of removing the stone, which was stuck in 15 feet of muck.

He planned to use the seasons to his advantage. Carburi would move the rock in winter, when the morass was frozen and he wouldn't be up to his neck in mud. But there was plenty to be done before he could lift the rock out of the swamp. The first task was to construct barracks in which 400 workmen would live for the next six months. Once they settled in, they spent the summer and fall preparing a road on which the rock could travel from the swamp to the Neva River, where it would be transferred to a barge for its final journey to Petersburg. The road was 120 feet wide; trees were felled, terrain was leveled, and logistics planned. Throughout the summer, mosquitoes plagued the men and several died of malaria. Count Carburi also contracted the disease, and suffered from it for the rest of his life. Many years after he had moved the rock, he mused that there was only one thing he would have done differently—he would have drained the swamp and thus alleviated a great amount of suffering.

By March the road had been prepared and the swamp was now frozen enough to raise the rock from it. A trench 100 feet wide and 15 feet deep was cleared around the rock to create a working area so levers could be positioned beneath it and workmen would have a place to stand. No one had ever seen the underside of the rock and Carburi's first task was to turn it over. Levers 65 feet long and 18 inches thick had been brought but, because the swamp didn't freeze completely, piles had to be driven into the marsh beneath the rock so the levers would rest on something solid. While one end of the huge levers rested on the piles, the long ends that protruded out of the swamp were attached to the capstans that would provide the mechanical advantage to turn the boulder. With thirty-two men working each capstan, Carburi rolled the rock over and had his first look at the underside. It was fine.

To pull the rock out of the swamp he constructed a path made of alternating layers of small fir trees and gravel extending from the swamp and onto the prepared road. Twelve pulleys and four capstans were used and, with two drummers posted on top of the rock to signal starting and stopping, the huge rock was slowly winched out of the marsh onto level ground. Phase one was complete.

Carburi was now faced with the problem of moving the 600-ton rock over uneven terrain. Something that large couldn't move on wheels. There was no material strong enough for an axle, and wheels would collapse under such a load. Carburi's solution was to build a rail system in which metal balls could roll—essentially giant ball bearings. Thus the rock could roll along relatively friction free. As the rock advanced, the rail system behind was pulled up and moved ahead of the rock.

With the rock on solid ground and sliding on metal balls, it moved easily with only two capstans, each manned by thirty-two workers. When hills were encountered, Carburi used six capstans, and the moving mountain proceeded towards the Neva River. Even with the short Russian winter days of five hours of light, the rock progressed between 100 yards and a quarter of a mile a day, depending on the terrain. At the end of six weeks of hard work, it rested on the banks of the Neva, ready for the next stage of its journey.

Carburi had designed a 180-foot barge to receive the rock. He filled the barge with water and sunk it to the riverbed, making it easier to get the rock on board. The side of the barge nearest the riverbank was removed and the stone loaded by means of two capstans fixed on board a ship firmly anchored on the far side of the barge. The side was then replaced and the men began pumping water out of the barge, but as it began to rise, the deck bent because of the incredible weight of the stone. Carburi added stones to the prow and stern of the ship to equalize the weight, and the barge, heavy cargo and all, floated safely to the surface. A boat was lashed to either side of the barge to stabilize it on its river journey. For several days the inhabitants near the banks of the Neva were treated to the extraordinary sight of a mountain of granite floating down their river!

When the barge reached St. Petersburg, piles were driven into the river to support the barge on beam and stern as the granite statue base was hauled on shore by the capstans. Once again, with its two drummers on top, the stone began a land journey, this time to the site where the statue of Peter was to be erected. On September 15, the anniversary of the coronation of Catherine the Great, the stone passed the Empress's palace and then continued its journey to the site where the statue of Peter the Great on horseback (striding up Carburi's rock) now greets millions of tourists to St. Petersburg.

A man, a plan, an obelisk!

When Gorringe read of Carburi's moving the rock on metal balls, he quickly decided that he would use cannonballs for moving his obelisk when it was on land. His plan was taking shape. He knew how he would move the obelisk on land and he knew that he would have a self-propelled ship that could navigate high seas with an obelisk in its hold. The last major part of his plan was how to lower the obelisk from its pedestal in Alexandria.

For this, he designed a structure that looked like two mini-Eiffel towers standing right next to the obelisk on opposite sides. An iron belt fitted around the obelisk was bolted to clamps (trunnions) projecting from the miniature towers. The obelisk would then be pivoted around its center of gravity until it was parallel to the ground. Once in this position it would be lowered to the ground by hydraulic jacks at both of its ends. All this ironwork would be fabricated in the United States, shipped to Alexandria, and assembled there. Once the obelisk was down, the equipment would be disassembled and brought back to New York with the obelisk so it could be used to re-erect it in Central Park. It was a well-thought-out plan based on years of experience; now Gorringe just had to convince those in charge that it would work.

This wasn't the only plan submitted. Another came from the owner of a ship that transported blocks of granite on its deck. The ship had never carried a block larger than thirty tons, but the owner was confident. He presented a photo of the obelisk, showing that it stood close to the water. "I will moor my vessel here, lower the stone down on her deck, and then sail. When we reach New York we will not be in any hurry to set it up, for we will cart it about the country and make a good thing of it exhibiting it to the country folks." Aside from the P.T. Barnum aspect, the plan's defects were obvious to all. While the obelisk is indeed close to the water, reefs and other navigational hazards make it impossible to moor a ship within a mile of the coast. Further, the ship to be used was only 400 tons and with a 230-ton obelisk on its deck it would easily capsize in difficult seas. Perhaps most important was the fact that there was no room on the deck for the 69-foot obelisk!

Another plan called for towing the obelisk all the way to New York, but after the difficulties the British had towing their obelisk, no one was eager to try that on the open sea. When Gorringe presented his plan, he had several things

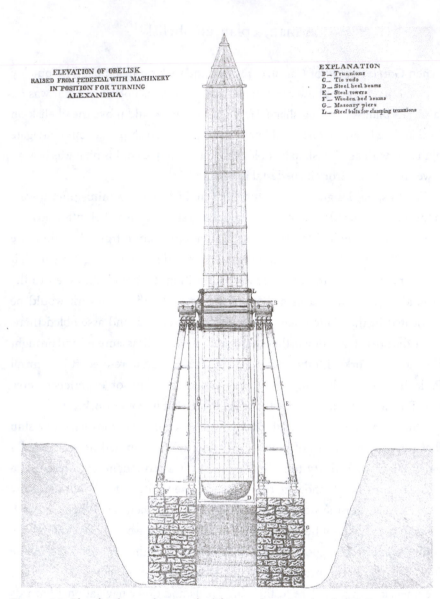

ELEVATION OF OBELISK
RAISED FROM PEDESTAL WITH MACHINERY
IN POSITION FOR TURNING
ALEXANDRIA

EXPLANATION
B — Trunnions
C — Tie rods
D — Steel heel beams
E — Steel towers
F — Wooden bed beams
G — Masonry piers
L — Steel bolts for clamping trunnions

Figure 6.1 Plan for the mechanism for lifting and turning the obelisk. It was manufactured by the Roebling Iron Works, who had just completed the Brooklyn Bridge.

going for him. He was a decorated naval commander who had never failed in any task that his government had given him. Those who had worked with him had nothing but praise, and he exuded a calm, reassuring confidence. Aside from his personal qualities, the plan impressed those who saw it as realistic and well thought out and they quickly concluded he was up to the task. When Vanderbilt was told of the plan and the man who would carry it out, he wrote to Gorringe with his proposal.

New York, Aug. 4, 1879

Lieut. H. H. Gorringe, U.S. Navy

Dear Sir: I have learned that you have or can procure the facilities to remove to the city of New York the obelisk now standing at Alexandria, in Egypt, known as "Cleopatra's Needle."

As I desire that this obelisk may be secured for the city of New York, I make you the following proposition: If you will take down and remove said obelisk from its present position to this city, and place it on such site as may be selected with my approval by the Commissioners of Parks, and furnish and construct at your own expense on said site a foundation of mason work and granite base of such form and dimensions as said Commissioners and myself may approve, I will, on completion of the whole work, pay to you seventy-five thousand dollars.

It is understood, however, that there is to be no liability on my part until the obelisk shall be so received and placed in position in the city of New York, and the same to be in as good condition as it now is. It is understood further, that this agreement binds also my executors and administrators; you to accept this proposition in writing on the receipt thereof, and agree to execute the same, and complete the work fully in every respect within one year from the date thereof.

Very truly yours,
W. H. Vanderbilt[6]

Gorringe had the job if he wanted it, but the terms were far from ideal. The money he was being offered was considerably more than what Dixon had asked for, but Gorringe would have far more responsibility. He would have to finance the project on his own and would only be repaid when the obelisk was safely erected in New York. He would have to procure a ship, move the obelisk, and erect a proper pedestal, all using his own money. As a naval officer, Gorringe didn't have the money for such a project, but he did have the reputation for being fearless and completely reliable. If he said he could do it, there were people who would back him. Lewis F. Whitin, an old New York friend, was one such person. He put up the money, secured only by the belief that his friend Henry Gorringe would succeed.

Full steam ahead

With his plan accepted and money in hand to execute it, Gorringe went full steam ahead. He immediately contacted Seaton Schroeder, his former navigator, who was now a lieutenant in the U.S. Navy, to see if he would help on the project. Schroeder was delighted and the State Department arranged for Gorringe and him to be given leaves of absence to bring America its obelisk. Gorringe then contracted with John A. Roebling's Sons to manufacture the iron parts for the turning mechanism. Roebling had recently completed the Brooklyn Bridge and clearly had the capability to produce large iron works. Though not of the magnitude of the Brooklyn Bridge, there would be large parts, some weighing as much as 12,575 pounds. Frank Price was hired by Gorringe as foreman of ironworks to oversee production, bring the parts to Alexandria, and assemble them.

As the turning mechanism was being forged, Gorringe attempted to charter an American steamer suitable for bringing the obelisk across the Atlantic. None was available. If America didn't have a ship, England would, so on August 24, 1879 he and Schroeder sailed for Liverpool on the *Arizona*. For two weeks the two attempted to charter a British ship, but when owners heard what cargo the ship would be transporting, and that the hull would be opened and then closed to load the obelisk below deck, they asked exorbitant fees, as much as it should have been to purchase the ship. Convinced that there were plenty of other ships to be had, Gorringe sailed for Alexandria without a ship for his obelisk.

As soon as they arrived at Alexandria, the European community began its opposition to the removal of the obelisk. Petitions were circulated for signatures, angry editorials appeared in newspapers, and Gorringe was called names as he walked through the streets. What Consul-General Farman had encountered was now intensified as it became clear that these Americans were serious about taking an obelisk. Gorringe thought it best to get the support of the new Khedive, Ismail's son Tewfik, so they took the train to Cairo for an audience with His Highness.

The Khedive was gracious and welcoming and the men talked frankly about the pressures that the European powers were putting on the Khedive. Tewfik was concerned that if the obelisk were damaged while being removed it would be a political disaster for him, but he was reassured when he heard Gorringe's detailed plan and by the calm manner in which it was presented. He would support the

Americans and instructed his secretary to see that orders were given to the Governor of Alexandria to formally hand over the obelisk to Gorringe and assist him in every way possible. The order echoes all the tribulations that Farman had experienced in his negotiations to obtain the obelisk.

TO HIS EXCELLENCY THE GOVERNOR OF ALEXANDRIA: In the time of the ex-Khedive the Egyptian government gave Cleopatra's Needle, now standing on the sea-shore of Alexandria to the United States of America, to be erected in the city of New York. His Excellency Cherif Pacha, who was then Minister of Foreign Affairs, communicated the fact to the United States Consul-General in a dispatch dated May 18, 1879. An American officer having been sent here to receive and remove said Cleopatra's Needle, and His Highness the Khedive having confirmed the gift by a decree, I hasten to instruct you to deliver the monument immediately to the said officer, and to offer him the same assistance for removing it from its site and embarking it as was offered at the time of removing the other obelisk that was given to the English government. All expenses will be paid by the officer of the United States.

(signed) MOUSTAPHA RAIZ, *Minister of Foreign Affairs*[7]

With the order in hand, Gorringe and Schroeder took the first train back to Alexandria and went straight to the Governor's office. They knew the protests would continue but wanted to be able to say: "Too late, the obelisk is now in the possession of an officer of the United States." The Governor immediately transferred the obelisk to Gorringe and a week later they began clearing the site. It soon became clear that opposition had not gone away; it had just taken a new form.

As the men began to clear the site, an Italian appeared and claimed that the land was his and they had no right to be on his property. The Italian didn't dispute that America now owned the obelisk; he was merely pointing out that they couldn't take it. Gorringe offered to lease the land, but the Italian refused. Gorringe responded with a letter to the governor, a remarkable document showing diplomacy and restraint while making it very clear that he would not back down.

ALEXANDRIA, Oct. 28, 1879

H.E. THE GOVERNOR OF ALEXANDRIA

SIR: I regret extremely that it has become once more necessary for me to have recourse to your good-will and your duty to assist me in prosecuting the work with which I am entrusted by the government of the United States. Yesterday, having received authority from you, I set some men to work to remove the paving stones that surrounded the obelisk, the owner of the stones making no objection whatever. Another individual arrived, however, and ordered the work stopped. Arriving myself a few moments afterward, I learned that the man claimed possession of the ground and would allow no one to work there. He also added that if we persisted he would apply to the Italian Consul, whose janissaries would be sent to eject us from the premises. Not recognizing his right to interfere, but not wishing to bring about a disturbance, I went to see the Italian Vice-Consul, accompanied by the Consul of the United States, to ask for an explanation. He informed me that any Italian subject occupying a property belonging to him had a right to his protection, and that he would protect him, even by force of arms. I thought it strange that he should dare prevent by main force what your Excellency had authorized me to do; but before notifying my government that the Italian Vice-Consul had defied the orders of the Egyptian government, and that I am thus stopped in the execution of a work with which I am charged, I though it best to try to arrange it amicably, so as not to trouble your Excellency. During the dispute on the ground I had offered to the *soi-disant* proprietor to pay him a rent, just as though it really belonged to him; but he refused point-blank to rent the ground to me, and informed me through his lawyer that he would not permit the operations for removing the obelisk. Nevertheless, I begged the Italian vice-consul to try his best to settle the matter, and he promised to give me an answer by four o'clock this afternoon. If he does not succeed I shall be compelled to telegraph my government that I have been forcibly ejected, and that Egyptian authority has failed to protect me.

I beg your Excellency to so direct affairs as to enable me to begin operations, because it is needless to say that if the matter should take official form between the two governments the situation would only become more grave.

I am, sir, with great respect, your obedient servant,

(signed) HENRY H. GORRINGE, *Lieutenant Commander, U.S. Navy.*[8]

Soon after he received the letter, the Governor explained that the Italian's claim to the land was far from clear, but court proceedings to settle the matter could take years. Gorringe took matters into his own hands and informed the Italian Consul-General that he would sue anyone attempting to hinder his work for 15,000 pounds in damages. He then offered to lease the land and added that the offer would expire at 4:00 p.m. that day. The offer was accepted. Gorringe had cleared the first hurdle, but the race was far from over.

The perfect ship?

When Schroeder and Gorringe landed in Alexandria they began prowling the port, looking for a suitable ship to purchase to transport the obelisk across the Atlantic. They arrived at the perfect time. Because the Egyptian government was bankrupt, it could not afford to maintain a fully active postal service and had decommissioned several of its postal steamers. Gorringe spotted one, the *Dessoug*, at dock and went on board to inspect it; the good news was that the hull was in perfect condition and was just large enough to admit the obelisk below deck. The bad news was that the engines and boilers were in poor condition and Gorringe, who was accustomed to the United States Navy, was shocked at how filthy the ship was and how badly it had been neglected. Still, Schroeder could work on refitting the ship while Gorringe focused on the obelisk itself, so they decided to make an immediate offer of 5,000 pounds sterling for the ship, knowing that it would cost an equal amount to refit. It was a low but fair offer and Gorringe knew there would be no other buyers for such a ship.

The Assistant Postmaster-General replied that the 5,000-pound offer was not serious enough to consider. This was followed by an offer from a shipbroker to sell the *Dessoug* to him at some unnamed price. He was looking to be bought off from bidding against Gorringe, but Gorringe refused to be held up. He informed the Ministry in Cairo that his offer of 5,000 pounds would be withdrawn at noon on December 3, 1879. He was convinced that the Egyptian government should be delighted to have 5,000 pounds for a ship that would otherwise rust to pieces at its mooring. In the meantime, the shipbroker had made an unsecured offer to the Assistant Postmaster-General that was accepted and now offered the ship to Gorringe for 6,000 pounds. Gorringe replied that he would not buy the *Dessoug* from him at any price. When the broker heard this, he backed out of the deal and the Assistant Postmaster-General quickly notified Gorringe that he could have the ship for 5,100 pounds sterling. On December 3 Gorringe transferred the funds. Soon after, he boarded the ship with a representative of the Postal Service who lowered the Egyptian flag. Gorringe quickly raised the American flag, making it clear to all who owned the ship. As Schroeder began refitting the *Dessoug*, Gorringe turned his attention to lowering the obelisk.

Scaffolding was erected around the obelisk so it could be sheathed in wood planks to prevent damage during the transfer operations. The planks were held together by iron barrel hoops, and attached to the top strap were several loops through which cables could be run to control the obelisk as it was turned. At the very top, a large American flag was flown, to emphasize who now owned the obelisk. One hundred local workers, ranging in age from ten to seventy, were hired to clear rubble and prepare the site. The middle-aged ones dug and filled baskets while the older workers lifted the baskets onto the backs of the young, who carried their loads to the sea and dumped them. It was a busy work area, but Gorringe treated it a bit like an archaeological excavation; after all, it was an ancient site. When fragments of bronze statues, ancient coins, scarabs, and amulets turned up as the men dug, Gorringe gave bonuses to those who discovered such objects and also sent men to the shore to search the beach for objects that might have escaped detection, been dumped, and later washed ashore.

Figure 6.2 Before lowering it, the obelisk was clad in wood to protect its surface.

While the turning mechanism was being manufactured in New Jersey, Gorringe prepared the foundation on which it would rest. Two masonry piers were constructed and then wooden derricks were erected to lift pieces of the turning mechanism onto the piers for assembly. The prefabricated turning mechanism, completed in early October, began its trip, accompanied by Frank Price, the master of ironworks, on the steamer *Nevada*, which arrived in Liverpool, England on October 19. There it was transshipped to the *Mariotis*, which arrived in Alexandria, Egypt on November 11, 1879.

In all of Alexandria there was no truck or cart large enough to transport the 12,000-pound trunnions from the port and through the streets of the city to the site where the obelisk stood. The best available cart was refitted and pulled by Gorringe's strongest workmen on a Sunday, when the streets were emptiest—Alexandria's population was largely European and Christian. As the cart inched its way through the streets, an American missionary denounced it as "the work of the Devil," not only because it was the Sabbath, but also because he felt his church could better use the money spent on the project. It seemed to Gorringe as if he were being fired upon from all sides!

Once the prefabricated pieces were on the site, they were quickly assembled on top of the masonry piers without the slightest difficulty. When the obelisk was fixed to the trunnions it was supported by the turning mechanism. Now the bronze crabs on which the obelisk rested could be cut free. By means of turnbuckles and screws (much like the mechanism in an automobile jack) the obelisk was raised straight up a few inches so it would clear the crabs that were still attached to the pedestal. The crabs are an important source for figuring out the obelisk's history. Originally the obelisk stood at Heliopolis but was later moved to Alexandria by the Emperor Augustus. When the obelisk was re-erected on its pedestal, four bronze crabs were placed at the corners of the bottom of the obelisk for stability. The crabs are inscribed with the details of the obelisk's re-erection. This is how we know not only that it was moved in the eighth year of Augustus's reign, but also that Barbarus was Prefect and Pontius was the architect. In Gorringe's time only two of the four crabs remained, and they can be seen today in the Egyptian Wing of the Metropolitan Museum of Art.[9] Unfortunately almost all the visitors walk right by this wonderful bit of history without noticing it.

Steel cables were run from both ends of the obelisk over the top of the scaffolding and into the masonry piers to take some of the weight off as it turned. Gorringe estimated that the cables supported only sixty of the obelisk's 230 tons and was afraid that when the obelisk went horizontal it might break under its own weight.

The obelisk turns

On December 4 Gorringe attempted to turn the obelisk by pulling on the cable at its top but, as it began turning, an iron beam on the bottom bent slightly and snagged on one of the crabs, so operations had to be suspended. European engineers in Alexandria took this as a chance to oppose the project and claimed the turning mechanism was not strong enough to support the obelisk. After all, it had bent when hardly any stress was put on it. Letters appeared in the newspapers stating that the Americans were going to damage a priceless antiquity. Throughout the criticism, Gorringe retained his faith in the turning mechanism and went forward. With great difficulty, similar to what Fontana had experienced three hundred years earlier, he removed the bronze crabs from the pedestal and on December 5, once again, attempted to turn the obelisk.

The obelisk swung effortlessly but when it reached an angle of about twelve degrees off vertical, Gorringe stopped the obelisk's motion, tied the cables, and left the 230-ton shaft of granite suspended overnight. He was making a statement. The system was clearly strong enough to hold the obelisk. In spite of his success, rumors were now circulating that there was going to be a demonstration by the European community when Gorringe attempted to bring the obelisk fully horizontal. These rumors reached Russian Rear Admiral Aslambekoff, whose flagship, *Minim*, was anchored in the port. Happy to assist Gorringe, a fellow naval officer, he disembarked a large force of his trained seamen to prevent the demonstration. With this help, Gorringe now was ready for the decisive moment. At 11:00 a.m. on December 6 he gave the order to his men to pull on the cables to bring the obelisk horizontal. Surrounded by a teeming crowd of Italians, Greeks, and Egyptians, the obelisk slowly and silently moved towards horizontal. Then disaster struck; a creaking sound

Figure 6.3 When the obelisk was turned to the horizontal, a cable snapped and the obelisk started moving past horizontal towards the ground. Gorringe had planned for such a contingency and the pile of timbers stacked on the left stopped the obelisk's descent.

came from the turning mechanism followed by a loud snap. One of the cables had separated. For a moment the obelisk's movement stopped, but just for a moment. Then it began moving again towards the horizontal, picking up speed as it went. The obelisk was out of control. Spectators began running in all directions, but Gorringe had planned for such a situation. He had stacked timbers almost as high as the obelisk would have been when it was horizontal; if the obelisk for any reason went past horizontal, continuing towards the ground, the timbers would stop it. Indeed, as the obelisk went past the horizontal, it crashed into the timbers, bounced up a few feet, moved downward again, only far more slowly, and came safely to rest on the timbers. Once the obelisk was safely horizontal, the Italians, Greeks, other Europeans, and Egyptians all sent up a great cheer, as if they had never opposed the project!

Lowering the obelisk—four inches at a time

The obelisk now had to be lowered to the ground. Gorringe positioned a stack of timber beneath its bottom end to match the one by the point that had saved the obelisk. Now, with the obelisk resting on timbers, the turning mechanism was dismantled to create more room to lower it. A notch was cut out of a beam on top of each stack and a hydraulic jack was placed in each notch. The two jacks were then raised a few inches so they supported the full weight of the obelisk. This enabled the workers to remove the top layer of timbers and then lower the obelisk onto the stacks again. This lowered the obelisk by four inches. Then another two notches were cut in the timbers of what was the new top level and the jacks were placed in them. When raised once again a few inches to support the obelisk, the new top level of timbers was removed and once again the jacks were lowered so the obelisk rested on the timbers. The obelisk was now another four inches closer to the ground. Slowly and methodically this cycle was repeated so that the obelisk was lowered about three feet each

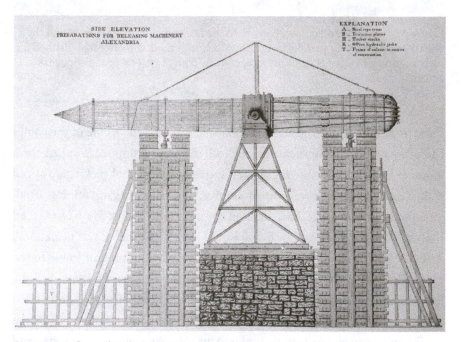

Figure 6.4 Once the obelisk was horizontal, it was lowered four inches at a time by hydraulic jacks.

day. While it was being lowered another very difficult operation was being conducted, one that Gorringe had not foreseen.

When Frank Price, the ironworks master, arrived in Alexandria with the turning mechanism, he also brought cannonballs and the iron channels they would roll in as the obelisk was transported through the streets of Alexandria. Gorringe knew that the water at the coast where the obelisk stood was not deep enough to bring a large ship close to shore and he had read about how rocks just beneath the surface had ripped a hole in the caisson containing the British obelisk. It would be far safer to move the New York obelisk one mile over land to Alexandria's port and load it on the ship there. As soon as Gorringe arrived in Alexandria he asked the Governor for permission to move the obelisk through the streets. The governor informed him that because the Egyptian government was bankrupt, it could neither clean nor maintain the streets, so it had given control of them to the European merchants in exchange for their maintaining them. The merchants refused to give permission to move the obelisk through the streets, claiming it might damage the sewers. Undaunted, Gorringe created a new plan for getting the obelisk to the port.

He realized that if he couldn't move the obelisk overland he would have to float it through the same treacherous waters that had ripped a hole in England's iron caisson. He immediately hired professional divers to clear an underwater route for the obelisk. Because of his interest in archaeology, Gorringe knew that the bottom of the shore was believed to be littered with blocks from Cleopatra's lost palace. He built piers in the water, on which he positioned lifting cranes. When the divers found blocks from the palace that were navigational hazards, they were lifted out of the water and placed on shore.

Diving in Alexandria is not an easy matter, especially in winter, and in 1880 it was even more difficult. Currents are strong, visibility is poor, and bad weather frequently makes diving impossible. For months, divers worked to clear the shore so the obelisk could be safely loaded and floated to the port. As the obelisk was slowly being lowered to the ground, they were still frantically working to prepare the path it would eventually take to the port. As all this was going on, Gorringe dismantled the masonry on which the turning mechanism had stood and focused his attention to moving the fifty-ton pedestal on which the obelisk had rested.

An iron bar was inserted beneath the pedestal, and with the help of hydraulic jacks it was raised off the three steps on which it rested. Iron channel rails with rows of cannonballs were positioned near the elevated fifty-ton pedestal and it was then lowered onto the rails. The channels and cannonballs formed giant skids, like the ones used by supermarkets to transport crates of goods from trucks being unloaded into the basements beneath stores. On these rails the pedestal was slid off to the side with the greatest of ease, which must have been a great relief for Gorringe. This was precisely the same method he was going to use for transporting the obelisk, which was five times the weight of its pedestal.

A message from ancient Freemasons

With the pedestal out of the way, Gorringe began removing the three steps on which it had rested. These steps were formed of several dozen large, rectangular limestone blocks and four of granite that fit together like a jigsaw puzzle. When the last step was removed, Gorringe made a surprising discovery that soon led to his obsession with how the blocks were configured.

The foundation beneath the steps had been filled with several large sandstone blocks and three of granite. Two of the granite blocks were polished and the third was rough. One of the granite blocks was a perfect cube and next to it was a limestone block on which rested a metal trowel and lead plumb bob. Gorringe, a Freemason and member of Anglo-Saxon Lodge 137 Brooklyn, New York concluded that he had found emblems of Freemasonry and proceeded to remove the foundation blocks, carefully numbering and recording their original positions. A committee from the Grand Lodge of Egypt was then called in to inspect the stones. Their report would eventually lead to one of the most incredible parades New York had ever seen.

The Committee, headed by Grand Master S. A. Zola, Sovereign Grand Commander of the Supreme Council of the Ancient and Accepted Scottish Rite, Chief of Symbolic Masonry of Egypt, examined the blocks Brother Gorringe had unearthed and concluded the blocks were indeed the handwork of fellow Masons. The polished cube was the Masonic perfect ashlar; the rough block, the rough ashlar. One of the blocks had two snakes carved on it that represented Wisdom. The trowel and plummet were clearly Masonic, intentionally left behind, to be found by brother Masons in the future. Gorringe immediately decided he must bring it all back to New York for his brother Masons to wonder at. Neither the French nor the English had brought their pedestals home. Gorringe's agreement with Vanderbilt said nothing about the pedestal, just the obelisk. Still, Gorringe felt New York should also have the pedestal; it was the right thing to do.

With the pedestal and steps cleared and the obelisk nearly on the ground, a caisson was built to receive the obelisk. The caisson was an 83-foot-long wood box resembling a giant coffin. Once the obelisk was secured inside the caisson, the plan was to launch it down a gangway that had been built right up to the water. Divers had continued the gangway underwater for quite a distance to protect the bottom of the caisson until it floated. The hope was that, with an initial shove provided by the hydraulic jacks, the caisson, with obelisk inside, would slide down the well-lubricated gangplank and into the water. Once afloat it would be towed to the port, where it would be loaded into the *Dessoug*. On March 18 they attempted to launch the caisson but it wouldn't slide and had to be inched along by jacks. This process took nearly two weeks, and when the obelisk finally reached the water, a gale stormed in. With the seaward end of the caisson rising and falling in the turbulent water and the landward side stuck on the gangway, Gorringe feared the obelisk might break in the storm, so he flooded the caisson to add weight to stabilize it. The storm raged during the night but subsided in the morning. The caisson was unharmed, the water was pumped out, and at 10:00 a.m. on March 31 the caisson was towed to Alexandria's port.

A ship fit for an obelisk

While the obelisk was being lowered and the pedestal removed, Schroeder had been overseeing refitting of the *Dessoug*, and it wasn't easy. First he strengthened the interior of the hull with steel beams to distribute the weight of the obelisk over the entire ship. Existing internal beams had to be cut out to make room for the obelisk and bolt-holes drilled so they could be refitted once the obelisk was inside. Thirty plates in the hull were removed as well as some above the waterline. Much of this was done while the ship was moored, but eventually a floating dock was required and there was only one large enough to accommodate the *Dessoug*. The government officer in charge made Schroeder wait five weeks before the *Dessoug* was permitted to use the dock, and time was running out. A foreman shipwright from Glasgow was brought to Alexandria to oversee the boiler and engine repairs and the final opening and closing of the hull. It was a massive and time-consuming job that was done by three teams of thirty Arab boilermakers who worked around the clock.

The obelisk was not the only heavy cargo the *Dessoug* had to be prepared to receive. There was also the pedestal weighing in at fifty tons, and it proved to be quite a problem. Bringing the pedestal to the port where the *Dessoug* was waiting was relatively easy. A lighter was chartered that could be sailed to the coast where the obelisk had stood. Following the path that had been taken by the caisson, only in reverse, it went towards shore through the path cleared by the divers and right onto the gangway that had been constructed. With the lighter beached, Gorringe used hydraulic jacks to lift the pedestal, set it on the lighter's deck, and then launched it down the gangway with a push from the jacks. The lighter then was towed to the port with ease, but Gorringe knew that loading it on the *Dessoug* was going to be difficult.

A delicate balancing act

To keep the pedestal from shifting during the ocean voyage it had to be secured to an iron frame that Schroeder had constructed. To get it onto the frame they had to raise the pedestal thirty feet above the deck of the *Dessoug* and lower it through a hatch. The problem was that the pedestal weighed fifty tons and the largest crane in Alexandria could lift only thirty tons. Gorringe's solution was complex and involved considerable risk. In addition to the thirty-ton shore crane, there was a floating steam-derrick that could lift twenty-five tons. If the weight of the pedestal could be precisely distributed between the crane and the derrick, the pedestal could be lifted above the *Dessoug* and placed in the hold. If, however, something went wrong and the pedestal fell on the *Dessoug*, it would destroy the ship and likely be lost forever at the bottom of the harbor.

Gorringe calculated how much water the derrick would displace when it supported twenty-two tons—less than its twenty-five-ton capacity. A mark was made on the derrick at the level it would sink into the water when it supported twenty-two tons. That mark could not be permitted to go underwater or the

Figure 6.5 Hoisting and then lowering the fifty-ton base into the ship's hold was a very difficult maneuver involving two cranes working in tandem.

derrick might be supporting too much weight and collapse. By keeping the mark right at water level (twenty-two tons) the shore crane would have to support twenty-eight tons, just within its operating capacity. It was a delicate balancing act and would require four steel cables, the derrick, and the crane all working in tandem, but Gorringe was confident.

The lighter with the pedestal on deck was towed between the floating steam-derrick and the shore crane, and four one-and-a-half-inch steel cables were attached to the pedestal, to the crane, and the derrick. The signal to lift was given and the crane and derrick began lifting in unison. Slowly the pedestal rose off the deck of the lighter, which was then quickly towed out of the way, and the pedestal was swung over the deck of the *Dessoug*. The water level of the floating derrick was perfect and all was going well when a loud cracking was heard and the pedestal began oscillating as it hung above the ship. If it fell, it was the end of the *Dessoug*. Afraid that the pedestal might come crashing down, the ship was maneuvered out from under the suspended block of granite. Once there was nothing between the pedestal and the water, the cables

Copyright 1882 by Geo. Wright.
of Benneman St. n.y.

The "Obelisk" in Dry Dock
Waiting Shipment.

Figure 6.6 The obelisk in dry dock at Alexandria.

were carefully inspected. One had snapped, but the pedestal was still supported by the other three. The lighter was quickly towed back beneath the pedestal, which was safely lowered onto its deck. Disaster was averted but now Gorringe was sure the plan would work; he just had to replace a cable.

The next day Gorringe and Schroeder replaced the broken cable with one from the *Dessoug* and once again the pedestal was lifted off the lighter, and swung above the ship. This time it was lowered through the hatch and into the frame designed to hold it. The pedestal was the largest object ever maneuvered onto a ship at Alexandria. Next up was the obelisk, weighing nearly five times as much as its pedestal.

When the obelisk was towed to the port, it was brought onto the floating dock and the caisson removed. There is a photo of the obelisk in the floating dock that is a bit of a mystery. The obelisk has been taken out of its wood cladding. Why? Shortly after the photo was taken, it was in its protective wood casing again, awaiting the *Dessoug* to be positioned to receive it. Had something happened to the obelisk and they were checking it?

Figure 6.7 The hull of the *Dessoug* was opened so the obelisk could be slid inside on cannonballs.

It had been calculated that the obelisk must enter the hold at a 21-degree angle and it was placed at this angle on the dock and the *Dessoug* brought in. A wood gangway was laid down from the bottom of the obelisk, entering the ship first at the aperture and continuing into the hold. On this gangway carpenters anchored the iron channels with their five-and-a-half-inch balls that would form the skids on which the obelisk would slide into the ship. These skids proved so efficient that the two hydraulic jacks that pushed the obelisk into the hold never had to exert more than five tons of force.

When the obelisk was completely inside, the two hydraulic jacks were repositioned to lift it a few inches so the channels and iron balls could be removed. Once the obelisk was securely resting on its bed of soft wood, teams of carpenters began wedging it in on all sides so it couldn't shift during the voyage. As the carpenters worked inside, ironworkers replaced the plates over the aperture. On June 1, 1880 the *Dessoug*, with its precious cargo stowed in the hold, was almost ready to sail.

How to insure an obelisk

The blocks from the steps beneath the pedestal were stowed below decks and secured as ballast, as were the parts to the turning mechanism. On June 8 the *Dessoug* took on 500 tons of coal, twice the weight of the obelisk, but just enough to get it as far as Gibraltar, where it would refuel. The last arrangement was to organize the ship's insurance and, like every other part of the project, this proved to be a trial. The usual rate for insurance of a vessel was two percent of its value, but when the underwriters heard about the obelisk as cargo, they wanted twenty-five percent! Gorringe refused and by June 11 the rate was down to five percent—better, but still more than twice the going rate. Gorringe told his London agent to inform the underwriters that he would sail the next day, without insurance, if the rate was not two percent. Offers of acceptance came flooding in; the *Dessoug* was insured. The crew was another matter.

As soon as Gorringe and Schroeder purchased the ship they began assembling a crew. The chief engineer was a Scotsman who had worked for the Egyptian Postal Service. He knew the *Dessoug* well and oversaw the refitting of the boilers and engines. The other officers were all British. The first and second mates were alcoholics, with the second officer so drunk he fell overboard twice before they ever left port and had to be fired for his own safety. Forty-eight of the locals who signed on as crew deserted before the ship sailed and Gorringe's description of the quartermasters wasn't encouraging: "They would do credit to a pirate crew."[10] It was quite a group, but that was only one small part of the difficulties Gorringe was facing.

Because of legal technicalities, the ship couldn't be registered as an American vessel and Gorringe wasn't about to sail under the Egyptian flag, nor under the flag of any European country. When the *Dessoug* finally entered international waters, Lieutenant Commander Gorringe was commanding an unregistered ship with no nationality displayed. This meant that any man-of-war could seize it while at sea or in any country when in port. It was a risk that Gorringe was willing to take.

At sea at last

Even with all the problems they faced, Schroeder and Gorringe felt a great sense of relief as they watched the coast of Alexandria recede. They had overcome great obstacles in Egypt and now were together again, in their element, the open sea, and knew they could overcome any future hurdles. The *Dessoug* behaved beautifully, only pitching and rolling slightly, like any other merchant steamer. The problem they encountered was that the supposedly refitted boilers leaked. When they put in at Gibraltar they stayed for three days, to allow the boilers to cool so they could be properly repaired. This done, they took on 500 tons of coal, enough to reach New York, and left at midnight on June 25/6 in good weather.

On July 6 they were 1,500 miles from New York when a loud noise emanated from the engine room, then the engines came to an abrupt stop. They had broken a crankshaft. Fortunately there was a spare on board, and that was due to Gorringe's meticulous planning and perseverance. The ship's purchase included "all equipments and spare articles on board and in store that properly belong to the *Dessoug*." An extra crankshaft for the *Dessoug* was in a government warehouse but the officials repeatedly ignored Gorringe's requests for it. Only because he didn't give up was it delivered to the ship five days before they sailed. It took six days to install the new crankshaft, but once again they were steaming towards New York. On July 10 they got the biggest fright of the trip.

It was then that they encountered squalls, which should have been no problem for the *Dessoug*, but Gorringe could see waterspouts forming in the distance. Usually these spouts form and dissipate quickly, rarely reaching a height of more than twenty feet. But here the crew watched in horror as a spout formed directly in front of the ship and kept growing and growing till it was fifty feet high. The weight of so much water could crush the deck of the *Dessoug* if it landed, and it was heading straight for them. Normally ships fired a cannon to dissipate a waterspout, but the Dessoug was unarmed. All they could do was batten down the hatches and wait. For nearly five minutes the spout slowly moved towards them and then, just as it was upon them, it turned and crashed back into the sea. The gale blew for the next three days, but the ship behaved beautifully and New York was straight ahead.

On July 19 they sighted New York and were met by the pilot-boat *A.M. Lawrence, No. 4*. After anchoring overnight off Fire Island, they were escorted to the Staten Island Quarantine Station where they were given a quick once over and released. Then they steamed around the southern tip of Manhattan, up the Hudson River, and docked at 23rd Street. Gorringe gave the officers

Figure 6.8 The pedestal was pulled through Central Park in a specially designed carriage by sixteen horses.

leave and opened the ship to visitors. The *Dessoug* and its ancient distinguished passenger were a New York sensation, attracting more than 1,700 visitors in one day. New Yorkers had been following the progress of the *Dessoug* in their newspapers and, now that it was here, it was like a Broadway star. As New York's curious traipsed through to see the obelisk, Gorringe made plans for erecting it.

For logistical reasons, the pedestal and obelisk had to be disembarked at different locations. The ship sailed north to 51st Street where a huge dock crane lifted the pedestal out of the hold and swung it onto shore with the greatest of ease—a marked contrast to the difficulties encountered loading it at Alexandria. It was next loaded onto a truck wagon specially rebuilt to bear the fifty-ton load. Pulled by sixteen pairs of horses, the pedestal started east on 51st Street towards Fifth Avenue. Several times along the way the procession had to halt because the wheels of the truck sank into the soft pavement and had to be freed. After reaching Fifth Avenue, it turned north and proceeded up to 82nd Street where it entered Central Park. The park terrain was too uneven for the wheeled vehicle, so the pedestal was placed on greased skids and hauled to Greywacke Knoll, the site selected for the obelisk.

There had been some debate about where to place the obelisk. Some favored prominent sites in the middle of the city, like Columbus Circle. However, there were concerns that tall buildings would eventually be erected, obstructing the view of the obelisk, so a park site was agreed upon. Greywacke Knoll, the park's highest point, near the city's new Metropolitan Museum of Art, provided a solid foundation and was selected. On August 5 Department of Parks workers began preparing the site by removing young trees and leveling the surface, but a few days later work stopped and didn't resume. The Department of Parks traditionally prepared the sites for new monuments but, in Gorringe's words, "In this case the custom was violated." Nothing as large as the obelisk had ever been erected in a city park before and perhaps the Department of Parks just didn't want the responsibility if anything went wrong. Gorringe offered to prepare the site at his own expense and finally was given permission to proceed. Throughout September the site was prepared, but a great deal more had to be done.

The Freemasons have their day

The ceremony for laying the foundation was be presided over by the Masons, and thousands of members of various lodges and their officers participated. On October 9, 1880, dressed in top hats, black coats and white gloves, 500 commanders of local Masonic lodges formed ranks on 15th Street, on the east and west sides of Fifth Avenue. As they converged onto Fifth Avenue in the cool October air, they marched north, six abreast with four-foot intervals between ranks, resembling a giant, black millipede with white legs. When the last row passed 16th Street they were joined by 500 more commanders converging from 16th Street onto Fifth Avenue, lengthening the giant insect to nearly a quarter of a mile. At 17th Street, members of the Brooklyn Masonic lodges and lodges from Suffolk and Richmond Counties joined them, and so it went, street after street adding to the flow up Fifth Avenue. At 21st Street they added French, Italian, Spanish, and German-speaking lodges until more than 8,500 masons in military ranks filled Fifth Avenue. Bands preceded many of the lodges, so the 30,000 spectators that lined the route were treated to music as well as pageantry. It was the greatest congregation of Masons the world had ever seen.

As the column marched north towards Central Park, three horse-drawn carriages left the Grand Masonic Temple on 23rd Street and 9th Avenue. The

Figure 6.9 A gold and amethyst baton was crafted by the Freemasons to be used at the installation ceremony for the obelisk's pedestal. This detail shows the miniature gold obelisk at its tip. Illustration courtesy of the Chancellor Robert R. Livingston Masonic Library of Grand Lodge, New York, N.Y.

carriages contained the officers of the Grand Lodge and Supreme Grand Master Jesse B. Anthony, who carried a baton of gold and amethyst specially crafted for the occasion. It was a thing of beauty, with a gold obelisk decorated with hieroglyphs just like the ones on the obelisk that Brother Gorringe, Anglo-Saxon Lodge 137, had brought all the way from Egypt to New York. (You can still see it today if you make an appointment at the Grand Masonic Lodge of New York.)

As the parade passed 23rd Street and the Masons marched by Madison

Square, towering above the landscape was an obelisk—not their obelisk, not the one Brother Gorringe had brought to New York, but a different obelisk. The 51-foot obelisk they encountered on this bright fall day was pure American Egyptomania. Carved of Massachusetts granite and erected in 1857, it honored General William Jenkins Worth, hero of the War of 1812 and the Mexican–American War, and Fourth Commandant of West Point Military Academy. It is not a thing of beauty; the sculptor got it wrong. Although carved out of a single piece of granite, there are no sleek unbroken lines emphasizing the obelisk's height. Four bands carved into the granite list significant battles from Worth's long career, but they make it seem as if the obelisk has been cobbled together from several pieces, depriving it of its majesty. Still, the Masons could compare their obelisk to Worth's. Unencumbered by battle scenes, their obelisk had something far better—mysterious ancient Egyptian hieroglyphs, far more appropriate for a Masonic monument.

At precisely 2:30 p.m. the column of marchers reached 33rd Street, halted, and was met by carriages from the Grand Lodge. The officials and Past Masters wore their jewels and white lambskin aprons, symbols of the Masonic trade. As the Masons stood at attention the officers reviewed the ranks, nodded approval, and the thousands continued their march up Fifth Avenue in the brilliant sunlight.

As they neared 40th Street they had one last Egyptian encounter. They could see it from several blocks away, massive and imposing—an Egyptian temple complete with thirty-foot-high walls and even taller entrance pylons. The Croton Reservoir had been built in "the Egyptian style" and when it went on line on July 4, 1842, it was the pride of New York City. No longer would people have to rely on rainwater caught in cisterns and barrels. Fresh, clean water from the Croton River upstate flowed through two aqueducts to serve the growing population. The reservoir remained operational until 1911 when it was taken down, the land filled in, and New York's famous 42nd Street Public Library was erected on the site.

After passing the reservoir on their march north, houses and buildings began to thin out. Northern Manhattan was still practically pastoral. The Dakota Apartment building on 72nd Street had not yet been built, but when it was, it was so far from the city's center that the building was called "The Dakota" because it was like living in the Dakota Territories.

At 82nd Street the column paused. By now it stretched more than a mile back to 60th Street, where the ranks opened their center and faced inward, permitting the Anglo-Saxon Lodge and Grand Lodge to march up the middle to be the first to enter Central Park. As they entered the park, to their right was the newly constructed Metropolitan Museum of Art, but they gave it hardly a thought as they made their way to the site that Brother Gorringe had prepared to receive them. A large elevated deck had been constructed for the Grand Master, Grand Officers, Masters, and Wardens of the Lodges. Once they took their places on the platform the other marchers closed ranks on the north, east, and west sides of the platform. The grassy knoll on the south, left open for visitors, quickly filled to capacity, swelling the crowd to more than 20,000.

In front of the crowd on Greywacke Knoll, the large limestone blocks of differing sizes and shapes had been fitted back together like a jigsaw puzzle, forming the steps that would support the obelisk's pedestal. It was this unique assemblage of blocks that had drawn the thousands of Freemasons to this spot. Months earlier, and 8,000 miles away, in Alexandria, Egypt, Brother Gorringe had noticed that the unusual arrangement of blocks suggested it was a Masonic monument. Gorringe and other brother Masons concluded that twenty centuries earlier brother Masons had prepared the obelisk base as a concealed message for the future. Later that day they would be told they were wrong.

But now he and his brothers crowded around this Masonic marvel to fit its last stone in place. The block was several inches smaller on all four sides than the void that received it, and Gorringe had ideas how to fill it. His choices give us a rare insight into his personality. Although he was now a celebrity, Gorringe remains an enigma to this day. Who were his close friends? What was his house like? What did he do in his spare time? We just don't know, but we do know that he intended to transform the base of the obelisk into a time capsule, and we know what he wanted to put in it.

He asked the American Bible Society for copies of the Bible in various languages. They told him where he could buy them, and he did! So we suspect he was religious. He tried to get an example of that amazing new invention, the telephone, but couldn't. That also shows us something about the man. My bet is he was a techie. He asked the United States Coast Guard and Geodetic Survey for samples of weights and measures. They refused, but he did have some successes with other government agencies.

The Treasury Department contributed a set of medals of the United States presidents and a proof set of 1880 coins. The Department of State gave a facsimile of the Declaration of Independence, a Congressional Directory for 1880, and some other documents. The Navy supplied a silver medal given to seamen and officers for Arctic exploration by Queen Victoria. All this hints at Gorringe's patriotism.

The Society for the Prevention of Cruelty to Animals provided some of their literature, suggesting Gorringe may have been an animal lover. Gorringe's Anglo-Saxon Lodge 137 gave a complete set of silver emblems and jewels of the Order of Freemasons. William Hurlbert, the editor of the *World* newspaper, who had helped so much to bring the obelisk to New York, supplied the most intriguing of the items placed in the time capsule. He "contributed a small box, the contents of which is known only to himself, and a gold plate on which is engraved the essential facts relating to the removal of the Alexandria obelisk to New York."[11] But this wasn't all. Into the base went *Webster's Unabridged Dictionary*, the works of Shakespeare, a New York City Directory and map, an *Encyclopedia of Mechanics and Engineering*, and even a hydraulic jack like the two that had lowered and moved the obelisk in Alexandria. The base was a compendium of knowledge deemed important for future generations.

The assembly bowed their heads as the Chaplain of the Grand Lodge said a brief prayer. Grand Master Jesse B. Anthony, Master of New York State's Grand Lodge in Troy, New York stepped forward. With a silver trowel he spread a thin layer of mortar on the three-foot limestone cube that was the final block and dropped a dab of mortar into the open central hole into which the block was to be lowered. Grand Master Anthony next took a wooden square, another Masonic symbol, and examined the corners of the stone and found them true. Stepping back, he was replaced by Acting Grand Senior Warden Edward H. Simmons, who tested the foundation blocks with a level. The Grand Junior Mason assessed the cornerstone with a plumb, and Grand Master Anthony returned to solemnly declare the stone fit to be installed. A small derrick slowly lifted the block, swung it over the hole and lowered it into place.

Grand Mason Anthony stood before the stone, now in place, and said, "I, Jesse B. Anthony, Grand Master of Masons of the State of New York, do find this stone plumb, level, and square, well formed, true and trusty, and duly laid." Deputy Grand Master Taylor placed a handful of grain, the emblem of plenty, on the stone. The Grand Senior Warden poured wine on the stone to symbolize joy, and the Junior Warden poured oil, representing peace.

Lieutenant Commander Gorringe, the man whose heroic efforts had brought them all to this spot, was formally presented to the Grand Master, who declared, "In the name of the Grand Lodge of the State of New York I now proclaim the cornerstone of this obelisk, known as Cleopatra's Needle, duly laid in ample form." He then repeated these words on the south, west, and east sides of the stone. When this was done, 8,500 Masons clapped in unison three times and the voices of 20,000 people rose in one great cheer. Cleopatra's Needle had been officially welcomed to New York.

It was now 5:00 p.m. and the sun was just beginning to cross the Hudson River to the west, a half-mile from the gathering. Grand Master Anthony stepped forward to formally address the crowd. His speech was a bombshell. It began by praising the ancient Egyptian builders for their skill and insight. OK so far. Then Master Anthony launched into a discussion of the Great Pyramid and how a record of past history had been coded into the measurements of the pyramid's blocks and passageways. If one measured carefully, perhaps one could use the pyramid to predict the future. This was a theory recently put forward by Charles Piazzi Smyth, Scotland's Astronomer Royal,[12] who was a fine astronomer but a bit of a new-ager when it came to the Great Pyramid. He had surveyed the pyramid and declared it to be a repository of ancient wisdom inspired by God. Soon he would be labeled a "pyramidiot" by scientists and archaeologists, but when Master Anthony gave his speech, there were still plenty of people who believed the theory. So the references to coded messages and prophecies were nothing shocking. Then, towards the end, came his real message.

Referring to the committee of Alexandrian Masons who declared the base had been built by fellow Freemasons, Master Anthony mentioned that many people believed there were Freemasons in ancient Egypt. Well, they were wrong. He explained that, indeed, modern Freemasons shared many principles in common with the ancient Egyptian builders, but when one looked at the history of Freemasonry, it simply didn't go back that far. There were no Freemasons in ancient Egypt!

It was a carefully reasoned, thoughtful presentation with a clear conclusion: Fellow Masons did not build the monument they were now inaugurating.

There is no record of the reaction of Commander Gorringe, or his fellow Masons. Were they shocked? Disappointed? We just don't know. All indications are that they were thrilled to be conducting the ceremony and delighted to be part of such a historic event. Besides, it wasn't over; this was just the base. There was still plenty to do before the obelisk could be erected.

On the following day, the fifty-ton pedestal was lifted into place on top of the three steps, to await the obelisk's arrival. It would take another three months. Well before Gorringe reached New York he had planned how to off-load the obelisk from the hull of the *Dessoug*. The ship would go into dry dock and then he would reverse the loading procedure: Remove all the wood struts that held it in place, jack it up a few inches with the hydraulic jacks so the channel irons and iron balls could be slipped under the obelisk, and then haul it out of the reopened aperture in the hull. As soon as he arrived in New York, Gorringe set out to find the right dry dock. Unfortunately there was only one that was suitable, and once its owner heard about the obelisk, he saw dollar signs and asked an exorbitant rate. Gorringe had seen this several times before, most recently with the insurance brokers who wanted to rob him when they heard about the *Dessoug*'s cargo. Gorringe offered the going rate, but the owner, knowing he had the only dry dock for off-loading the obelisk, refused to budge. Gorringe walked out. Now he needed a new plan for off-loading the obelisk.

His first thought was to take the *Dessoug* to either Baltimore or Philadelphia, use their dry docks, disembark the obelisk and then tow it to New York via canals. But as he ran the details through his mind he saw the flaw in this plan. The *Dessoug* was unregistered and could be seized. New York City was happy to be getting an obelisk and he had connections there. Who knew what Baltimore or Philadelphia might do? No, the obelisk had to be off-loaded in New York. There was an alternative to a dry dock—a marine railway at Staten Island.

How to float an obelisk

A marine railway is basically a cradle on pilings next to a shoreline. A ship is sailed into the cradle and the cradle lifted above the high-tide level so the ship can be worked on and repaired. The problem is that marine railways are not usually used for unloading large objects; Gorringe had to figure out how to make it work. It would take a great deal of skill to execute, but he had a plan. The obelisk had gone into the *Dessoug*'s hull at an angle of 21 degrees and it would have to come out at that angle. Gorringe sank pilings into the water and built what looked like a boardwalk right next to the marine railway, at a 21-degree angle. When the obelisk exited the hull, it would go onto the boardwalk. After two weeks, everything was ready. The hull was opened, iron railings and balls were placed under the obelisk, and fifty minutes after a hydraulic jack began tugging on the obelisk it was resting safely on the boardwalk. Then came the hard part.

The obelisk was resting safely on its pier but the 230-ton monolith still had to be lifted onto some sort of barge that could be towed to Manhattan, and the question was how to lift it when no cranes were available. Gorringe's solution was as brilliant as it was simple: Let the tide lift it. He had designed the pilings of the pier so that two pontoons could be brought under the pier and thus under the obelisk. When the tide came in, the pontoons rose, lifting the pier's crossbeams with the obelisk on them. It was ingenious and it worked perfectly. The two pontoons were towed free of the pier and lashed together to form a kind of catamaran with the obelisk fixed to the deck. The plan was to tow it twelve miles around the southern tip of Manhattan, up the Hudson River to 96th Street, where a landing stage had been prepared to receive the obelisk. The journey to the west side of Manhattan was delayed a day because of bad weather, but at 5:00 p.m. on September 6 the obelisk began moving slowly towards its new home. All along the way boats tooted their steam whistles, welcoming New York's newest and most celebrated resident.

Ninety-sixth Street was just about the only place on the Hudson where the obelisk could have been off-loaded. All along the Hudson River cliffs line the shore with the only break at 96th Street. The obelisk reached the loading stage at 7:15 p.m., during high tide, just as planned. The pontoons were floated between pilings that had been sunk into the water so that the crossbeams on which the obelisk rested almost formed a boardwalk, like the one at Staten Island; but because of high tide they were floating a few feet above the pilings. As planned, valves in the pontoons were opened to fill them with water. As the pontoons sank lower in the water, the crossbeams and obelisk settled on the pilings. The obelisk had now officially landed on Manhattan Island and was about to begin its remarkable journey to Central Park.

The long journey to Central Park

Gorringe had already planned the route the obelisk would take to the park and knew the first few hundred feet were the most difficult. The Hudson River Railway ran along the riverside, so its tracks were between the obelisk, as it lay on the boardwalk, and 96th Street, where the obelisk would begin wending its way through the New York City streets. The obelisk would first have to cross the railroad tracks along the Hudson River, where trains packed with commuters ran frequently. Somehow Gorringe had to move the huge obelisk across the tracks quickly. He had a team of workers lay timbers from the boardwalk across the tracks and onto 96th Street. On this he would lay the iron channels that held the cannonballs on which the obelisk would roll. The wood pathway was designed so it could rapidly be taken apart and reassembled. For days the workers practiced putting it together and taking it apart till they knew every timber and its place intimately. Finally, on September 25, it was show time.

Fortunately Vanderbilt, who was paying to move the obelisk, also owned the railroad. His officials were instructed to stop all incoming trains at 11:00 a.m. and, soon after, the workmen skillfully assembled the wood path, laid the iron channels on top of it, and attached the obelisk by an enormous iron chain to one of the pile driver engines that had been repositioned to pull the obelisk

Figure 6.10 The obelisk was off-loaded from the Hudson River at 96th Street, where it was hauled across the railroad tracks.

over the tracks. The men had been so well prepared that the entire operation, including disassembling the iron channels and wood path, took only one hour and twenty minutes. No passenger train was delayed, and only one freight train had to wait for twenty-five minutes. This was the last time the iron channels and cannonballs would be used. Under the extended pressure the channels split in two and for the two-mile journey to Central Park something even stronger was necessary.

Gorringe adapted something he had seen when the *Dessoug* was at the marine railway in Staten Island. The obelisk would sit in a steel cradle with rollers attached underneath and a pile driver engine would winch the cradle containing the obelisk. Tracks were laid along the first leg of the obelisk's journey, from 96th Street to West Boulevard, today's West End Avenue. There was a sixty-foot climb from 96th Street by the Hudson River to West Boulevard and even the best of engines can't pull heavy loads up steep grades, so skilled men were put to work laying tracks so that the grade would be as gentle as possible. Holes were drilled into boulders, permitting cables to anchor the tracks and stabilize the mini-railroad. This difficult piece of engineering required considerable precision and it took over a month for the obelisk to travel its first quarter-mile to West Boulevard, but the system was working. Now the difficulty was going to be turns.

Turning something as large as an obelisk is not easy. The plan was to use hydraulic jacks to lift the bottom end of the obelisk a few inches, push it sideways and then repeat the maneuver as many times as necessary. By the time the obelisk was finally pointed south on West Boulevard, six days and nights of constant labor had passed and there were eleven more turns ahead. This would not do.

As the obelisk slowly moved south towards its next turn at 86th Street, Gorringe began designing and then creating a turning mechanism that was basically a giant lazy Susan. Concentric circles of iron channels held the old familiar cannonballs. A hydraulic jack attached to the system could push the end of the obelisk around, making turns far quicker than before; at least that was the hope. It took the obelisk six days to reach 86th Street and by that time the new turning mechanism was in place. It had taken twenty-two hours to position the concentric circles and cannonballs but only four hours to turn the obelisk, a great improvement. Since the turning mechanism could be laid prior

Figure 6.11 Newspapers and magazines fanned interest in the obelisk's journey.

J. & P. GOATS'　Best Six-Cord
SPOOL COTTON
AND
CLEOPATRA'S NEEDLE

THE GREATEST THREAD AND NEEDLE IN THE WORLD.

over

Figure 6.12 To capitalize on interest in the obelisk, tradesmen gave out souvenir cards to customers.

to the obelisk's arrival, turns would hardly slow the obelisk's progress towards its pedestal in Central Park.

All of New York read about or came out to see the progress of the huge monolith through the city's streets. As it slowly made its way towards its pedestal, everyone was caught up in the event. Storeowners gave out trade cards with pictures of the obelisk. Since the obelisk was called "Cleopatra's Needle," it was a natural for sewing stores to capitalize on the obelisk's fame. Many created wonderful images of the obelisk being used in conjunction with their products. Some showed the obelisk being towed or raised with thread while others showed Cleopatra herself threading a needle produced by John English & Co. It was all very exciting.

The obelisk proceeded east towards Central Park and at Eighth Avenue, 86th Street became Transverse Road No.3, cutting through the park. Steep grades and difficult terrain meant the obelisk couldn't go in a straight line, directly to its pedestal, but rather had to go all the way east thorough the park via the Transverse Road to Fifth Avenue. Even with the longer gentler route, the trip across Central Park became a battle with the forces of nature. The progress across Central Park slowed as a bitter December cold wave hit New York and heavy snows fell for days. Soon members of Gorringe's handpicked team began

Figure 6.13 One merchant's card showed Cleopatra threading her needle.

dropping out, victims of exposure to the elements. Gorringe formed those that remained into two teams that worked round the clock, replacing each other at 6:00 a.m. and 6:00 p.m. Each day the foreman was asked to estimate a reasonable distance that could be covered; if the men exceeded it, they were paid bonuses. To encourage his crews and show solidarity, Gorringe spent six hours with each day crew and five with the evening crews. He was a man who knew how to lead, and his men willingly followed. After nineteen brutal days exposed to the elements, the obelisk had completed the half-mile journey across the park and turned south on Fifth Avenue. The goal was almost within sight.

Figure 6.14 When the obelisk entered Central Park, a trestle was built so the obelisk would be high enough to be lowered onto its base. Just as the trestle was completed, a blizzard struck in December, suspending operations for several days.

It was a short gentle downhill to 82nd Street, where the obelisk was to re-enter the park. The final leg of the journey through the park to the pedestal was just eight hundred and ninety feet, but required tremendous advance preparation. The obelisk had to be lowered onto the pedestal that rested on the highest point in Central Park. This meant that it had to gain about fifty feet of elevation. Knowing this, in October Gorringe began constructing a railroad trestle from Fifth Avenue to the final site of the obelisk. Thus as one team of Gorringe's workers was fighting the elements, hauling the obelisk through the Park in November and December, another team was building a massive trestle out of timbers as thick as seventeen inches. On December 28, just as the obelisk was to begin its journey on the trestle, a blizzard hit New York and all work was suspended for several days. When the snows finally let up, the obelisk continued its odyssey, arriving at Greywacke Knoll on January 5, 1881. The obelisk was stopped when its center of gravity was directly above the pedestal. Now all that remained was to turn it vertical and lower it.

Erecting the obelisk

Gorringe had previously prepared the masonry base on which the Alexandria turning mechanism now rested. Using seven hydraulic jacks, the obelisk was raised out of its cradle to a position above the trestle, permitting it to be clamped to the turning mechanism at its center of gravity. Now the long process of dismantling the trestle began and on January 15 the obelisk, supported solely by the turning mechanism, was swung slightly to the right and then slightly to the left to give the system its first test. All looked good. The obelisk was to be set on its pedestal at noon on January 22. By January 20 almost all the trestle had been taken apart and that evening, near midnight, Gorringe and a small team of trusted workers quietly entered Central Park where, in the frigid cold, under the light of a quarter moon, the obelisk floated, suspended horizontally over its pedestal. Gorringe wanted a secret test before the public turning. The team stealthily went to work. Several workers pulled on the cables attached to the obelisk's base while others gave slack to the cables at the tip and, as planned, the obelisk began to pivot on its center of gravity, silently coming to rest in a vertical position above the pedestal.

The next day another violent storm tore through New York, causing extensive damage throughout the city, but the obelisk remained unmoved, suspended high above its pedestal. Throughout the morning of the 22nd New Yorkers filed into Central Park, seeking good vantage points to see the obelisk erected. The park was covered in snow with punishing winds blowing, but by 11:30 a.m. there were more than ten thousand people crowding the site. A grandstand had been built for dignitaries and a little before noon a Marine Band marched into the park and took its place beside it. Soon after, the carriages of William Evarts, the Secretary of State, of William Hurlbert, the editor of the *New York World*, and others pulled up to the grandstand. The officials descended and took their seats in the stands.

A signal had been arranged with the workmen so that when Gorringe raised his hand they would begin working the cables to turn the obelisk and would continue turning till he put his hand down. With no fanfare—it was bitter cold—Gorringe raised his hand and, as an unnatural silence fell over the crowd, the massive shaft of granite began to move effortlessly. When the obelisk reached 45 degrees, he lowered his hand to allow the well-known photographer,

Figure 6.15 When the obelisk was at 45 degrees Gorringe halted the turning so a photograph could be taken, preserving the moment. This artotype is based on the photograph.

Edward Bierstadt, to record the moment and, after a very brief pause for the photo, the obelisk continued turning. This broke the spell of silence and, much like for the New Year's Eve ball descending in Times Square, the crowd began cheering until the obelisk was perfectly vertical above its pedestal. The turning and photography had taken only five minutes and at its completion the military band played patriotic tunes. With the obelisk successfully turned, the crowd, eager to get out of the cold, quickly dispersed, but they didn't go away empty-handed. Gorringe had thoughtfully printed five thousand souvenir cards with a photo of the obelisk in Alexandria on one side and on the reverse the announcement that he would place it on its pedestal in Central Park at noon on January 22, 1881. As everyone happily headed indoors, Gorringe still had a long, cold day of work ahead of him.

The obelisk was vertical, but was not resting on the pedestal and still had to be lowered onto it. Gorringe's method of seating the obelisk on its pedestal was the third technique that the obelisk had experienced in its three-thousand-year history. In the time of Tuthmosis III, when it was carved and erected in Heliopolis, the Egyptian masons placed it directly on its pedestal with no support other than gravity. The obelisk was so precisely crafted that it could balance. Fifteen hundred years later, when the Romans moved the obelisk to Alexandria, they felt they had to anchor it somehow to its base. They crafted four bronze crabs with poles protruding from their bodies that slipped into slots cut in the pedestal and the bottom of the obelisk. We do not know why they chose this method, but a clue may be the corners of the obelisk, or, more accurately, the lack of corners. The four corners at the bottom are missing, broken in antiquity, we know not how. Perhaps the Romans, in lowering the obelisk from its pedestal, damaged the corners; we can't be sure. What is certain is that the bottom of the obelisk now has only about two-thirds of its original surface area. The Romans may have been afraid that this reduced surface area was not enough for the obelisk to safely balance on and thus they added the extra support of the crabs. This second method gave the obelisk a slightly different look because it now rested on the crabs, not the pedestal, with space between the pedestal and the bottom of the obelisk. This is how the obelisk stood for nearly two thousand years till it was once again moved, this time to Central Park. With the crowd now dispersed, Gorringe began to implement yet a third method of placing the obelisk on its base, a combination of the ancient Egyptian and Roman methods.

The plan was to spread a thin layer of cement on the pedestal and then lower the obelisk onto it by using the turning mechanism. Cement, however, doesn't pour in cold weather and the team of workers had to repeatedly heat

Figure 6.16 The obelisk in 1882, resting on the four modern crabs.

the surface and spread the cement before one pour finally set. It wasn't till 8:00 p.m. that night that the obelisk was finally balancing on its pedestal, looking much as it had in ancient Egyptian times. Over the next ten days the turning machinery was dismantled and the various workshops on the site were removed, but completing the process of fixing the obelisk to the pedestal would take ten more days of hard work. To ensure the stability of the obelisk, Gorringe also wanted to use the Roman method of bronze crabs. Over the previous months, craftsmen at the Brooklyn Navy Yard had made plaster casts of the broken Roman crabs, carved the missing parts, and cast four replica crabs in bronze weighing more than 900 pounds each. Working in the bitter cold of Central Park, it took Gorringe's workers more than a week to install the crabs at the corners of the obelisk, but in the end the New York obelisk rested directly on its pedestal, anchored by the crabs. Gorringe calculated that it would take a wind exerting a force of 78 tons at the obelisk's center of gravity to topple it, whereas the maximum generated by a hurricane is about 15 tons. Finally Gorringe could relax; his job was done.

The official ceremony to welcome the obelisk to New York was held on February 22 in the Grand Reception Gallery of the newly built Metropolitan Museum of Art. The event was by invitation only, but by 2:00 p.m. more than twenty thousand people crowded around the museum, wanting to be part of the festive occasion. Park police were called upon to clear a path up the museum's steps for those with invitations. The remaining twenty thousand joyously gathered around the obelisk for a kind of nineteenth-century Woodstock, looking up and marveling at Cleopatra's Needle.

Inside, Secretary of State Evarts began the proceedings from a platform on which sixty distinguished guests were seated. He thanked the Khedive for his generous gift and William Vanderbilt for paying to bring the obelisk to New York. Secretary Evarts pointed out that New York's obelisk, unlike France's or England's, was not a trophy of war. He also mentioned Consul E. E. Farman's brilliant and persistent negotiations for the obelisk that made it all possible. Evart's praise for Gorringe was lavish and extensive, chronicling the journey of the obelisk and all the difficulties that had to be overcome. At the end he summed it up perfectly: "Whatever Lieutenant Commander Gorringe undertakes to do he will accomplish." When Evarts completed his remarks, Mayor William Russell Grace came forward to receive the obelisk on behalf of

Figure 6.17 The medal given to 100 schoolboys to commemorate the obelisk's installation.

the City of New York. He was followed by Mr. A. S. Sullivan, representing the American Numismatic and Archaeological Society of New York. The Society had struck a commemorative medal for the occasion showing the obelisk and seals of New York and the United States on the front. Surrounding the obelisk and seals is a Latin motto stating: "Let the future learn from the past." The front of the medal is a bit busy, but nothing compared to the reverse, which reads like a billboard: "Presented to the United States by Ismail, Khedive of Egypt" (not quite right; the obelisk was presented to the City of New York); "Removed to New York through the liberality of W. H. Vanderbilt, and the skill of Lieu. Cm. H. H. Gorringe U.S.N." Aside from thanking everyone, the medal's reverse also presents a brief history of the obelisk: "Quarried at Syene and Erected at

Heliopolis by Tothme—Re-Erected at Alexandria Under Augustus." Quite a bit of text for a medal smaller than a silver dollar. Silver copies of the medal were presented to Gorringe and Vanderbilt in beautifully crafted wood boxes. In addition, one hundred aluminum copies were to be presented to schoolboys (yes, no girls) who were selected to attend the event. It was intended to have them come up to the platform but the room was so packed that no one could move, so the medals were given to a teacher to distribute later. After the ceremony, everyone strolled out into the cold to look at the obelisk standing tall behind the Metropolitan Museum. Gorringe could be proud of what he had accomplished, overcoming seemingly endless obstacles to bring New York its obelisk.

He did not live very long to enjoy his marvelous accomplishment. A few years after placing Cleopatra's Needle on its pedestal, he tripped while boarding a moving train, hit his head, and died from his injuries at the age of 45. He was buried in a private ceremony attended by his mother and sister Blanche at

Figure 6.18 On October 12, 1886 a special train brought Gorringe's friends and family to Rockland Cemetery, where the obelisk above his grave was unveiled.

Rockland Cemetery, just twenty miles from the obelisk he erected. Friends donated $2,500 to erect a suitable marker above his grave, and on October 12, 1886 a special train brought friends and admirers to the dedication. The marker, a beautiful thirty-foot Vermont granite obelisk, is a miniature of the one he worked so hard to bring to Central Park. One face of the pedestal bears a bronze portrait of Gorringe; another side shows the turning mechanism he designed. On the north face is the eulogy:

> By his courage, skill, and patriotism in the naval
> service of his adopted country in her time of need,
> he rose to distinguished rank.

> His crowning work was the removal of Cleopatra's
> Needle from Egypt to the United States—a feat of
> engineering without parallel.

> Brave, tender, and true, he passed away lamented
> by those who knew his worth, whose loving hands
> have raised this obelisk to his memory.

Postscript on the Obelisks

It is more than 130 years since the last obelisk left Egypt and we now have some perspective on the achievements of those who moved these monoliths. Surprisingly, it seems that as technology advanced, moving obelisks became more difficult. For the Romans, who moved dozens of them, it was an event almost not worthy of mentioning, so they have left us no real records of how they erected those taken to Rome. Fifteen hundred years later, when Fontana moved the Vatican obelisk, it was one of the engineering triumphs of the Renaissance. When we fast-forward to the nineteenth century and the transportation of the Paris, London, and New York obelisks, the achievement and drama seem even greater. This only increases my admiration for the ancient Egyptian engineers who erected dozens and dozens of obelisks with just rope, wood, and sand.

Today it is unimaginable that Egypt would permit more obelisks to be lowered from their pedestals and sent to foreign shores. The political and social climate has changed since the days when the Khedive of Egypt could casually say, "Well, if America wants an obelisk, she can have one." Egypt is now much more protective of her heritage, and the obelisks still standing in Egypt are admired with reverence by millions of tourists each year. The two still standing at Karnak Temple—one erected by Hatshepsut, one by her father, Tuthmosis I—are wonderful stopping places for guides to tell their groups the story of the female pharaoh and her remarkable family.

The lone obelisk remaining at Luxor Temple is also a star. It is the only obelisk in Egypt that stands in front of its original gateway and gives us an idea of how the ancient Egyptians saw it. Originally, of course, there were two; the missing one, once on the right, now stands in Paris. Of all the objects that have left Egypt, this "obelisk on the right" is the one I would absolutely love to see back in Egypt. It would be fabulous to have both obelisks standing in front of the entrance to Luxor Temple, as they did 3,500 years ago. It is almost certain that this will never happen, so I would be happy just to see a good replica of the Paris obelisk placed on the empty base at Luxor Temple so everyone could experience the glory of Egypt as it was.

While millions of tourists visit the Karnak and Luxor obelisks, there are others in Egypt that hardly anyone sees. Egypt's oldest monumental obelisk, erected by King Sesostris I, sits quietly isolated in a garden in Heliopolis, now a fashionable suburb of Cairo. It is within walking distance of the Marriott, a popular tourist hotel, but few take the trouble to see it. There are bigger fish to fry—the Great Pyramid at Giza, the Sphinx, the Egyptian Museum, the Step Pyramid of Saqqara, etc., etc.—so the obelisk goes unvisited. This is not only true in Egypt.

The Paris obelisk stands right in the middle of the Place de la Concorde, so it is well known and seen by all of Paris. The same is true of the Vatican obelisk, presiding over St. Peter's Basilica and surrounded by crowds every Sunday when the Pope celebrates Mass. The London obelisk, however, is not so well known. It has a beautiful location on the Thames, but one has to cross a major road to visit it, so most Londoners pass it by, ignorant of the heroics that brought it to England.

Save the obelisk!

Similarly, the New York obelisk is unknown to most New Yorkers. When it arrived it was a celebrity, with newspapers covering every step of its journey, and everyone was concerned about it. During its first four years in New York, chips of granite began flaking off its surface. New York winters with their freezing and thawing cycles are notoriously hard on the roads. When rain or melted snow enters cracks in the road, it freezes and expands, causing potholes. The obelisk suffered a similar fate. Water entered through small cracks and when temperatures dropped, the water froze and expanded, causing chips of the obelisk to fall to the ground. The obelisk was clearly in danger and there were cries of "Save the obelisk!"

In an attempt to protect the obelisk from more damage, it was waxed to stabilize the surface and keep water out. At the time of its waxing, the obelisk was in such bad condition that two-and-a-half barrels (780 pounds) of granite chips were removed from its surface. The waxing treatment had a good effect for many years. For forty years, starting in the 1970s, I visited the obelisk at all times of the year and never found a chip of granite on the ground. People calmed down, trees grew up around it, making it less visible than when it first was erected, and slowly the obelisk fell into relative obscurity. While many New Yorkers know that we have an obelisk, few have visited it. Recently people have claimed it is in terrible condition and in danger of falling, but this is not based on evidence. In danger of falling, no; dirty, yes. By the 1960s the obelisk was filthy, in need of a good cleaning thanks to New York's pollution.

In the late 1970s I thought it would be a good idea to have the obelisk cleaned for its hundredth anniversary in Central Park, but didn't get much support for the idea. However, in 1983 a team from New York University and the Metropolitan Museum of Art did a thorough study of the obelisk's history and condition, and it became clear when, where, and how the damage had occurred. Evidence replaced speculation.[1]

It is almost certain that when Tuthmosis III erected the obelisk in Heliopolis around 1450 BC, it was in perfect condition. The next account of the obelisk's condition is from the Geographer, Strabo, who visited Heliopolis around 24 BC. He mentions the well-documented invasion of Egypt by the Persian King Cambyses around 525 BC. Cambyses was infamous for disrespecting the monuments and customs of Egypt and Strabo says Cambyses "did very great injury to the temples, partly by fire, partly by violence, mutilating in some cases and applying fire in others. In this manner he injured the obelisks" (*Geography*, Book XXVII, I).

A simple visual inspection of the obelisk seems to confirm what Strabo tells us. The bottom twelve or so feet is the part most damaged—what one would expect if a fire were set at the base. Alexis Julien noted that the obelisk's pedestal is undecorated, while most other obelisk pedestals are highly ornamented.[2] For example, Hatshepsut's obelisk bases had historical inscriptions; Ramses the Great's at Luxor Temple had baboons adoring the sun and other scenes, etc. Julien suggests that the pedestal of the New York obelisk originally was decorated. These scenes were damaged in the fire, and when the Romans later moved the obelisks and pedestals to Alexandria, they cut away the damaged surfaces, leaving the pedestals bare.

If we want to understand where all the problems are coming from, it is important to note that the damage around the bottom is to all four sides, while the major damage to the upper portion is extreme on one side and more moderate on two other sides. The upper damage is probably from something other than the fire. A possible scenario is that Cambyses toppled the two Alexandrian obelisks when they were in Heliopolis and then for 500 years they lay partially buried in the ground until the Romans moved them. During the period while they were partially buried, the exposed surface suffered much of the wear and tear that we see today. Much of this was probably due to salt crystallization. This is not to say that no damage has happened in New York. As mentioned above, 780 pounds of granite came off the obelisk in its first four years in New York.

Modern scientific examination of the obelisk showed that the New York damage was, indeed, primarily due to thermal changes during the thaw–freeze cycles of bitter winters. Once the obelisk was waxed, this helped to protect the surface. The waxing, unfortunately, wasn't applied soon enough to prevent damage. This is supported by a comparison with the obelisk's twin in London. That one was waxed the first year it arrived and has had no problems worth noting. We must remember, however, that London has a much milder winter than New York.

The black soiling coating the obelisk was not a danger to the obelisk's well-being but it was unsightly, so in 2014 a Central Park Conservancy team carefully cleaned it. They decided to use lasers calibrated to vaporize the soiling but never touch the stone. In the few places where fragments of the obelisk were in danger of falling, conservation grade adhesives were used to stabilize it.

To enable conservators to remove the stains and consolidate fragile portions, a scaffold was erected around the entire obelisk. This gave me the chance to observe the tip of the obelisk up close, something I had always wanted to do. After a few minutes of climbing the spiral staircase surrounding the obelisk, I was at the top and was met with a surprise. The tip of the obelisk was not one piece as it should have been. All obelisks are carved from a single piece of stone. This obelisk had been damaged and repaired sometime during its very long life, but when? Close-up inspection showed that the top eight inches or so of the pyramidion was attached to the rest of the obelisk by means of a modern (late nineteenth-century or later) threaded rod about one inch in diameter.

After my initial shock wore off, I looked closely at the rest of the pyramidion and discovered that on all four sides, towards the bottom of the pyramidion were two drilled holes, one with a bolt still inside it. In all my reading about the

Figure 7.1 The very tip of the obelisk was broken and repaired, but we don't know exactly when. The arrows point to three of the bolt-holes that once held cladding.

obelisk, I had never seen the broken tip or bolt-holes mentioned. What was the function of the eight bolt-holes? My mind started filling with scenarios. Had Gorringe broken the tip in transport, reattached it, and then intended to cover up the break by cladding the tip with copper or bronze? It was difficult to tell if the attached tip was the original reattached or a replacement; the stone was certainly pink Aswan granite. The edges of the obelisk continue almost unbroken even with the attached tip. It is hard to imagine the tip breaking so cleanly and with no loss of stone, so my bet is that it is a replacement. But when did the damage occur?

My first thought was to look at old photos of the obelisk when it was standing in Alexandria. Perhaps I could see if the tip was missing then. Ambiguous! I just couldn't tell. Even with a trip to Staples to enlarge the images, I couldn't be certain. Sometimes it looked as if it *could* be missing, but from other angles it looked complete.

I next went to Gorringe's book to see the photos there. Perhaps they could answer the questions of when it was broken and when it was repaired. The problem with most of these photos is that Gorringe clad the obelisk in wood to protect it, so we don't see the tip. However, the book contains two beautiful photos by the well-known photographer Edward Bierstadt—one of the obelisk standing in Alexandria before Gorringe moved it and one after its erection in Central Park. The photo taken in Alexandria seems to show the obelisk missing the tip, but is not 100 percent clear. I needed a photo form a different angle. I sent out the word to friends who collect nineteenth-century photos of Egypt, explaining what I needed. One friend, William Joy, wrote back that he had just ordered some photos from France and one was of the standing Alexandria obelisk taken around the 1870s. When it arrived he e-mailed me the photo (Figure 7.2). He also enlarged the top for me and there it is, no doubt, the tip is missing (Figure 7.3). So the first part of the mystery is solved. The obelisk lost its tip in Egypt some time ago. Now the question is, when was it repaired?

The Bierstadt photo of the obelisk safely erected in the park (see Figure 6.16), I believe, shows an obelisk with the tip attached. Again, it isn't perfectly clear—I had to use a magnifying glass—but it seems as if Gorringe had a replacement cut and attached it in Alexandria. If this is true, why didn't he mention the restoration? And what about the bolt-holes? They were definitely used. When was the cladding put on and when was it removed? That remains a mystery.

With its conservation completed, the obelisk is safely nestled behind the Metropolitan Museum of Art in Central Park. Like other obelisks, it was erected to perpetuate the glory of a pharaoh. To some extent it has failed to do this. The great warrior pharaoh, Tuthmosis III, erected it and carved *his* titles boldly down the center of all four sides of the monolith. Two centuries later, Ramses the Great elbowed his way in and proclaimed his glory by carving his

Figure 7.2 The New York obelisk in its squalid surroundings in Alexandria around 1870. This photo seems to show that the obelisk had a broken tip while it was standing in Alexandria.

names and titles in columns on either side of Tuthmosis' inscriptions. Several centuries later a minor pharaoh, Osorcon, wanted to be remembered with the great ones, but by this time uncarved space on the obelisk was scarce, so he squeezed in just his name on a small spot on one side of the obelisk. But the truth is, these pharaohs' associations with the obelisk are largely forgotten. It is the obelisk people remember, not the inscriptions.

Figure 7.3 The enlargement of the tip shows it was broken before Gorringe moved it.

There is something about the obelisks themselves, not their history, that calls to us. Walk through any cemetery and you will see dozens of obelisks marking graves. They have become symbols of endurance and eternity. Soaring skyward, with their tips pointing straight up, they draw the eye heavenward. It doesn't matter who the hero was who erected it, or in what year. The obelisk is a thing-in-itself, not a monument to a particular person, but a tribute to the human spirit.

Notes

Chapter 1 How to Quarry an Obelisk
1   Partridge, p. 65.

Chapter 2 Rome's Obelisks
1   Finden, p. 22.
2   Towards the end of his long career, Kircher was ridiculed for his flights of fancy into the realm of hieroglyphs. After reading one of Kircher's learned works on hieroglyphs, the German mathematician Leibniz concluded, "He understands nothing." But it would be unfair to conclude that Kircher was merely a fraud. Misguided, certainly, but he did, indeed make a contribution towards the decipherment of hieroglyphs. In his *Prodromus Coptus sive Aegyptiacus* he is the first to note that Coptic is related to the language of the ancient Egyptians. Perhaps one reason he was so often wrong is that he was just spread too thin. He was interested in everything. As a young man he was lowered by rope into an active volcano so he could study its eruptions. When the plague struck Rome in 1667 he looked at Rome's water through his microscope to find the cause—early germ theory! When he was named curator of the Collegio Romano's museum, he added considerably to its holdings, creating one of the greatest cabinets of curiosities in the world.

Chapter 3 God's Architect
1   Parsons, p. 156.
2   Fontana, *Della Transportatione Dell'Obelisco Vaticano* (Oakland: Octavo, 2002), pp. 12–13.

Chapter 4 Napoleon's Obelisk
1   Lebas, p. 13.
2   Ibid., p. 18.
3   Ibid., p. 11.
4   De Joannis.
5   Lebas, p. 24.
6   Norden, Vol. I, plate VII
7   Lebas, p. 45.
8   Ibid.
9   Ibid., p. 84.
10 Ibid., pp. 132–3.

11 Joannis, p. 49.

12 Lebas, pp. 143–4.

13 Joannis, p. 11.

14 Lebas, p. 155.

15 Ibid., pp. 155–6.

Chapter 5 Cleopatra's Needle Sails for London

 1 Cooper, p. 130.

 2 Ibid., p. 140.

 3 Ibid., p. 141

 4 Baker, p. 234.

 5 Letter from Captain Henry Carter to John Dixon, October 17, 1877. London
   Metropolitan Archives, item Q/CN/4. I am indebted to Ian Pierce for this reference.

 6 Anon, p. 157.

Chapter 6 The Oldest Skyscraper in New York

 1 Yeates, p. 19.

 2 Farman, *Cleopatra's Needle*, pp. 162–3.

 3 Ibid., p. 163.

 4 Schroeder, p. 76.

 5 Ibid., p. 127.

 6 Gorringe, p. 5.

 7 Gorringe, p. 10.

 8 Ibid., pp. 10–11.

 9 Molds were made of the two remaining bronze crabs and four replica bronze crabs
   were fashioned at the Brooklyn Navy Yard. These are the crabs that visitors to the
   obelisk see today.

10 Gorringe, p. 28.

11 Ibid., p. 33.

12 Smyth.

Chapter 7 Postscript on the Obelisks

 1 Lewin, Wheeler, and Charola.

 2 Julien, pp. 93–166.

Bibliography

Anon. *Chicago Daily Tribune*. Dec. 28, 1962.

Anon. *Harper's Weekly*. Feb. 23, 1878.

Anon. *Time Magazine*. Jan. 4, 1954.

Arnold, Dieter. *Building in Egypt*. Oxford: Oxford University Press, 1991.

Baker, Benjamin. *Proceedings of the Institution of Civil Engineers, Vol. 61*. London: Institution of Civil Engineers, 1880.

Brinton, Jasper Yeates. *The Mixed Courts of Egypt*. New Haven: Yale University Press, 1930.

Budge, E. A. Wallis. *Cleopatra's Needles and Other Obelisks*. Chicago: Ares Publishers, 1979.

Carter, Captain Henry. *Letter form Carter to Henry Dixon*. London, Metropolitan Archives, Item Q/CN/4. Oct 17, 1877.

Clark, Somers and Rex Engelbach. *Ancient Egyptian Masonry*. London: Oxford University Press, 1930.

Cooper, William R. *A Short History of Egyptian Obelisks*. London: Samuel Bagster and Sons, 1877.

Curran, Brian A. et al. *Obelisk. A History*. Cambridge, Mass.: Burndy Library, 2009.

D'Alton, Martina. *The New York Obelisk*. New York: Metropolitan Museum of Art, 1993.

De Joannis, Léon. *Campagne Pittoresque du Luxor*. Paris: Huzard, 1835.

Engelbach, Rex. *The Problem of the Obelisks*. London: T. Fisher Unwin Ltd., 1923.

Farman, Elbert E. *Along the Nile*. New York: Grafton Press, 1908.

Farman, Elbert E. *Cleopatra's Needle*. New York: Grafton Press, 1908.

Farman, Elbert E. *Egypt and its Betrayal*. New York: Grafton Press, 1908.

Ficoronii, Francisci. *Gemmae Antiquae Literatae*. Rome: Monaldini, 1757.

Finden, Paula. *Athanasius Kircher: The Last Man Who Knew Everything*. London: Routledge, 2004.

Fontana, Domenico. *Della Transportatione Dell'Obelisco Vaticano*. Rome: Bassa, 1590.

Fontana, Domenico. *Della Transportatione Dell'Obelisco Vaticano*. 1590. Translated with notes. Oakland: Octavo, 2002.

Gorringe, Henry H. *Egyptian Obelisks*. London: John C. Nimmo, 1885.

Habachi, Labib. *The Obelisks of Egypt*. New York: Charles Scribner's Sons, 1977.

Hayward, R. A. *Cleopatra's Needles*. Derbyshire: Moorland Publishing, 1978.

Iversen, Erik. *Obelisks in Exile*. Copenhagen: G.E.C. Gad Publishers, 1968.

Julien, Alexis A. *A Study of the New York Obelisk as a Decayed Boulder*. Annals N.Y. Acad. Sci. VIII, 1893.

Julien, Alexis Anastey. *Notes of Research on the New York Obelisk*. New York: Alexis Julien, 1893.

Lebas, Apollinaire. *L'Obelisque De Luxor*. Paris: Libraires des Corps des Ponts et Chaussees et des Mines, 1839.

King, James. *Cleopatra's Needle*. London: Religious Tract Society, n.d.

Lewin, S. Z., G. E. Wheeler, and A. E. Charola. *Stone Conservation and Cleopatra's Needle: A Case History and an Object Lesson*. Unpublished report.

Moldenke, Charles E. *The New York Obelisk*. New York: Anson D.F. Randolph and Co., 1891.

Naville, Edouard. *The Temple of Deir El Bahri. Part VI*. London: Egypt Exploration Fund, 1908.

Newberry, Percy and F. L. Griffith. *El Bersheh, Part I*. London: Egypt Exploration Fund, 1890.

Norden, Frederick. *Travels in Egypt and Nubia* London: Davis and Reymer, 1757.

Oberg, Erik and F. D. Jones. *Machinery's Handbook*. New York: Industrial Press, 1942.

Parsons, William. *Engineers and Engineering in the Renaissance*. Cambridge, Mass.: MIT Press, 1968.

Partridge, Robert. *Transport in Ancient Egypt*. London: Rubicon Press, 1996.

Raynolds, William. "Finding a Needle in a Very Large Park: Reconsidering the Significance of the New York Obelisk." New York: Columbia University MS Thesis, 2015.

Schroeder, Seaton. *A Half Century of Naval Service*. New York: D. Appleton and Co., 1922.

Selim, Abdel-Kader. *Les Obelisques Egyptiens*. Cairo: Government Printing Office, 1991.

Smyth, Charles Piazzi. *Our Inheritance in the Great Pyramid*. London: W. Isbister, 1880.

Sorek, Susan. *The Emperor's Needles*. Exeter: Bristol Phoenix Press, 2010.

Tompkins, Peter. *The Magic of Obelisks*. New York: Harper & Row, 1981.

Young, John Russell. *Around the World with General Grant*. New York: American News Company, 1879. Reprinted with introduction. Baltimore: Johns Hopkins University Press, 2002.

Index